2004

Young People, Risk and Leisure

Young People, Risk and Leisure

Constructing Identities in Everyday Life

Edited by

Wendy Mitchell
Social Policy Research Unit
University of York, UK

Robin Bunton
School of Social Sciences and Law
University of Teesside, UK

and

Eileen Green
Centre for Social and Policy Research
University of Teesside, UK

First published 2004 by
PALGRAVE MACMILLAN
Houndmills, Basingstoke, Hampshire RG21 6XS and
175 Fifth Avenue, New York, N.Y. 10010
Companies and representatives throughout the world

PALGRAVE MACMILLAN is the global academic imprint of the Palgrave
Macmillan division of St. Martin's Press, LLC and of Palgrave Macmillan Ltd.
Macmillan® is a registered trademark in the United States, United Kingdom
and other countries. Palgrave is a registered trademark in the European
Union and other countries.

ISBN 1–4039–0116–3 hardback

This book is printed on paper suitable for recycling and made from fully
managed and sustained forest sources.

A catalogue record for this book is available from the British Library.

Library of Congress Cataloging-in-Publication Data
    Young people, risk and leisure : constructing identities in everyday life /
    edited by Wendy Mitchell, Robin Bunton & Eileen Green.
        p. cm.
    Includes bibliographical references and index.
    ISBN 1–4039–0116–3 (hardback)
        1. Youth with social disabilities – Great Britain – Case studies. 2. Risk –
    Sociological aspects. 3. Risk perception – Social aspects. 4. Leisure – Social
    aspects. 5. Identity (Psychology) I. Mitchell, Wendy, 1969– II. Bunton,
    Robin, 1954– III. Green, Eileen, 1947–

HV1441.G7Y54 2004
302'.12—dc22   2003064667

10 9 8 7 6 5 4 3 2 1
13 12 11 10 09 08 07 06 05 04

Printed and bound in Great Britain by
Antony Rowe Ltd, Chippenham and Eastbourne

Contents

306.12
Y75

List of Tables

Acknowledgements

This book evolved from the research and ideas surrounding the Action Risk project (1997–2000) conducted in the Centre for Social Policy Research (CSPR), University of Teeside. The editors would like to thank the Action Risk research team, specifically, Paul Crawshaw, Anne Foreman and Tamara Seabrook and also Sharon Dickenson and Barbara Cox, who provided unceasing administrative support. Throughout Action Risk, a small number of additional researchers worked upon specific aspects of this and other related projects in CSPR. In particular, we would thus like to acknowledge the work of Alan France for his professional ideas and guidance, Wendy Dewhirst for co-ordinating the initial stages of Action Risk, Di Parkin for co-ordinating and training community interviewers and her help with analysing the school questionnaire. We would also like to acknowledge the work of the following individuals who were involved with the Empowering Young Parents Project; Jan Douglas who co-directed the project (now Executive Director of Middlesbrough Social Services), Patricia Bell and Tamara Seabrook for co-ordinating and conducting the fieldwork, Jane Kochanowski for co-ordinating the parenting programmes and the Sexual Exploitation of Children on the Streets (SECOS) project for enabling access to specific case study communities.

The editors would also like to thank the community of Townville, where Action Risk was located. Without their help and support, the project would and could not have existed. The young people and many adult residents were extremely generous with their time, explaining their ideas and feelings, often at short notice and in their own leisure space to the researchers. In addition, we could not have gained the trust of many residents without the support and backing of Townville's numerous community development workers and professionals. Everyone played an important role, however, we would like to particularly acknowledge the hard work and enthusiasm of Sue Anderson, Beth Lindley, Salma Castle and Peter Jones.

The Single Regeneration Budget (SRB), Department of the Environment funded the Action Risk and Empowering Parents projects. We are grateful for the support and interest of the SRB, however, the facts presented and views expressed by the Action Risk and Empowering Parents researchers are those of the authors and not necessarily those of the Department of the Environment.

This collection is however, much more than an analysis of Action Risk, as it draws upon a wide and diverse range of empirical youth research, theoretical and methodological ideas. The editors would thus like to thank all the authors for their contributions, especially their understanding and co-operation throughout the editing process. Finally, we also wish to thank our publishers, Palgrave Macmillan for their patience and helpful comments, especially, Jennifer Nelson and Briar Towers.

List of Contributors

Cara Aitchison is Professor in Human Geography at the University of Bristol, West of England, where she leads research in human geography, leisure and tourism. She is author of *Gender and Leisure: Social and Cultural Perspectives* (2003) lead author (with Nicola Macheod and Stephen Shaw) of Leisure and Tourism Landscapes: Social and Cultural Geographies (2001). She is currently Chair of the Leisure Studies Association and World Leisure's Commission on Women and Gender.

Maura Banim is Principal Lecturer in Foundation Studies at the University of Teesside. She has undertaken research into social policy and social exclusion covering a number of topics including young people's health and disability. She has also researched the area of identity and clothing.

Robin Bunton is Professor of Sociology at the University of Teesside. He has undertaken research and published in the sociology of health. His recent books are, *The New Genetics and Public Health* (2001) with Alan Petersen and *Health Promotion: Disciplines, Diversity and Developments* (2002) with Gordon Macdonald. He is editor of the international journal *Critical Public Health* (Taylor and Francis).

Eilzabeth Burn is a Senior Lecturer in Primary Education at London Metropolitan University, with a particular interest in gender issues. Her doctoral research is concerned with male primary school teachers and she is increasingly concerned at the way football is being employed as a way of tackling educational exclusion.

Fred Cartmel is a Senior Research Associate in the Youth, Education and Employment Research Unit based at the University of Glasgow and has written extensively on the labour market experiences of young people. He is presently involved in an investigation into long-term unemployment among 26 to 30-year olds, using a life biography approach.

Paul Crawshaw is currently Principal Lecturer for Postgraduate Programmes in the School of Health and Social Care at the University of Teesside where he also teaches public health and research methods. His research and teaching interests include; the critical study of men's health, the evaluation of community based health improvement programmes with a particular focus on the use of qualitative and action research methods and the sociology of risk.

Anne Foreman is a Research Associate at the Centre for Public Policy, University of Northumbria where she leads on the Centre's children and young people portfolio. In addition to previous academic posts, Anne has also worked at both community and corporate levels in local government, experiences that continue to inform and ground her research activities.

Kate Gillen is currently Director of Educational Development for County Durham and Tees Valley NHS Workforce Development Confederation. Prior to this, she has lectured in psychology at the Universities of Durham, Teesside and Sunderland. Her research interests have focused upon examining young people's perceptions of risk-taking and exploring health inequalities and the impact of strategies designed to address these, such as Health Action Zones and the NHS Modernisation Agenda.

Eileen Green is Professor of Sociology and Director of the Centre for Social and Policy Research at the University of Teesside. She has publications in the areas of risk, women's leisure, women and health, gender and IT and the meaning of clothes. Her most recent books include (with Alison Adam) Gender, Society and ICTS special issue of *Information Communication and Society* (1999), *Virtual Gender: Technology, Consumption and Identity* (2001) and with Ali Guy and Maura Banim, *Through the Wardrobe, Women, Identity and their Relationship with Clothes* (2001). She is also co-editor of the journal *Leisure Studies*.

Alison Guy is Psychology Subject leader at Teesside University. She has carried out research with young people and young disabled people and their families in relation to sexual health needs. Her current research focuses on women's everyday relationships with their clothes.

Deborah Lupton is Professor of Sociology and Cultural Studies at Charles Sturt University, Australia. Her latest books are *Risk* (1999), the edited collection, *Risk and Sociocultural Theory: New Directions and Perspectives* (1999) and, with John Tulloch, *Risk and Everyday Life* (2003).

Wendy Mitchell is a Research Fellow in the Social Policy Research Unit at the University of York. Her research interests focus upon children, young people and their families. Her doctoral research explored the transition experiences of young people with learning disabilities. She has published a range of articles exploring the lives of young mothers and services provided for families with disabled and chronically ill children.

Simon Pratt is Senior Lecturer in Education Studies at London Metropolitan University and he also teaches at the State University of

New York. His specialist areas include primary education, the urban context and gender issues. Prior to his university appointment he was deputy head of an inner city primary school. His doctoral research on the education and social development of young males has included a study of the construction of male identities in organised team sport.

Tamara Seabrook is a Researcher in the School of Health at the University of Bradford. She has researched and written in the area of young people, gender and community regeneration and is currently carrying out research exploring the experiences and perceptions of young problematic drug users in Bradford.

John Tulloch is Professor of Media Communication, Cardiff University, Wales and Director of the Centre for Cultural Research into Risk, Charles Sturt University, New South Wales, Australia. He has published several books on film history and theory, television, drama, audience methodology and theory (in television and theatre) and risk. His most recent book (with Deborah Lupton) is *Risk and the Everyday* (2003).

Rebecca Watson is a Senior Lecturer in the School of Leisure and Sports Studies at Leeds Metropolitan University. She is currently building upon her doctoral research, which explored young motherhood and difference and is more generally involved in research on gender and equity issues. In particular, her interests include feminist analyses of leisure and sport and the interrelationships between gender, race and class.

1

Introduction: Young People, Risk and Leisure, an Overview

Robin Bunton, Eileen Green and Wendy Mitchell

Risk appears to have become central to our understanding of childhood and adolescence. Recent sociology has plotted the arrival of this perspective (Jenks, 1996; Scott *et al.*, 1998; Brownlie, 2001) in which the unfinished selves and bodies of the young are viewed as precarious and in need of guidance and governance. In modern Western societies, risk has largely lost its neutral 'scientific' status and become almost synonymous with notions of hazard (Fox, 1999). Young people appear to have been framed as 'risky', as they were previously conceived as 'dangerous' or 'trouble', and this concern is intimately linked to social techniques for governing populations of young people. Concern for 'risky youth' has become a feature of general adult anxiety surrounding young people and their personal development. This collection of chapters reflects the growing interest in young people and risk and offers reflection on the different ways of conceiving young people and risk. It includes a number of studies that address everyday understandings of risk, providing insight into the ways that risks are routinely encountered and managed and the complex ways in which risk manifests itself for young people living in contemporary Western society.

The study of risk has been of central sociological interest for over a decade, the interest coming from various quarters. In relation to youth in particular, one can identify a strand of research that derives from what might be said to be general efforts of modern societies to enhance the health and well-being of their populations and to exert increasing control over our lives and our environments. Development of science and technology would appear to offer us more opportunities to prevent threats to our health and well-being and allow us more prediction and intervention to curtail harmful future events (Alaszewski and Horlick-Jones, 2000). This concern has underscored a number of policy developments, policy and

1

planning on social, economic and technical change with the introduction of a 'precautionary principal' (European Environment Agency, 2001). Since the 1970s, the precautionary principle has entered policy dialogue, as governments and trans-national organisations attempt to formulate policies to deal with scientific uncertainties and potential hazards, particularly in relation to the environment. Alongside policies, methods are being developed to involve the public in decision-making about global risk taking (European Commission, 2000). At the time of writing, the UK government is conducting a nation-wide debate about the future of genetically modified (GM) crops. It is facilitating local discussion about the nature of the threats and the promises of these new crops, prior to further formulating national policy. Such developments could be interpreted as support for Ulrich Beck's thesis that contemporary society is fundamentally a 'risk society' and requires increasing reflexivity to manage modern social processes (Beck, 1992, 1999).

Concern for the risks encountered by young people, similarly, reflects a general concern for their continued well-being in relation to a number of potential threats. Often academic and policy concerns of this sort are based upon technical and scientific knowledge taken from disciplines such as: epidemiology, medicine, economics and engineering. Dispositions towards the assumed 'objective' risks ascertained by these expert knowledges have informed a number of psycho-social approaches to risk which attempt to ascertain what factors determine 'subjective' risk perceptions, and ultimately influence behavioural choices. An endemic assumption within much of this literature is risk-taking behaviour is frequently fundamentally irrational and that individuals can be assisted in overcoming such behaviour with the help of professional intervention (Bloor, 1995a). Young 'risk takers' may be helped to recognise the 'error' of their risk-taking ways, and to adopt more 'rational' behaviours (Plant and Plant, 1992). There is increasing dissatisfaction with such approaches to risk behaviour not least because of it's rather naïve epistemological treatment of risk itself (Rhodes, 1997). Risk often appears as an obdurate reality lying beyond historical, cultural and social processes. More reflective and theoretically informed work on risk has problematised such assumptions, and it is mainly this work that has informed the approach of the chapters included in this volume.

Lupton has identified at least three commonly recognised approaches to sociological theorising about risk in recent years: the cultural/symbolic treatment of risk associated with Mary Douglas, the discussion of 'risk society' in the work of Ulrich Beck and also Anthony Giddens, and also work on governmentality, drawing on ideas influenced by Michael

Foucault (Lupton, 1999a,b). The chapters presented here represent and take issue with this range of theory in relation to the study of young people. A number of key issues recur, though perhaps the most common focus is the relationship of young people to the professed onset of the 'risk society'.

Studying risk society and inequality

Considered as an increasingly important organising principle of late-modern industrial society, risk has far-reaching effects on the assumption of contemporary identity (Giddens, 1991; Beck, 1992, 1999). Contemporary risk theorists have argued that identity is increasingly articulated through differing dispositions towards risk. An outcome of the onset of 'risk society' is that a number of traditional features of industrial society, such as class, community and family are decreasing in influence and relationships with strangers, encountered through greater national and global flows of people and cultures, are taking on greater significance. Features of this change are said to be increased reflexivity and 'individualisation' in the processes of identity formation (Beck and Beck-Gernsheim, 1996), resulting in individuals experiencing more choice and determination in the construction of the 'project of self'. Contemporary individuals are said to be more able to build identities through self-monitoring and choice drawing on increasingly pervasive secular knowledges which constitute the human sciences and which provide the grounding of 'technologies of the self' (Foucault, 1986; Martin, 1989).

Furlong and Cartmel (1997) have addressed Beck's central thesis of the onset of risk society in relation to young people in a study of young people and risk in the UK. They attempted to identify whether features of 'risk society' were part of broader changes that young people encountered in their transition to adulthood. They argued that risk becomes a determinant of social relations and that consequently within late modernity young people must, 'negotiate a set of risks which were largely unknown to their parents', irrespective of class and gender (Furlong and Cartmel, 1997, p. 2). They suggest that in the last twenty years or so, under the conditions of 'disorganised capital', young people have encountered less certainty as a result of the restructuring of the labour market, an increased demand for an educated labour force, flexible specialisation in the workplace and social policies that have extended the period of family dependency. The processes of individualisation engendered by risk society in late modernity, they argue, produced a type of misrecognition in which social actors fail to recognise the 'real' social structures and forces shaping them. Consequently, young people mistakenly see the world as unpredictable and filled with risks that must be addressed individually, rather than through the collectivist struggles such as class or other politics. They contest, to some extent, the extent of the 'real' individualising processes brought on by risk society. The realities of class inequalities are still determining these young people's lives, though not recognised as such.

Furlong and Cartmel's (1997) analysis provides a useful grounding of some of the more abstract theoretical analyses of risk, though the study highlights another problem; that the ontological status of risk is unclear. Within such discussions it is uncertain whether we should see risk as a member's category or as some type of 'objective' institutional discourse, as risks manifest at broader societal and institutional levels may be experienced differently at a local or individual level. Furlong and Cartmel (1997) draw largely upon 'objective' data sources, using secondary analysis of official statistics to characterise the worlds of young people in the UK, in the areas of leisure, changing patterns of family dependency, labour market transitions, health risks, crime and insecurity and politics and participation. This approach is not unproblematic but Beck's thesis has also come under attack for his lack of clarity on the epistemology of risk. Alexander (1996) found Beck's perception of risk to be 'objectivist'. Lash and Urry (1994) have criticised Beck's 'cognitive realism' and his failure to account for the aesthetic aspects of reasoning and subjectivity. Summarising these problems, Elliot has recently argued that Beck has failed to grasp, 'the hermeneutical, aesthetic, psychological and culturally bounded forms of subjectivity and intersubjectivity in and through which risk is constructed and perceived' (2002, pp. 300–1). In other words the routine interpretation and construction of risks, danger and hazard is difficult to ascertain, which undermines broader macro statements that are made about risk, such as the claim that the modern world contains risks that have never previously been encountered and that risk is engendering forms of reflexivity and anxiety.

Clearly, far more understanding is needed of the situated, 'everyday' reasoning and management of risk to begin to address some of these problems with the 'risk society' thesis. Some of the studies included here have attempted to ground risk theorising in just such a way, by describing the everyday risk reasoning and risk management strategies of young people, based around specific concerns. They are operating with a broad range of epistemological standpoints. Lupton has identified a continuum between the 'realist', 'weak constructionist' and 'strong constructionist' approaches to risk in the literature (1999a). The authors in our collection would appear to favour the latter two categories. Five of the authors of chapters in this volume have worked together on one project. The resulting five chapters included here are drawn from one area study of risk and young people in the UK. The concern of this study was how young people 'construct' risk within their own socially embedded and culturally meaningful discourses – a recurring theme in recent UK youth research. A sixth chapter is also authored by one of this team and draws upon a parallel study of young parents in the same region. Such young parents have been represented as constituting families who are potentially 'at risk' and are also the subject of recent government interventions, which have taken the form of parenting classes. Some recent studies of risk have considered how young people often reject 'objective' definitions of risky behaviour in favour of constructing their own 'risk hierarchies' (see Abbott-Chapman and Denholm, 2001) and have recognised the situated nature of risk within the life worlds of young people (Lawy, 2002). Here risk becomes something of a contested concept, to be negotiated and managed with reference to complex and diverse social and cultural influences such as education, the family and the peer group. The chapters based upon these two projects examine 'risk' as an everyday meaningful category. The studies gathered accounts of dangers, concerns, worries and anxieties, as well as notions of fate, chance and luck. We discovered that dispositions to risk are manifest in everyday discourse and that such discourses run alongside other means of dealing with uncertainty and the unpredictability of contemporary life, by reference to fate and chance, for example. Whilst analysing and writing up the data we discovered similar concerns being addressed by others working in this field. This volume grew out of an awareness of the need to examine and ground some of the interesting theoretical work on risk, and to test, operationalise and develop this work, particularly with reference to current debates about the impact of gendered experiences of leisure.

In situated risk discourses we are particularly interested in the ways that risk calculation and risk management strategies are socially located and represent and reproduce social inequalities. Beck (1992) has acknowledged that lower classes will bear a disproportionate burden of risks. We would concur with this and are particularly interested in the distribution of risk and risk perception across class, gender, ethnicity and age groups. The nature of risk analysed in the chapters, which form the core of the book, relates specifically to the 'risk communities' in which these studies were carried out and requires some description.

Our own two studies were based in two districts of a large industrial town in the North of England, which we have here called Townville.

Both three-year projects took place between 1997 and 2001 and were funded under the UK Department of Environment's Single Regeneration Budget. They were conceived as action/research projects and formed part of a broader strategy on economic regeneration. This collection draws upon data from both studies, which involved qualitative interviews and a quantitative survey of young people's accounts of risk, risk taking and management. Focus group interviews were carried out with over 25 groups of young people, including young parents, and with adult stakeholders. Five hundred and eleven school children were surveyed in two of Townville's schools (constituting approximately 25 per cent of young people in Townville).

Townville exhibits a range of features of recent economic and social transformation in the industrial regions of the UK that is in many ways at the forefront of transformed late modern industrial society. Consequently, the economic uncertainties of 'risk society' are highlighted in this community. Townville has had an employment tradition in steel, chemical and other 'heavy' industries. Employment compares very unfavourably with other areas in the UK. Since 1979, 140 000 jobs have been lost in the steel industry and since 1981, 3000 from the chemical industry. The overall rate of unemployment is currently 22.9 per cent compared to 8.8 per cent nationally. Male unemployment is 30 per cent compared to 11.9 per cent nationally and female unemployment is 10 per cent compared to 4.7 per cent nationally. The employed residents of Townville are less likely to be in full time, non-manual employment and more likely to be unskilled (20.4 per cent compared to 4.3 per cent nationally). Car ownership, often regarded as a good indicator of class and income, is low, with over half population (57 per cent) having no car compared with a national figure of 32.4 per cent. In 1991 13.5 per cent of the population were single parent families compared with the national figure of 3.8 per cent. The population is mainly white working class, though since the 1960s a small number of Asian people have moved into the area. Levels of public amenities are low. The indicators of poor health and social deprivation in the area have scored so high that it has featured in a number of UK national studies (Townsend *et al.*, 1998). This profile of social and economic deprivation has involved national and local government in investment programmes of regeneration.[1]

Socially situated risk

The setting for the majority of these chapters then is socially specific and the accounts that we have described here are highly socially relative.

Mary Douglas's work on risk was amongst the first to draw attention to the social and cultural relativity of risk. She pointed out the ways in which risk was related to politics and to attributing blame and danger to certain social groups (1992). Risk, Douglas argues, is used as a resource to assist groups attribute cause to the existence of certain causes and dangers. Danger can be attributed to the activities of 'outsider' groups who are made responsible for misfortunes. Young people, similarly, can be blamed for the entry of dangers or 'pollutants' into a community. Constructed as 'risky youth', young people can be maintained as outsiders and the 'purity' of the insider community maintained. Douglas's approach suggests a more grounded, empirical and phenomenological approach to risk. The meaning of risk for young people, adults and others may be uncovered and described in flight, as it is called upon as a resource to manage broader social dynamics. Mary Douglas' writing on risk is a part of her broader concern with the self and the body. The embodied aspect of risk is another aspect of Beck's account that is left underdeveloped (Turner, 1994).

A feature of individualisation and 'risk society', according to Giddens (1991) is increased concern for the body as a potentially controllable element of self-production and realisation. Embodiment also appears to be a feature of theoretical interest in risk from the perspective of governmentality. Self-actualisation through the management of risk is a life-long accomplishment because the body, as a social product, is always 'unfinished' (Shilling, 2003). Adolescence or the period of 'youth' is likely to be a particularly intense period for the management of risk and identity (Lupton and Tulloch, 1998; France, 1998; Abbott-Chapman and Denholm, 2001; Lawy, 2002). For example, adolescent concern with the 'unfinished body' in relation to HIV/AIDS, is claimed to illustrate something of young people's, 'heightened sense level of agentive reflexivity in relation to the health of their bodies ...' (Lupton and Tulloch, 1998, pp. 31–2). Consequently, it has been argued that contemporary youthful identities are *sin qua non* postmodern identities (Miles, 1998). As such they offer a useful entry point for a more detailed analysis of the modern body and the construction of self and identity in risk cultures.

Through risk profiling, individuals construct enterprising, calculating and prudent selves appropriate to the rationality of advanced liberalism (Petersen, 1996; Rose, 1996; Petersen and Lupton, 1996). The pursuit of the body that exhibits health, fitness, 'youthfulness' and beauty has taken a particular moral form, and Gillick (1984) has pointed out that the incentives for such self-care have come from a number of quarters including sport, leisure industries and a more general economic rationale. The emergence of employee assistance programmes, stress management courses and reduced insurance premiums for those with healthier lifestyles are clear examples of this encouragement. Studying risk, then, offers a vantage point on newer processes of governance, in particular, the governance of youth. Taite (1995) amongst others has argued that 'youth' can be conceived of as an 'artefact of government' (Taite, 1995; Kelly, 2000) underpinned by academic discourses in sociology, psychology, criminology, education, leisure studies and cultural studies, which inform 'youth studies'. These discourses have helped construct populations of 'youth at risk' and facilitated the call for the regulation of youth identities through schooling, training, cognitive skills and newer 'initiatives'. A pertinent example of this is the recent UK Labour government led 'New Deal', which focuses on the development of employment skills (Office of the Deputy Prime Minister, 1998). Also relevant here is the Connexions programme for young people (Department of Education and Employment, 2000), which attempts to provide 'holistic' services across the welfare, education and employment sectors as well as offering personal support in the form of counselling and alcohol and drugs advice. Such critiques of the 'sociology of youth' have added a valuable reflexivity to the study of young people. Drawing on Foucault's notion of 'governmentality', this critique has reiterated critical feminist work on the sociology of 'youth culture' which has privileged class and age over other structural analysis such as gender and space (Walkerdine 1997; McRobbie, 1980). Walkerdine in particular is critical of an apparent romanticisation of spectacular male working class youth sub-cultures in left wing intellectual analysis. Similarly, in these chapters we draw upon a range of empirical work on young people, and in particular, upon data from the North of England to examine young people's notions of risk, safety and danger in relation to some general socio-cultural conceptions of risk, leisure and the gendered body.

The chapters in this collection all attempt to situate risk by adopting methodologies that immerse risk in various social contexts. Fred Cartmel in Chapter 5, for example, pursues his longer term interest in the 'risk society thesis', investigating Scottish rural labour market integration and social exclusion of young people. The 'risk' of unemployment for young people, it is argued, is based upon local social conditions and lack of contact with informal networks rather than global and individual factors that has been posited by Beck in 'Risk Society'. Rather than the old social cleavages disappearing under conditions where individuals have to create their own biographical trajectories, structural factors continue to affect young people's integration into the labour market. Informal networks provide a valuable source of information for young people living in rural communities on employment opportunities. For the socially included and excluded, social and informal networks play an important part in creating employment opportunities. The risk of unemployment associated with global influences and poor educational qualifications are minimal in rural areas compared with structural influences, such as connections to informal networks which provide information about employment. Cartmel's research is able to ground broad abstract statements about risk society in concrete everyday settings, using conventional research methodologies.

In Chapter 3 Gillen, Guy and Banim start from familiar assumptions about the nature of risk and adolescence. Health promoters in Western societies are in the main concerned to reduce adolescent risk taking and control their leisure where it may affect health. As the authors point out, however, any initiatives aimed at reducing risk must address issues that directly impact on young people's lives and must engage young people if they are to have any chance of success. Risk analysis takes us directly into the lives of adolescents including their risk-taking behaviour and their social networks. Gillen, Guy and Banim start from the assumption that social and cultural factors determine the type of social networks an individual belongs to, and ultimately their risk perceptions. Furthermore, social networks impact on behaviour via four primary psychosocial mechanisms; social support, social influence, social engagement and attachment and access to material resources (Berkman *et al.*, 2000). This chapter reports on a study of risk in a town in North Eastern England and used focus groups to explore reasons for risk taking among young people. Like Townville, the area suffers from complex social problems including unemployment, poverty, illegal drug use and crime and there are also high levels of mortality and morbidity. The authors conclude that adolescents show a complex and subtle framing of risk taking, involving several thematic strands. These include: the perceived personal and social consequences of risk taking, parents' behaviours (both as risk encouraging and risk discouraging factors) and societal rules that seem to act as a spur to risk taking. Although it adopts a social psychological focus, like other works cited in this volume, this study contextualises risk and young people's leisure and argues for a complex understanding of context and social 'networks' in designing health prevention activities.

Whilst addressing substantive areas of concern, such as social context, space, work, leisure and gendered identity, many of the chapters in this volume also address central epistemological issues. Crawshaw (Chapter 13) problematises methods of studying risk in his exploration of Bourdieu's work in relation to the analysis of risk. He argues that Bourdieu's own elaboration of sociological method offers us a guide on how to approach risk in social context. Bourdieu's epistemology offers a pathway between objectivist and subjectivist treatments of risk, which seems to offer possibilities for avoiding some of the problems inherent in the 'risk society' thesis. Beck's lack of clarity over the epistemological status of risk, noted earlier, might be dealt with the help of Bourdieu's method. This chapter illustrates how such an approach might be applied to notions of (gendered) masculine identities and risk.

Gender issues are key to the collection and threaded through theoretical debates from within the social sciences and leisure studies, both areas have benefited from feminist critiques which highlighted the importance of difference and diversity (Green *et al.*, 1990; Wearing, 1998; Scraton and Watson, 1998). Central to feminist leisure studies, for example, has been the recognition that leisure is constituted through a variety of meanings and experiences. It is an important site for the analysis of complex social relations that include the development of subject identities related to the consumption of space and place, as demonstrated in the data introduced by Seabrook and Green in Chapter 8. Informal leisure is also significant in creating and maintaining a sense of identity and belonging (Green, 1998). In Chapter 6, Cara Aitchison considers the relationships between identity construction, risk, adventure and the 'testing of boundaries' that are a feature of leisure in a number of academic disciplines. Leisure studies, she notes, has frequently offered critiques of the ways in which public policy has attempted to regulate both risk and leisure for young people. The chapter evaluates the subject field of leisure studies as an increasingly complex and contested site of social and cultural critique and outlines the ways in which leisure studies has responded to theories of leisure relations developed within gender studies and geography, whilst also evaluating leisure studies' contribution to theories of gender and spatial relations. Drawing on geography, as an underpinning or 'parent' discipline to the subject field of leisure studies, the chapter highlights contrasting and, at times, competing discourses of gender and leisure whilst also seeking to address the extent to which 'risk' is accommodated in these discourses. Aitchison argues that recent theoretical developments in social and cultural geographies have provided a meeting ground for critiques of gender, leisure and place. These analyses of cultural production and consumption have accommodated critiques of gender; sexuality and identity, which were previously, marginalised within orthodox leisure studies. Social and cultural geographies have explored risk as an everyday, and frequently sought after, aspect of contemporary leisure, particularly for young people; everyday risks that are embodied and perceived as connected with specific (gendered) spaces.

Risk, gender and the body

The concept of embodied experience has emerged as a key issue linking debates within medical sociology, the sociology of the body and feminist theory. We argue that it also illuminates the analysis of risky leisure pursued by many young people. Despite the current interest in embodiment, there is an absence of both theory and narratives about bodily experience (Nettleton and Watson, 1998). Although there is now an expanding corpus of sociological research on the body, the bodies in question are implicitly white and male and without voices (Green, 2001). Women's accounts of bodily experience that might, for example, assist us in understanding the experience of adolescence, are noticeably absent. Drawing upon data from young women's narratives of embodied experience, as girls or mothers striving for and resisting respectability and social acceptance, this collection highlights the need for more qualitative studies that explore the impact of differences such as gender, ethnicity and sexuality. In addition, we need to know more about the significance of the 'local', whether it be socio-cultural context or local biologies, upon perceptions and experience. Pivotal to our understanding of young women's experiences of risk, are the ways in which they are represented as bodies which need to be carefully managed, whether it be by medical experts or by themselves through a mixture of personal care and 'self surveillance'.

The concept of self-surveillance stems from Foucault's work which has been widely adopted by both sociologists and feminists alike, in particular his concept of the individual self created by surveillance (Foucault, 1982). Such surveillance practices, it is argued, constitute the body and invite individuals to govern themselves, observing and monitoring their own behaviour through the operation of disciplinary power (Nettleton, 1997). However, as Howson (1998) observes, this work fails to address the gendered nature of both power and the bodies concerned. Reviewing theorisations of bodily surveillance, it seems that apart from Bordo's work (1993), few theorists have addressed either the ways in which regulation creates specific identities or the processes through which these identities are negotiated and internalised. It is also important to notice, as we know from cultural geographers' accounts of the significance of place (Massey, 1994) local, embodied knowledges (Howson, 1998).

Feminists, such as Skeggs (1999) explore the theme of space and identity and remind us that most women learn that they do not belong in many public spaces and that public spaces are masculine. They are maintained as such by the fear of male violence which encourages women (and some men) to regulate their behaviour by avoiding particular spaces and places. Actual male violence or fear of it operates what Stanko (1997) has referred to as a 'technology of self' whereby women guard their behaviour. The empirical data from our studies of Townville supports this thesis, although the data also demonstrates interesting differences both within and between genders, in terms of their management and perceptions of embodied risk. For heterosexual women, safety and legitimacy are key issues and keeping themselves safe involves self-exclusion from 'dangerous' public spaces, regardless of whether it is their reputation or physical safety which are at risk (Valentine, 1989, 1992). Even those women who deliberately inhabit risky spaces and related identities as street prostitutes (explored by Green in Chapter 4) adopt strategies to minimise risk which include dividing punters into safe or risky categories and managing them accordingly.

Interrogating how young women in Townville use and think about the meanings and use of space, enables us to construct an analysis of the ways in which individuals and, in particular young women, think or reflect 'through the body' as a process for understanding and coping with risk and change. Feminist, qualitative research reminds us that, social expectations and cultural discourse have always mediated women's relationships with their bodies. Since individuals are subject to embodied experience, as Davis argues, we need to 'tackle the relationship between the symbolic and the material, between representations of the body and embodiment as experience or social practice in concrete social, cultural and historical contexts' (1997, p. 15). Drawing upon perspectives which stress the importance of gender as process, we can see that identity is linked to the continual and at times contradictory, re-working of individual subjectivities via a complex interaction between personal agency and social context. This enables an understanding of how young women can both actively construct their identities (Green, 1998) and yet continue to be constrained by dominant discourses which represent them as submissive *bodies* 'striving for respectability'. At a theoretical level, it would seem that the themes of risk and body management are crucial concepts to explore in relation to providing a framework though which to understand women's experiences. Feminist perspectives on the sociology of the body (Bordo, 1993) and embodiment (Howson, 1998) appear to provide the most promising framework here, given the focus upon personal experience and the centrality of concepts such as agency and subversion.

This collection provides data on discourses of individualised risk, gendered bodies and self-surveillance, as the background against which young women (and men) manage their bodies in risky spaces and situations. We argue for the inclusion of approaches that draw upon the sociology of the body and embodiment and address the importance of embodiment to the ongoing process of identity construction, this enables us to conceptualise women 'thinking through their bodies'. At a theoretical level, this achieves three things, first it allows us to ground theoretical discourses which construct women as fragmented subjectivities, by drawing upon their own accounts and second it addresses the commonalities of gendered, embodied experience. Three chapters in this volume address the experience of embodied, young motherhood, a key example of the impact of moral discourses of gendered responsibility and respectability which is centred around the maternal body.

Young mothers managing risk

Young mothers and children frequently occupy ambiguous even contradictory positions in relation to risk. They are frequently seen as 'at risk' and vulnerable in official discourses. Drawing upon qualitative data exploring the lives of 14 young mothers in Townville, Mitchell (Chapter 11) examines young mother's ever-present strategies to manage risk, in relation to safe spaces and leisure experiences for their children. The chapter demonstrates the importance of getting inside individual accounts of risk, whilst simultaneously recognising that these understandings are socially, economically and culturally grounded in specific concrete local contexts. This data illustrates the ways that management strategies demonstrate a complex interweaving of three discourses within late modern society. The first centres upon accounts of a society pervaded by ever-present risk anxiety, and demonstrate attempts to control or manage 'risk'. A second discourse discusses ideologies of motherhood, and the experience of being perceived as a 'responsible and respectable mother'. The third discourse focuses upon the historically fluid and often contradictory concept of childhood, particularly with regard to children's leisure. The chapter examines how these discourses are interwoven within the mothers' lives their children's lives and the mother's sense of 'self'.

The social position of these mothers may at times seem bleak, as unrelenting poverty and deprivation are added to by persistence of negative social stereotypes associated with young motherhood. Moreover, the threat of danger on Townville's streets clearly impacts upon their own and their children's lives. However, we are once again cautioned against the assumption of structural determinism in relation to the experience of risk. Mothers are not passive victims of their circumstances. The often heightened awareness of risk and attempts to externalise or 'other' risk are illustrative of attempts to manage risk symbolically and practically. Pressure to secure safe, risk-free play space by the community was indicative of these attempts. In a similar vein, Rebecca Watson in Chapter 12 begins from insights offered into young mothers' experiences of 'risk' by feminist analysis of dominant discourses on lone motherhood and young mothers. Acknowledging that the public sphere, including leisure is subject to transformation due to global social change, she examines the micro effects of such change on everyday contexts of 'risk' with a sample of women living in Leeds and in the late 1990s. This in-depth qualitative study provides analysis of shifting identities of young women as they become mothers and face a number of risks and uncertainties in relation to caring for and bringing up children. These women negotiate, create and achieve time and space for themselves despite their everyday experiences being shaped by the axes of gender, race and class. Their strategies can be seen to resist dominant forms of 'respectability' that remain evident in everyday discourse on mothering. Young mothers are frequently constructed as the 'other' in relation to risk, both as '*a* risk' to moral values surrounding marriage and the family and '*at* risk', as vulnerable and welfare dependent – a point that both Green and Mitchell develop in Chapters 4 and 11. Becoming a mother is risky in itself, and many other risks surround these young women, such as: uncertainty in relation to close relationships, housing and financial instability. These women must calculate risks in order to protect and achieve their own time and space for leisure, thus creating and re-creating identities that enable them to see themselves as more than (just) 'being a mum'. Leisure as risk is where these mothers engage in situations that offer excitement, exhilaration, something different. The meanings of risk are multiple and intertwined with leisure and escape. As risky leisure appears to be gaining significance as a contemporary form of conspicuous consumption (Rojek, 1995), it is interesting to see how such everyday risk remains a negotiable aspect of women's everyday experience at the public/private interface.

Identity, difference and the calculation of risk

The chapters in this volume report upon and explore the ways that gendered risk characteristics and debates about difference intersect with class, ethnicity and other social factors in situated discourses. Analysis of risk will inevitably spill into other areas of research. Human ability to calculate, reason or even to deny and make contra-judgement in relation to the future, cuts across many aspects of life. It is clear from many of these chapters that young people attach multiple meanings to specific types of bodily risks that they and their peers are exposed to – either physical or social. They also have strategies for managing these risks. In this volume, we draw upon work conducted on young people in a variety of circumstances: on the roads, on the streets, at home, at leisure and at work. Throughout, risk reasoning, calculation and management are being considered. As the grand theorists of risk have reminded us, these small acts of calculation and apparently personal judgement are part of broader macro social processes and global changes in world governance (Crook, 1999; Dean, 1999). Though apparently focusing on young people we are also examining social life in general. Complex risk calculation is apparent in the data drawn upon by Green in Chapter 4, which explores how motherhood is both a source of safety and risk for young mothers working in street prostitution. Women and children are routinely warned to guard against risk, to keep themselves safe and to be cautious of strangers, but for women making a living by selling sex, risk taking with strangers is routine. Focusing upon the experience of prostituted mothers, Green explores the ways in which young women working in street prostitution manage what they perceive to be 'normal, everyday risks'. This chapter draws upon a qualitative case study of the role and importance of motherhood in the lives and identities of a group of young women working in prostitution in the North East of England. In managing their family lives these young women present a challenge to traditionally conceived boundaries between 'work', 'family' and 'home'. Their accounts of everyday risks are interwoven with narratives of motherhood and 'family'. In order to understand such accounts, we must ground them in the specific social and economic contexts in which they are embedded: local spaces and places where risk taking is perceived as part of the 'normal everyday'. The dangers involved, and the personal anxieties are experienced as part of a complex negation of the often conflicting identities of good mother and streetwise prostitute.

This chapter, in particular, highlights the complexity of young people's risk narratives. It explores the inter-related themes of multiple identity and risk management and the risks and benefits attached to crossing the boundaries between the identities of 'risky bodies' and mothers who care. These young women's narratives confirm that they are not passive victims, but rather that they actively engage with both public discourses of 'good mothering' that impact upon their sense of self and identity as mothers, and with discourses of 'fallen women', or 'dirty', street prostitutes.

Simon Pratt and Elizabeth Burn also deal with gender identity in Chapter 14. Here, attention to risk, masculinity and leisure in the context of current integration of football into school education initiatives, is used to address the issue of 'disaffected' young men. Their chapter offers a critique of current uses and constructions of football in England. Whilst presented as educationally enriching, football is supposedly inclusive of class and racial differences. Yet, the authors argue, this discourse of football appears to be actively re-establishing traditional forms of hegemonic masculinity. The chapter draws upon a range of data, including media coverage and research into school practice. It explores how class, race and gender are embedded in a football culture and how young male identities are affected by developments in a society where risk-taking is increasingly a part of young men's experiences.

Research on masculinity cannot ignore 'risk-taking' amongst young men and women. Pratt and Burn examine how cultural definitions of hegemonic masculinities are both maintained and reconstituted through the 'ritualised' performance of football and its place in the formal and informal school curriculum. Young men and women are not cultural dopes subject to such constructions but, rather, actively define and negotiate, oppose or resist such received artefacts. This chapter points out the complexity of risk management for young people and the schools involved. Mills (2001) has suggested that boys take risks by resisting dominant masculinising practices such as football. By drawing football into the curriculum, schools run the risk of excluding girls, female teachers and some boys. In relation to gender, then, this chapter also examines the location of risk within particular social structures of inequality, gender, class and ethnicity and socially contextualises risk.

Risk, place, leisure and pleasure

In putting risk in context, a number of papers in this collection focus on the social space of risk and problematise traditional understandings of leisure. Space and place are important dimensions of both risk and leisure. Young people in the Townville study had an acute awareness of risky and safe places to play, walk and hang-out. They were aware of space that was 'inside' and 'outside' of their own community. This issue is explored in Anne Foreman's chapter which is based around a community action programme to re-design space. In Chapter 9 Foreman describes Townville's efforts to re-design leisure spaces in relation to risk. For communities such as Townville redefinition of space and community has become part of what might be considered post-industrial local policy development. Foreman's data illustrates how concerns for risk and safety become intimately linked to the re-defining of community. In the study of risk from which this chapter draws, risk analysis became a resource for reflection and debate about the nature of community and community identity. The reputation of the district as 'risky', unsafe or dangerous was addressed in local planning and regeneration strategy. Visions of new urban spaces emerged with new dictates for citizen's participation. As Foreman illustrates, public space became a battleground for competing attempts to manage risk.

Seabrook and Green's chapter also addresses the issue of 'inside' and 'outside', bringing space, identity and time into focus. In Chapter 8, they examine the ways in which girls, who belonged to a local girls group, managed and/or reduced risks. The data suggests that the girls encounter and manage risk on a daily basis. Constructions of time and space are based upon, not simply the structural design of spaces, but are also a focus for feelings, fears and anxieties depending upon where they are situated in the locality. Such feelings and emotions are described as embedded in local discourses and knowledge, which are linked to gender and power. In these accounts, risk is depicted as an organising principle of daily routines and risk dictates young women's diverse use of time and space. The girls perceived certain times and spaces as risky and thus their own position/place in time and space were continually under self-surveillance and negotiation. Being perceived as streetwise or a part of the 'in' crowd could coincide with simultaneously being perceived to be 'outside' by others, seen as tarts or 'slappers', for example. Being seen 'outside', especially after dark, was to court and embody risk and danger for themselves and for the extended families' collective honour and reputation of women. This leisure, space and representations of respectability as located in women's bodies theme, is also explored in Watson's chapter. Being *out* and expressing non-conformity to traditionally 'respectable' female roles and dress could mean being *in* with the boys but made them visible to the male gaze. Risk and place were features of a dynamic status negotiation that was multidimensional and fluid.

In Chapter 7, John Tulloch explores another area of space and risk, risk perception during train travel. Travelling on train is between spaces, literally neither here nor there. In the chapter on Youth, Leisure Travel and Fear of Crime, Tulloch draws upon study of fear of crime among three generations of respondents (teenagers, parents of teenagers, older people) in Australia. The data here is primarily qualitative and focuses on 'teenagers' experiences of risks on trains. It also attempts to provide in-depth insights into how people construct their fear of crime as *situated* everyday experience. As such this data presents a study of 'lay criminological' knowledge, using teenage concerns about leisure-time travel after dark. Young people are the most likely victims of crime. Even though older people may fear teenagers and young men in particular, teenagers themselves are acutely aware of the reality of teenage aggression to other teenagers. Teenagers (especially girls) often fear to travel by train at night but, unlike older people, tend to travel anyway. This means that like the girls in Townville, many devise strategies for making themselves feel safer at night.

Due to the greater likelihood of using public space for leisure activities, or for travelling to them, young people in this Australian study often went out alone, even when they did not feel safe. Young women were more fearful of unpredictable 'stranger danger' than males, being frightened of sexual and physical assault from men of all ages, and were subject to more endemic sexual harassment. Like many of the other young women in the research reported upon in this collection, these girls adopted a wide range of surveillance and avoidance strategies when travelling. However, they accepted this as routine and by and large did not feel disempowered from travelling by these fears. Again place is important here. The young people had different experiences in different parts of New South Wales; constructing different 'landscapes' coloured by different perceptions of risk. These respondents also had various solutions to the problems of risk.

Deborah Lupton, in Chapter 2, takes up the notion of risk and pleasure in relation to travelling in cars. Drawing upon a qualitative study of Sydneysiders' experiences of driving with a particular focus on 'road rage'/aggressive driving, she examines narratives about driving experiences and the pleasures of risk taking. Discourses on young people and driving, both in popular and official forums, tend to represent young drivers (particularly those who are male), as risk-taking, inexperienced, impatient, even reckless and enamoured of speed at the sake of safety. The qualitative data presented here suggests that many young women, as well as young men, experience pleasure by 'taking risks' when driving, engaging in such behaviours as speeding and driving aggressively. Both young women and young men appeared to enjoy the sense of freedom, mobility, independence and often the exhilaration they felt when driving, particularly when not impeded by city traffic. The chapter adds to a very limited body of work that examines the place of driving in youth cultures and also adds to our understanding of the relationship between risk and pleasure. The research suggests that aggressive approaches to driving may be becoming less a product of gender than of position in the life-course. Driving in such a manner is not necessarily now limited to notions of hegemonic masculinities privileging risk-taking and aggression, but is being incorporated into discourses and practices related to particular kinds of femininities as young Australian women take them up.

Chapter 10 also focuses on the pleasure to be taken in risk. Bunton, Crawshaw and Green draw upon data from the UK 'Townville' study to explore some of the ways in which girls and boys, and young men and women perceive and manage risk in their communities. They draw upon a survey of school children as well as qualitative data. Like Lupton, they question a somewhat 'received wisdom' assumption that male risk taking is more significant than female risk taking. By examining the type of risk taken and the social circumstances of risk, they argue that the relationship between gender and risk is far from straightforward. Girls and young women frequently excel in risk taking in particular areas, albeit that the consequences of such behaviour are more punitive in terms of damage to their reputations than to those of their male peers. The association of risk taking with 'boyish' or 'laddish' behaviour reflects, perhaps a broader male bias in studies of youthful behaviour patterns.

All chapters in this volume, in one way or another, attempt to locate risk socially and culturally. They do this by adopting a variety of methodologies and epistemological stances. The social study of risk has to date, offered little coherence in methodological or theoretical approach and, whilst focusing on youth and leisure, this volume represents a diversity of both approaches. In our view, the studies included are representative of a range of contemporary work that is attempting to ground the more abstract theorising of risk within empirical study and 'middle-range' theorising. Although the volume is divided into three broad sections or themes, these themes are also referred to in chapters placed under different headings. For example, while Mitchell's chapter on Risk, Motherhood and Play Spaces and Watson's chapter on young mothers' experiences of motherhood and leisure are located in the part on Leisure Pursuits and Gendered Identity, both discussions also refer to issues of space and place. In our view the theoretical ideas and new data contained in this collection make a key contribution to debates within and across a broad range of academic disciplines, whilst also contributing to the expanding field of youth studies.

Note

1. We note that the study itself forms part of a broader 'risk management strategy'. In the early discussions of the project with local government officials we were made aware of the ubiquity of risk discourse. Young people were identified as a risky population in need of local policy intervention.

References

Abbott-chapman, J. and Denholm, C. (2001) 'Adolescents' risk activities, risk hierarchies and the influence is Religiosity'. *Journal of Youth Studies*, Vol. 4, No. 3, pp. 279–297.

Alaszewski, A. and Horlick-Jones, T. (2002) *Risk And Health: Review of current Research And Identification of Areas for further Research.* University of Kent; Centre for Health Service Studies.

Alexander, J. C. (1996) 'Critical reflections on "reflexive modernization" '. *Theory, Culture and Society*, Vol. 13, No. 4, pp. 133–8.

Beck, U. (1991) *Ecological Enlightenment: Essays on the Politics of the Risk Society.* Amherst, NY: Prometheus Books.

Beck, U. (1992) *Risk Society: Towards a New Modernity.* London: Sage.

Beck, U. (1994a) *Ecological Politics in an Age of Risk.* Cambridge: Polity.

Beck, U. (1994b) *Ecological Enlightenment: Essays in the Politics of the Risk Society.* Atlantic Highlands, NJ: Humanities Press.

Beck, U. (1999) *World Risk Society.* Cambridge: Polity Press.

Beck, U. and Beck-Gernsheim, E. (1996) 'Individualization and "precarious freedoms": Perspectives and controversies of a subject-orientated sociology' in Heelas, P., Lash, S. and Morris, P. (eds) *Detraditionalization: Critical Reflections on Authority and Identity.* Oxford: Blackwell.

Berkman, L. F., Glass, T., Brissette, I. and Seeman T. E. (2000) 'From social integration to health: Durkheim in the new millenium'. *Social Science and Medicine*, Vol. 51, pp. 843–57.

Bloor, M. (1995a) 'A user's guide to contrasting theories of HIV-related risk behaviour' in Gabe, J. (ed.) *Medicine, Health and Risk: Sociology Beyond Structuralism and Hermeneutics.* London: Harvester Wheatsheaf.

Bloor, M. (1995b) *The Sociology of HIV Transmission.* London: Sage.

Bordo, S. (1993) *Unbearable Weight: Feminism, Western Culture and the Body.* Berkley: University of California Press.

Brownlie, J. (2001) 'The "being-risky" child: governing childhood and sexual risk'. *Sociology*, Vol. 35, No. 2, pp. 519–37.

Cranny-Francis, A. (1995) *The Body in the Text.* Melbourne: University Press.

Crook, S. (1999) 'Ordering risks' in Lupton, D. (ed.) *Risk and Sociocultural Theory: New Directions and Perspective.* Cambridge: Cambridge University Press.

Davis, K. (ed.) (1997) *Embodied Practices: Feminist Perspectives on the Body.* London: Sage.

Dean, M. (1999) 'Risks: calculable and incalculable' in Lupton, D. (ed.) *Risk and Sociocultural Theory: New Directions and Perspectives.* Cambridge: Cambridge University Press.

Douglas, M. (1986) *Risk Acceptability According to the Social Sciences.* London: Routledge.

Douglas, M. (1992) *Risk and Blame: Essays in Cultural Theory*. London: Routledge.

Douglas, M. and Wildavsky, A. (1982) *Risk and Culture*. Oxford: Blackwell.

Elliott, A. (2002) 'Beck's sociology of risk: a critical assessment'. *Sociology*, Vol. 36, No. 2, pp. 293–315.

European Commission (2000) Communication from the Commission on the Precautionary Principle, Com (2000) 1, Brussels.

European Environment Agency (2001) *Late Lessons from Early Warning: the Precautionary Principle 1996–2000*, European Environment Agency Issue Report No. 22. Luxembourg: Office for Official Publications of the European Communities.

Foucault, M. (1982) 'The subject and power' in Dreyfus, H. and Rabinow, P. (eds), *Michel Foucault*: Beyond structuralism and hermeneutics: with an afterthought by Michel Foucault. Brighton: Harvester Press.

Foucault, M. (1984) *The Use of Pleasures*. New York: Pantheon.

Foucault, M. (1986) *The Care of the Self*. New York: Pantheon.

Fox, N. (1999) Post-modern reflections on risk, 'hazards' and life choices, in Lupton, D. (1999b) (ed.) *Risk & Sociocultural Theory: New Directions & Perspectives*. Cambridge: University Press.

France (1998) 'Why should we care?': young people, citizenship and questions of social responsibility in *Journal of Youth Studies*, Vol. 1, No. 1, February.

Furlong, A. and Cartmel, F. (1997) *Young People and Social Change: Individualisation and Risk in Late Modernity*. Buckingham: Open University Press.

Giddens, A. (1991) *Modernity and Self-Identity: Self and Society in the Late Modern Age*. Cambridge: Polity Press.

Gillick, M. R. (1984) 'Health promotion, jogging, and the pursuit of the moral life'. *Journal of Health, Politics, Policy and Law*, Vol. 9, No. 3, pp. 369–84.

Gilman, S. (1993) 'Touch, sexuality and disease' in Bynum, W. and Porter, R. (eds) *Medicine and the Five Senses*. Cambridge: Cambridge University Press.

Green, E. (1998) 'Women doing friendship': an analysis of women's leisure as a site of identity construction, empowerment and resistance. *Leisure Studies*, Vol. 17, pp. 171–85.

Green, E. (2001) *'Leaky Bodies or Drying Husks?' Menopause, Health and Embodied Experience*. Brighton: Leisure Studies Association.

Green, E., Hebron, S. and Woodward, D. (1990) *Women's Leisure, What Leisure?* London: Macmillan.

Holland, J., Ramazanoglu, C., Sharpe, S. and Thompson, R. (1998) *The Male in the Head: Young people, Heterosexuality and Power*. London: The Tufnell Press.

Howson, A. (1998) 'Embodied obligation: the female body and health surveillance' in Nettleton, S. and Watson, J. (eds) *The Body in Everyday Life*. London: Routledge.

Jenks, C. (1996) *Childhood*. London: Routledge.

Jones, A. (1993) ' "Defending the border", men's bodies and vulnerability'. *Cultural Studies from Birmingham*, No. 2, pp. 77–123.

Kelly, P. (1998) *Risk and the Regulation of Youth(ful) Identities in an Age of Manufactured Uncertainty*, Unpublished PhD, Deakin University, Faculty of Education, March.

Kelly, P. (2000) 'Youth as an artefact of expertise: problematising the practice of Youth Studies in an age of uncertainty'. *Journal of Youth Studies*, Vol. 3, No. 3, pp. 301–15.

Lasch, S., Szerszynski, B. and Wynne, B. (eds) (1994) *Risk, Environment and Modernity*. London: Sage Publications.

Lasch, S. and Urry, J. (1994) *Economies of Signs & Space*, London: Sage.
Lawy, R. (2002) 'Risky stories: youth identities, learning and everyday risk'. *Journal of Youth Studies*, Vol. 5, No. 4, pp. 407–23.
Lupton, D. (1999a) *Risk*. London: Routledge.
Lupton, D. (ed.) (1999b) *Risk and Sociocultural Theory: New Directions and Perspectives*. Cambridge: Cambridge University Press.
Lupton, D. and Tulloch, J. (1998) 'The adolescent "unfinished body", reflexivity and HIV/AIDS'. *Body and Society*, Vol. 4, No. 2, pp. 19–34.
Martin, E. (1989) *The Woman in the Body: A Cultural Analysis of Reproduction*. Milton Keynes: Open University Press.
Massey, D. (1994) *Space, Place and Gender*. Blackwell: Oxford.
McRobbie, A. (1980) 'Settling accounts with subcultures: a feminist critique'. *Screen Education*, Vol. 10, No. 4, pp. 127–42.
McRobbie, A. (1996) 'Different youthful subjectivities' in Chambers, I. and Curtis, L. (eds) *The Post-Colonial Question: Common Skies, Divided Horizons*. London: Routledge.
Miles, S. (1998) *Consumerism as a Way of Life*. London: Sage.
Mills, M. (2001) 'Pushing it to the max: interrogating the risky business of being a boy' in Martino, W. and Meyenn, B. (eds) *What about the Boys?* Buckingham: Open University Press.
Nettleton, S. (1997) 'Governing the risky self: how to become healthy, wealthy and wise' in Peterson, A. and Bunton, R. (eds) *Foucault, Health and Medicine*. London: Routledge.
Nettleton, S. and Watson, J. (1998) *The Body in Everyday Life*, London: Routledge.
Office of the Deputy Prime Minister (20 A New Commitment to Neighbourhood Renewal: A National Strategy Action Plan. www.neighbourhood.gov.uk
O'Malley, P. (1999) 'Governmentality and the risk society'. *Economy and Society*, Vol. 28, No. 1, pp. 138–48.
Petersen, A. (1996) 'Risk and the regulated self: the discourse of health'. *Australian and New Zealand Journal of Sociology*, Vol. 32, No. 1, pp. 44–57.
Petersen. A. and Lupton, D. (1996) *The New Public Health: Health and Self in the Age of Risk*. London: Sage Publications.
Plant, M. and Plant, M. (1992) *The Risk Takers*. London: Routledge.
Rhodes, T. (1997) 'Risk theory in epidemic times: sex, drugs and the social organisation of "risk behaviour"'. *Sociology of Health and Illness*, Vol. 19, No. 2, pp. 208–27.
Rojek, C. (1995) *Decentring Leisure: Rethinking Leisure Theory*. London: Sage.
Rose, N. (1996) 'Re-figuring the territory of government'. *Economy and Society*, Vol. 25, No. 3, pp. 327–56.
Scott, S., Jackson, S. and Backett Milburn, K. (1998) 'Swings and roundabouts: risk anxiety in the everyday world of children'. *Sociology*, Vol. 32, pp. 689–705.
Scraton, S. and Watson, B. (1998) 'Gendered cities: women and public leisure space in the "postmodern" city'. *Leisure Studies*, Vol. 17, pp. 123–37.
Seymour, W. (1998) *Remaking the Body: Rehabilitation and Change*. London and New York: Routledge.
Shilling, C. (1993) *The Body and Social Theory*. London: Sage Publications.
Skeggs, B. (1999) 'Matter out of place: visibility and sexualities in leisure spaces'. *Leisure Studies*, Vol. 18, No. 3, pp. 213–32.

Stanko, B. (1997) 'Safety talk: conceptualising women's risk assessment as a "technology of the soul" '. *Theoretical Criminology*, Vol. 1, No. 4, pp. 479–99.

Taite, G. (1995) 'Shaping the "at-risk youth": risk, governmentality and the Finn Report'. *Discourse*, Vol. 16, No. 1, pp. 123–34.

Townsend, P., Phillipmore, P. and Beattie, A. (1998) *Health and Deprivation: Inequality and the North*. London: Routledge.

Turner, B. S. (1994) *Orientalism, Postmodernism and Globalization*, London: Routledge.

Valentine, G. (1989) 'The geography of women's fear'. *Area*, Vol. 21, No. 4, pp. 385–90.

Valentine, G. (1992) 'Images of danger: women's sources of Information about the spatial distributions of male violence'. *Area*, Vol. 24, pp. 22–9.

Walkerdine, V. (1997) *Daddy's Girl: Young Girls and Popular Culture*. Basingstoke: Macmillan Press.

Watson, J. (1998) 'Running around like a lunatic: Colin's body and the case of male embodiment' in Nettleton, S. and Watson, J. (eds) *The Body in Everyday Life*. London: Routledge.

Watson, J. (2002) *Male Bodies: Health, Culture and Identity*. Buckinghamshire: Open University Press.

Wearing, B. (1998) *Leisure and Feminist Theory*. London: Sage.

Wynne, B. (1994) 'May the sheep safely graze? A reflexive view of the expert-lay knowledge divide' in Lasch, S., Szerszynski, B. and Wynne, B. (eds) *Risk, Environment and Modernity: Towards a New Ecology*. London: Sage Publications.

Part I

Danger, Uncertainty and Pleasure: The Management of Everyday Risks

2
Pleasure, Aggression and Fear: The Driving Experience of Young Sydneysiders

Deborah Lupton

Introduction

Discourses on young people and driving, both in popular and official forums, tend to represent young drivers – particularly those who are male – as risk-taking: reckless, inexperienced, impatient and enamoured of speed at the sake of safety. These characterisations have taken on a new aspect with the emergence of the phenomenon of 'road rage'. The term 'road rage' is used somewhat loosely in popular discourse. It is used to refer to a wide range of driving behaviours, from the fairly innocuous and common practices of tooting one's horn or flashing one's lights to display displeasure at others' actions, to the more dangerous practices of tailgating or suddenly swerving one's car in front of another vehicle and at the most extreme including assaults or homicides upon other motorists or other road users as a result of anger at an incident that has occurred while using the road.

The term emerged in the news media in the mid-1990s, generating a public debate over the ways in which drivers use their vehicles in an aggressive or dangerous manner to express the emotions of frustration and anger. In the research I carried out examining representations of road rage in the Sydney press (Lupton, 2001), I noticed that accounts tended to portray it as perpetrated by young male drivers above all social groups. Thus, for example, the 'typical road rager' identified in an article published in one Sydney newspaper was described as a 'Young male aged 18–24. Liking for speed. Probable convictions for driving offences. Extremely aggressive driving style. Impatient with other motorists' ('Daily Telegraph', 30 October 1996). Importantly, however, it was also suggested in these media that any driver could potentially be a 'road rager' by losing control over her or his emotions at the wheel. Indeed, one dominant theme of accounts appearing in Sydney newspapers was that young women were becoming equally as aggressive and risk-taking on the road as their male counterparts.

These media accounts have drawn upon reports such as the market research on Australians' driving behaviours conducted by a local motorists' association (NRMA, 1996). The research, using data from focus groups, noted that many young women, as well as young men, described the pleasure of 'taking risks' when driving, engaging in such behaviours as speeding and driving aggressively. Both young women and young men said that they enjoyed the sense of freedom, mobility, independence and often the exhilaration they felt when driving, particularly when not impeded by city traffic. Their idea of a 'good driver' was someone who drove fast and aggressively while maintaining control of the car. This research suggests that such an aggressive approach to driving may be becoming less a product of gender than of position in the life-course. That is, it implies that driving in such a manner is not necessarily now limited to notions of hegemonic masculinities privileging risk-taking and aggression, but is being incorporated into discourses and practices related to particular kinds of femininities as they are taken up by young Australian women.

While such studies of driving provide useful data, very little in-depth socio-cultural research has been published in the academic literature concerning the phenomenon of 'road rage'/aggressive driving, or even of the driving experience more generally. Despite the prominence of the car in western societies as a major vehicle of transport, its dominance of the urban streetscape and more than that, its importance as a commodity bearing a variety of symbolic meanings (Stallabrass, 1996; Graves-Brown, 1997; Lupton, 1999), there is a conspicuous lack of writing in sociology or cultural studies on the subject of the car and the driving experience. Further, very little detailed research has sought to examine the place of driving in youth cultures, despite the importance to many young people of the car as a medium of self-expression, risk-taking and rebellion (Groombridge, 1998).

This chapter draws upon a qualitative study of Sydneysiders' experiences of driving which had a particular focus on 'road rage'/aggressive driving. The research, conducted in 2000, involved one-to-one interviews carried out with 77 people from a wide range of socio-economic circumstances and ages.[1] Interviewees were encouraged to recount narratives about their driving experiences which allowed for the exploration of how they related to their cars and viewed themselves as drivers and in relation to other drivers. Specific questions towards the end of the interview explored the participants' experiences of and opinions about aggressive driving behaviours. Interviews took place in participants' own homes, at their convenience. All interviewees were regular drivers (for the purpose of the study, defined as driving at least once a fortnight).

Forty of the 77 participants were from socio-economically disadvantaged suburbs and 37 from advantaged suburbs (40 interviews were completed but three were found to be unusable because of tape malfunction). Somewhat more men (42) than women (35) were interviewed. The age range of the interviewees was from 18 to 87, with 32 aged under 40 and 45 aged over 40. A total of 15 people were aged between 18 and 25 years (eight women and seven men). Table 2.1 gives the demographic details of these young people. This chapter draws on the interviews with these young drivers to explore the ways in which youth and gender intersect in the experience of and meanings given to driving. In what follows, I examine three rather different aspects of the driving experience for the young drivers: pleasure, aggression and fear.

Table 2.1   Demographic details of the young drivers

From advantaged suburbs
Jessica, 19, university student, some university education, Anglo-Celtic ethnicity
Nicole, 24, accounts clerk, completed final year of high school, Anglo-Celtic ethnicity
Peter, 19, university student, some university education, Taiwanese ethnicity
Tony, 21, car detailer and driver, completed final year of high school, Anglo-Celtic/Maltese ethnicity
Johanna, 24, e-business manager, completed university degree, German ethnicity
Luke, 19, university student, some university education, Anglo-Celtic ethnicity
Sarah, 19, university student, some university education, Anglo-Celtic ethnicity
Emma, 18, university student, some university education, Anglo-Celtic ethnicity

From disadvantaged suburbs
Jason, 24, hotel manager, completed final year of high school, Anglo-Celtic ethnicity
Danielle, 24, childcare assistant, final year of high school completed, Anglo-Celtic/Maltese ethnicity
Mike, 19, university student, some university education, Greek ethnicity
Atyen, 23, university student/administration worker, some university education, Turkish ethnicity
Mohammad, 24, unemployed, completed less than final year of high school, Iraqi ethnicity
Joe, 21, car mechanic, completed less than final year of high school, Assyrian ethnicity
Maria, 25, social worker, completed university degree, East Timorese ethnicity

Pleasure

All the interviewees were asked whether they enjoyed driving. The majority of them, regardless of age, said that they did. When asked to explain what they found enjoyable, most interviewees described such attributes as freedom and the opportunity to relax inside one's own special space, cocooned, as it were, from others. Driving, therefore, represented not only a means of transport, but a way to exert control over one's environment.

It is not surprising, given the lack of freedom many young people face, that these types of explanations were also evident among the young people who were interviewed. When talking about driving and the cars they owned or used to do so, most of the young people described the importance of freedom, the opportunity to control their travelling environment, to move about at will and avoid the vagaries and inconveniences of public transport. While both young men and young women said that they enjoyed driving, it was the young men who went into most detail about the pleasures afforded them by driving. Young women tended to discuss the convenience of driving, the flexibility it offered them and the independence it gave them. As Johanna, a 24-year-old business manager from an advantaged suburb (German ethnicity) commented:

> I like being able to drive because it gives me my freedom. It gets you places quickly. It means you don't have to tackle public transport.

Several young men went further in their articulation of their enjoyment of driving and of car culture generally. One example is Mike, a 19-year-old university student living in a disadvantaged suburb (Greek ethnicity). Mike had very recently purchased the car of his dreams, a Subaru WRX. When asked if he enjoys driving, Mike replied that 'I love it'. He explained his pleasure in the following terms:

> Because driving first of all is like a sense of freedom. I mean, you're in your house all day long, trapped whatever. You know that you've got [your car] in the driveway, it's yours, you've got the keys to it, you own it. So I mean, as soon as you jump in it you know it's there. I love driving because I can feel the car – you know, I can control it, I can go wherever I want, whenever I want. I can do whatever speeds I want. I can break the law if I want, you know. I just, I really enjoy driving, yeah. 'Specially when you've got a decent car.'

Tony, a 21-year-old car detailer and professional driver living in an advantaged suburb (Anglo/Maltese ethnicity), talked about the sense of release and opportunity to take a break from the pace of his life that driving offered him. For Tony, the space of his car moving from one location to another represented a liminal space, in which nothing was required of him. As he said:

> It's a release sometimes, just to be able to get onto the road and put some music on and just chill out and be in between doing things in your life. It just gives you a bit of time to prepare your thinking or your thoughts for what's about to happen next.

For Peter, a 19-year-old university student living in an advantaged sub-urb (Taiwanese ethnicity), it was the sense of control as well as the solitude offered by driving that he most enjoyed: 'I think it's just the pure control, and you're by yourself.'

Driving, as these comments suggest, while serving a predominantly utilitarian activity as a means of transport, also served a leisure or relax-ation function in itself for several interviewees. For the young people, most of whom still lived at home with their family of origin, the space of the car allowed them time to themselves, when they could play their own music as loudly as they wanted without interference from parents or others and just be by themselves. They saw their cars as offering them 'pure control' over their environment.

Aggression

Many interviewees singled out young men as the subgroup most likely to behave aggressively and to engage in risky driving. This characterisation was evident across the whole interviewee group, including younger as well as older participants. For example, Joe, 21 and an engine recondi-tioner from a disadvantaged suburb (Assyrian ethnicity), said that he thought that 'younger people, about my age, maybe older' were more likely to be aggressive and to take risks while driving 'because they're basically show-offs'. Peter commented that: 'Young people at night they are very aggressive. So I don't know whether it is the alcohol or what is causing them, but they do drive fast and they scream and they yell and they rage.'

Jason, a 24-year-old hotel manager from a disadvantaged suburb (Anglo-Celtic ethnicity) asserted that when it came to aggressive driv-ing: 'P-platers[2] are the worst.' Jason went on to admit that he himself engaged in aggressive driving when he was younger: 'Like I was one as well, so I'm guilty – guilty as charged!' He said that now he was 24 he no longer was the 'hoon' (delinquent) he was at 18. But later in the interview, when asked whether he had ever engaged in road rage, Jason recounted a recent incident in which he had been an aggressor, engaging in threatening behaviour after being disgruntled by another motorist's actions:

> A cab like nearly took me out off a roundabout coming home from work, so I caught up to him, pulled in front of him, pulled him over, tapped on his window, asked him to wind it down. I tried to explain to him what he did, and all he kept saying was "Oh, I'm sorry I'm sorry, I'm not from this place", you know. I said that wasn't the point, I said, you know, "We were on a roundabout and you cut me off. That's the whole thing. It doesn't matter if you're not from here or whatever." And he ended up just driving back off again. So yeah, guilty.

It is evident from Jason's account that he feels as if he has a right to his space on the road, and that someone who violates this space is regarded as in the wrong. He displays little chagrin at his behaviour, recounting his story in such a way as to represent the other driver as culpable and therefore deserving of his aggression.

Two other young men recounted experiences in which they had been involved in road rage. Mike, for example, said that he often felt angry and aggressive when driving. He went on to recount in detail an incident in which he had retaliated aggressively:

> Another car, like, they were driving and threw a bottle out on the front of the road, and it was glass and shattered, and I had to swerve just so I wouldn't get it on my tyres. And when they did that I went really close to them and wound my window down and said, "If yous [sic] are smart," – you know, I was by myself and there was four of them – I said, "If yous [sic] are smart", you know, "yous [sic] funny clowns pull over and I'll break all your heads", you know? And I grabbed a car lock like I was trying to hit their car for nuts and I went really crazy. I was telling them to pull out and you know. They were driving along as well. And they were just going like that, but they wouldn't pull over. And I pulled over a couple of times and then I catch [sic] up to them 'cause I wanted to pull over, I really wanted them to pull over. I would have just run up and started trying to hit the driver, and then take his friends on. I probably would have got myself hurt or, you know, bashed or in trouble. But some people don't think, you know, of the consequences and you just want to

attack. Because I mean it's stupid what they did and I mean, why throw the bottle out in front of me, you know? They know it's going to piss me off and drive me psycho.

As was outlined above, Mike is extremely proud of his new Subaru, the source of strong feelings of freedom and power over his life. In his account of his aggressive behaviour, his response to the other young men's action in throwing the bottle in front of his car (it is difficult to know whether this was a deliberate aggressive act or simply thoughtlessness on the part of these other men) is presented as a completely just response. These men threatened his precious car, and Mike was stirred to rage, going 'crazy' and 'psycho' in his desire for vengeance.

Like Mike, Tony derives a great sense of pleasure from driving, and indeed works with cars professionally. When questioned about aggressive or risky driving, he admitted that two or three years ago he had been 'quite an angry young man' who had frequently engaged in aggressive acts while driving:

> You know, [I would] just pursue anyone who took after me, and I have done it before in the past, but my way of doing it was just to drive fast after people and stuff like that, and just scare them. I never really wanted to do it – it was just more of a bully tactic, but not any more. I don't feel the need for it. It's unnecessary.

When asked why he had behaved in this manner, Tony replied:

> I felt great. I felt empowered by it. It made me feel a bit stronger. But then after doing it I just thought that it was a bit silly and that I could have hurt someone and they could have done something back.

Tony is candid in admitting that aggressive driving practices, at least in the past, contributed to his enjoyment of driving. Intimidating other drivers by retaliating for what is seen to be an incursion upon his use of the road gave him a thrilling sense of power and strength.

The three young men quoted above, therefore, display attitudes to aggressive driving that fit the stereotype of the reckless young male driver. Although like the others interviewed for the study they were reluctant to condone aggressive or risky driving, these men presented a narrative that portrayed their aggression as a justified response to the actions of others. It is perhaps no coincidence that two of these men (Jason and Mike) are from disadvantaged suburbs; and while the third

(Tony) lives in a more salubrious area, he is employed in manual labour and did not go to university. It is likely that, like many other working-class men (Connell, 1995; Canaan, 1996), they tend to seek empowerment and a sense of identity through pursuits and encounters linked to displays of power and masculinity through aggression and violence.

It is important to emphasise, however, that the four other young men in the study (two from advantaged and two from disadvantaged suburbs) did not represent themselves in such a manner, choosing to portray themselves as more emotionally contained drivers who did not give way to feelings of anger and frustration by acting aggressively. Joe, for example, described himself as a 'cautious' and 'fairly good' driver: 'I don't speed or anything like that.' When asked if he ever felt angry or aggressive when driving, he admits that he sometimes did: 'Like when I say I get cut off or – yeah I do get angry. But I don't go causing a fight over it. It's just idiots. I usually let them go.' He had been involved in car culture for several years, working as a mechanic after leaving school. But he noted that 'you just get sick of [cars] when you're around them all day, every day', and therefore he did not feel the need to 'show-off' when driving. Joe described people who engage in road rage as 'stupid', adding that 'there's no need for it'. Peter, for his part, described himself as a 'patient' and 'average driver', who rarely loses his temper on the roads: 'I mean I'm not a road rager and I don't like people who are raging. You know, I probably felt a bit angry sometimes but not as much that I like to get out there and bash that person.' He went on to add that he thought of road ragers as 'people who are rough and tough and I don't think they're nice people at all'.

What of the young women interviewed? It is notable that not one woman in the study, whatever her age, admitted to having engaged in 'road rage' or aggressive driving, although several women did acknowledge that they sometimes took risks, such as speeding. Most women also admitted to feelings of anger or frustration, although they emphasised that these feelings were not expressed overtly, as aggressive action, but rather were internalised. Several women interviewed, including young women, argued that men were more likely to lose their temper and become aggressive while driving than were women. Maria, a 25-year-old social worker from a disadvantaged suburb (East-Timorese ethnicity), for example, said that she noticed impatience and aggression more often in male than female drivers, including her own relatives:

> I've had experiences where, you know, I've been driving with a male friend and something has happened and they've wanted to get out

of the car and harass the person in front of them. Like my male cousins, I've seen them on the roads and I've seen how they can try and intimidate other drivers because they did something wrong.

As argued above, some research has suggested that young women were taking up such behaviours. Although a small number of older intervie-wees claimed that young women were becoming more aggressive and risk-taking in their driving, none of the young women themselves admitted to these behaviours. Emma, an 18-year-old university student (Anglo-Celtic) from an advantaged suburb, noted that: 'I know that there's a general perception that young female drivers have become more aggressive', but went on to say she herself did not behave aggres-sively. She said that she never toots her horn or responds in an aggres-sive manner, although she admitted to speeding sometimes:

> I generally raise my hands in disbelief and sometimes will say some-thing out loud. But that's about the extent of it. I don't toot my horn or anything like that.

At the most, women might toot their horn or flash their lights to display anger. Jessica, a 19-year-old university student from an advantaged suburb (Anglo-Celtic), described an incident of anger towards another driver:

> I was on my way to uni and I was really late, and I was going up the road behind [suburb name]. And there's a lane there – this sounds really stupid now – but there's a lane there that turns right, but you're not allowed to turn right unless it's in specific hours. And this person was just blatantly ignoring the hours and just waiting there to turn, and I was so late. No one would let me in because everyone saw what was happening. So I was flashing [my headlights] and I was getting cross then.

Jessica went on to say:

> I think like aggression, if you get a fright or aggression, if someone really does the wrong thing, its okay to a point, but obviously the peo-ple that get out and start screaming and yelling and bashing on win-dows and stuff, I mean that's ridiculous. I mean, there's never any justification for that. But, you know, I can understand getting a fright and getting cross about it. Well, I mean, I can see how it happens, but I think that it's just like anything. Like you have to control yourself.

Like the traffic's horrible and driving people do, do stupid things but it just happens, so it's not really an excuse.

As these comments suggest, for the young women in this study at least, aggressive and risk-taking driving was not regarded as appropriate, as part of their own constellation of driving practices. Like the non-aggressive young men interviewed, these women valued self-control over the open displaying of emotions such as anger and frustration, and condemned displays of aggression or violence.

Fear

Of the small minority (five interviewees) across the whole interviewee group who said that they did not enjoy driving, all but one were women. These women did not fall into a particular age, ethnicity or socio-economic group. What they shared was a representation of the self as a nervous (but not necessarily incompetent) driver, prone to small accidents or lapses of judgement. While more confident drivers seemed to feel able to laugh off their indiscretions, these women considered them to be emblematic of their negative driving experiences. They were also more likely than others to see driving as a dangerous activity. Danielle, a 24-year-old female childcare assistant (Anglo/Maltese, disadvantaged suburb), said, for example, that she disliked driving because:

I just think, it's just a scary thing to do really. I just think maybe because I've had a few accidents. I ran up the back of things when I was younger. I ran into a pylon in a shopping centre – I reversed into it. So I just think, you know, those sort of slip-ups if I was out on the road and did it then I could endanger my life. So I don't enjoy driving. So many people die from driving. They weren't at fault, like the other person's crashed into them or whatever else. So I guess it's just sort of – to me, like you're taking your life into your own hands every time you step behind the wheel.

Danielle was one of the few interviewees of the entire participant group who discussed the dangers of driving – the risk of a car accident causing serious injury or death. When talking about the negative aspects of driving, nearly every other participant identified such aspects as the stress and frustration of sitting in traffic jams, or the cost of cars and petrol, but rarely did they raise the issues of injury or death, even though they recounted having been a participant in or witness of road accidents.

Danielle had also experienced verbal abuse while driving:

> I get hollered at sometimes – like I got hollered at the other week for something, and called a stupid bitch. I was pulling out of somewhere and I was taking my time to do it, and as I went out, the car came out behind me and around it and [the driver] said 'stupid bitch!' or something, and I wasn't doing anything wrong.

This young woman's views on driving might be contrasted with those of a young man of a similar age, ethnicity and driving experience, Tony, who was quoted above referring to his enjoyment of driving and the 'release' it offers him. Yet Tony also admitted that 'I've had some terrible driving experiences.' In one of these, which occurred three years prior to the interview, he had been involved not merely in a minor accident, as had the young woman, but a serious accident involving a crash with a taxi. Although Tony was not injured, his car, which was brand new, was written off. Tony admitted that the accident was his fault, caused by careless driving. While he was shaken and angry with himself for a while afterwards, his confidence in and enjoyment of driving have not been undermined. In fact, his working life continues to revolve around cars and driving.

It is likely that gendered ideas about driving are influencing the ways in which this young woman and man have reacted to their negative driving experiences. The young man has been acculturated into the expectation that he will enjoy driving and perhaps even take risks as part of his subject position as a young man. This may involve experiencing accidents, but as long as these accidents do not cause injury, they are accepted as part of the risk-taking driving experience. In contrast, the young woman has assumed that her involvement in an accident reflects a lack of skill that is often attributed to female rather than male drivers. Such slips have revealed to this young woman her vulnerability as a driver at risk from possible injury or death on the road, rather than bolster a positive view of herself as a risk-taking individual.

Many other women interviewees recounted experiences in which they had felt intimidated by other vehicles when driving. Ayten, a 23-year-old university student from a disadvantaged suburb (Turkish ethnicity), for example, gave an account of an incident in which a truck driver had encroached upon her driving space:

> There was a truck – you see, I think some of the roads in Sydney, they're too narrow, and some trucks are very wide – and I got caught

by a truck. I was on the left lane and there was like a left lane bend, so what happened was this guy came onto me, and I was like, 'oh!' and he was like – he was using my lane, plus his own lane. One lane wasn't enough for him. I still, up to today, I feel very cautious when I see trucks. I just let them go past me. I slow down when I see one coming, approaching the lane near me, or behind me. I get very – especially when [the trucks are] oversized – I get very, I guess, frightened.

Similarly, Jessica described a time in which she was the victim of road rage, and how vulnerable this had made her feel:

There was a car on the freeway that goes out to Canberra, the big multi-lane one. And somebody – I think I was going too slowly because I'd just got onto the freeway from a normal kind of road so I hadn't sped up yet – and this person started honking at me. So I was, okay, sorry, sorry, and started speeding up, but then they like started weaving in and out and then pulling in front and stopping and like, you know. That was like a bit scary because they were yelling at me and stuff. So that stressed me out.

Very few men, young or otherwise, articulated such attitudes about driving and other drivers. Descriptions of feeling 'frightened' or 'intimidated' were rare in men's accounts of their driving experiences. For them, although the road might have been portrayed as a space incurring negative feelings of anger, frustration and stress, and for some as a battleground involving displays of aggression, it was far less often represented as a space in which they felt vulnerable or victimised.

Conclusion

It is clear from the interviews with these young people that notions of power are at the centre of the driving experience for many of them. Owning or having access to a car is a means by which they feel they can escape the bounds of their lives, an environment in which they feel they can relax, 'be themselves' and behave as they want to. Driving, therefore, may be experienced as empowering, the car both malleable to the driver's wishes and also extending his or her feelings of power, via, its own technological capacities for speed. Unlike the home, work or study environment of young people, which they often experience as overly restrictive, they are able to exert 'pure control' in their own cars. The car offers them a hermeneutic environment, a world unto itself, in which they feel powerful: even able to break the law, according to one of them, if he so wanted.

This 'pure control' is an illusion, of course, given the constraints exerted upon motorists by the choked motorways of the large metropolis in which these young people live and the incipient dangers of driving at fast speeds on busy roads. While the interior of the car may feel like a protective cocoon, the exterior world is replete with risks, including those posed by other motorists' or the young driver's own incompetence, inexperience or aggression.

It was evident from the interviews that for at least some young men, displays of driving involving aggression and risk-taking is part of their construction of the masculine self. Such men are often closely involved in car culture: they love their cars, they enjoy the driving experience, they derive positive feelings of strength, pride and power from driving. The expression of aggression to other road users who are perceived as encroaching on their space is represented as a justifiable act, which in itself contributes to the positive meanings of driving for these men. In abusing other drivers, they see themselves as defending their territory, their right to the road. Even negative experiences such as being involved in an accident because of one's own risk-taking fail to detract for long from the driving experience, with its intrinsic rewards for masculine self-identity. Such youths bolster and contribute to the stereotype of the swaggering young man, 'showing off' in his much-loved car, taking many risks and behaving aggressively to other road users. As previous research into 'unsafe' drivers and joyriders has found (Groombridge, 1998), young men who take such risks tend to be far more involved in car culture than others: that is, they are interested in and enthusiastic about cars and see their own cars as extensions of their selves.

For other young men, and for the young women interviewed in the study, the opposite was true. While they may have enjoyed driving, they did not position themselves as drivers in the same way as did the aggressive youths. Driving was not as important to their self-identity, and they did not display the same notion that the road was their space. Indeed, several women reported feelings of intimidation and fear, of being made to feel almost as they were trespassing on this space. For these young people, the control and repression of feelings such as anger and frustration was valued, and the aggressive expression of these feelings to other road users condemned. The young men did not seem to draw upon a form of hegemonic masculinity that represented driving as an aggressive practice and a means of empowerment. Rather, they preferred a bourgeois form of masculinity that privileges self-control over the emotions and disdains aggression and public displays of anger. Such a version of masculinity is itself powerful, because it underpins dominant cultural notions of the ideal 'civilised' body/self as emotionally contained (Lupton, 1998, 1999).

There was little in the young women's interviews to suggest that aggressive or risk-taking driving was becoming incorporated into contemporary femininities, despite claims to the contrary by the news media and some market research.[3] Indeed the interview data suggest that the space of the road, like most other public spaces (Pain, 1997), is still coded as a masculine space, and one in which young women are more likely to feel vulnerable and intimidated by others' actions than to position themselves as aggressors and intimidators of others. The meanings surrounding car culture tend to be inextricably intertwined with masculinities that conform to the ideals of power, risk-taking and brute strength. The car itself may be seen as standing as a symbol of this kind of masculinity. Although inanimate, cars are frequently anthropomorphised in popular culture as possessing such traits as aggressiveness (sexual and otherwise), domination over others and forcefulness, all traits which tend to be championed not only as masculine virtues but as profoundly anti-feminine masculinity (Richards, 1994; Stallabrass, 1996; Graves-Brown, 1997; Lupton, 1999). For women, therefore, and perhaps particularly young, inexperienced female drivers, driving may be experienced as both empowering (in allowing them the exhilaration of freedom and access to the world) and disempowering (by arousing feelings of vulnerability and fear).

To conclude, the car and the act of driving have multiple meanings for young people, meanings that are clearly phrased through such factors as gender and social class (although ethnicity appears to be less important, at least in this study). For some young people, particularly men from disadvantaged backgrounds; these meanings include an embracing of risk-taking in the form of aggressive acts as part of the pleasure and feelings of empowerment associated with driving one's own car. Such youths are far more likely to be involved as perpetrators of road rage. Other young people, particularly those who are female or from a more bourgeois background, or both, privilege a form of self-control which requires the internalisation of anger and frustration produced through interacting with other road users. As victims of others' aggressive driving, however, these youths may find themselves positioned as vulnerable, and feel themselves 'at-risk' of aggression. This has implications for the sense of power they derive from driving, and detracts from their pleasure in the act.

Acknowledgement

This research was funded by an Australian Research Council Large Grant awarded to the author.

Notes

1. The participants were recruited using the following procedure, designed to achieve a degree of randomisation in the selection of participants but also allowing for some stratification by socio-economic status (SES), gender and age. Using the latest edition of the 'Sydney: A Social Atlas' (Australian Bureau of Statistics, 1998) those Sydney suburbs of extremely high SES disadvantage and high SES advantage (based on such indicators as average income, education level, car ownership, home ownership and unemployment rates) were identified. From these, eight suburbs (four of high SES advantage and four of high SES disadvantage) were randomly selected. Research assistants travelled to those suburbs and recruited participants by door-knocking, with the goal of obtaining ten interviewees from each suburb.
2. 'P-platers', in the state of New South Wales, are drivers who have passed their driving test and are on probation for a period of two years. They must display P plates on their vehicles at all times when driving, and must conform to road rules specifically for them relating to such aspects as their speed and blood alcohol level.
3. Perhaps this is an artefact of this particular study, for only small numbers of young people were involved. However, as noted above, the interviewees were chosen randomly, and the young women's responses are similar to those of the larger group of female interviewees, none of whom admitted to aggression while driving.

References

Canaan, J. (1996) 'One thing leads to another: drinking, fighting and working-class masculinities' in Mac an Ghaill, M. (ed.) *Understanding Masculinities*. Buckingham: Open University Press, pp. 114–25.

Connell, R. (1995) *Masculinities*. St. Leonards: Allen and Unwin.

Graves-Brown, P. (1997) 'From highway to superhighway: the sustainability, symbolism and situated practices of car culture'. *Social Analysis*, Vol. 41, No. 1, pp. 64–75.

Groombridge, N. (1998) 'Masculinities and crimes against the environment'. *Theoretical Criminology*, Vol. 2, No. 2, pp. 249–67.

Lupton, D. (1998) *The Emotional Self: A Sociocultural Exploration*. London: Sage.

Lupton, D. (1999) 'Monsters in Metal Cocoons: "Road Rage" and Cyborg Bodies'. *Body and Society*, Vol. 5, No. 1, pp. 57–72.

Lupton, D. (2001) 'Constructing "road rage" as news: an analysis of two Australian newspapers'. *Australian Journal of Communication*, Vol. 28, No. 3, pp. 23–36.

NRMA (1996) *Women, Men, Cars and Driving*. NRMA Limited: place of publication unspecified.

Pain, R. (1997) 'Social geographies of women's fear of crime'. *Transactions of the Institute of British Geography*, Vol. 22, pp. 231–44.

Richards, B. (1994) *Disciplines of Delight: The Psychoanalysis of Popular Culture*. London: Free Association Books.

Stallabrass, J. (1996) *Gargantua: Manufactured Mass Culture*. London: Verso.

3

Living in my Street: Adolescents' Perceptions of Health and Social Risks

Kate Gillen, Alison Guy and Maura Banim

Introduction

Problems associated with adolescent risk-taking activities such as substance misuse and early pregnancy have become key social issues in many Western societies and impact on government policy. However, health promotion methods currently in use in the UK appear to have little impact on adolescent risk-taking in health arenas. Any initiatives aimed at reducing risk-taking in adolescence, either in health, social or other domains, must address issues that directly impact on young people's lives and must engage young people if they are to have any chance of success. Therefore, exploring adolescent perceptions of risk provides a good basis for designing strategies to address risk-taking behaviours.

Early work on adolescent risk-taking focused on problem behaviours (e.g. Jessor and Jessor, 1977) including delinquency, early sexual activity and drug and alcohol use. Since that time the problem behaviour field has rapidly expanded to include health-threatening activities such as smoking, dangerous driving and substance misuse. However, there has also been an acknowledgement that other areas of adolescent behaviour as diverse as low achievement in school, eating junk food and taking part in criminal behaviour compromise optimum development (Jessor, 1998).

Research has identified factors that both encourage and discourage risk-taking behaviour in adolescents. These include the perceived benefits of risk-taking (Moore and Gullone, 1996; Moore *et al.*, 1997), psychosocial resources (Maggs *et al.*, 1997) and the effect of the home environment (NeumarkSztainer *et al.*, 1997). In addition a persuasive model of Social Networks and their health effects (Berkman *et al.*, 2000) suggests that the social environment at macro and micro levels powerfully affects physical and mental health. This model is pertinent to a debate on risk-taking in adolescence. According to the model, social and cultural factors determine the type of social networks an individual belongs to. Furthermore, social networks impact on behaviour via four primary psychosocial mechanisms; social support, social influence, social engagement and attachment and access to material resources (Berkman *et al.*, 2000).

Embodied in the description of an activity as a risk behaviour is the tacit acceptance that the behaviour has (at least potentially) injurious or negative outcomes for the person concerned. Such outcomes can be in the personal, social and developmental domains and can have far-reaching consequences. For example, poor achievement in school can lead to unemployment and in turn to poverty with its adverse consequences for mortality and morbidity (Department of Health, 1999). Gaining adolescent perceptions of risk is important since perceptions, for example, of the personal dangers of a particular risk, are likely to influence decisions about whether or not to take that risk. Exploring the reasons for risk-taking may also provide key data for facilitating change and encouraging safer life choices for young people and for developing more effective health intervention strategies.

The study reported here investigated adolescent perceptions of risk in a North Eastern England town and used focus groups to explore reasons for risk-taking among young people. The area suffers from complex social problems including unemployment, poverty, illegal drug use and crime and there are also high levels of mortality and morbidity (Tees Health, 1997).

The study

The aim of the study was to explore adolescent perceptions of risk-taking behaviour through focus group discussions. Sixty participants were drawn from two schools and one young person's club in the area of study. Permission to carry out the study was granted by the head teachers of the schools and the steering committee of the young people's club. Sixty per cent of the total sample were boys. Sixty per cent of the sample were aged 11–12 years and 40 per cent of the sample were aged 14–15 years. Participants were randomly selected to choose whether to take part in the focus groups by their year tutor. Adolescents from the young persons' club volunteered themselves to take part in one mixed focus group session. All adolescents were volunteer participants in this study. Both focus group interviewers were female.

Nine focus groups were held with small numbers of adolescents. In each school, two single sex focus groups were held for both years seven and ten, giving a total of eight school focus group sessions. A single focus group consisting of both boys and girls was held at the young people's club. Interviewers used a prompt sheet to begin and facilitate the discussion. Data from the focus groups were analysed using Thematic Analysis (Hayes, 1997).

Focus groups took place during Personal and Social Education (PSE) lessons in the schools and during a supervised recreational session at the young people's club. Teachers and club supervisors were not present during focus group discussions. After a short introduction focus groups sessions were facilitated by the semi-structured rapport interview technique (Massarik, 1981) and, with the permission of participants, were tape-recorded for later transcription. Following transcription of the data the tapes were destroyed. A list of organisations providing support for young people was distributed at the end of each focus group. Focus groups lasted about 40 minutes.

Results and discussion

Thematic Analysis was used to organise respondents' comments into several themes. Examination of the data revealed that individual themes were often perceived as both an encouraging and a discouraging factor in risk-taking. Themes included Personal Consequences, Social Consequences, Parents' Behaviours and Social Rules and examples of each theme are presented and discussed below. Participants' language is preserved but the authors have used their own phrases in square brackets ([ ]) where appropriate to provide clarification.

Results indicated that adolescents' perceptions of risk appear to depend on an evaluation of the potential consequences of taking the risk in terms of the potential rewards and penalties, a pervasive theme in the data. The perceived costs of taking a risk included, for example, injurious health consequences and the perceived benefits included, for example, affiliation with the peer group. Conversely, the costs of not taking a risk included losing status with the peer group and the benefits included avoiding ill health. Such perceived costs and benefits often co-exist, but results strongly suggest that young people will take a risk even though they are aware of its potentially severe consequences (e.g., smoking) so long as taking that risk has the potential to provide a valued benefit (such as, being accepted by others).

So, for young people it appears taking a risk is worth doing if the potential benefits outweigh the potential costs. For participants in this study, the primary motivation for risk-taking appeared to be the personal gains that accrue from such actions, in line with Moore and Gullone's (1996) findings. The following quotes are illustrative of the point:

> Drinking [is a risk worth taking]. Most people look old enough to get into clubs, so they go in and if you enjoy it you go in again and again. Nobody says anything unless you cause loads of trouble and everything. (Girl, year 10)

> Some people, smoking helps them if they are stressed, they have one then it helps them to calm down so yeah it's worth it for them. (Girl, year 10)

> You get the buzz type feeling when you know you are doing something wrong. (Boy, year 10)

Moore and Gullone (1996) provide support for this cost/benefit hypothesis. The researchers found a strong and consistent relationship between risk participation and perception of outcome; positive outcomes were associated with risk involvement and negative outcomes were associated with abstention from risk. A later study (Moore *et al.*, 1997) supported these findings using a story completion task. The perceived short-term outcomes of risk-taking predicted risk involvement, which was more likely when positive outcomes were described. Long-term consequences were less likely to be described by adolescents than short-term consequences, and were not predictive of risk involvement. However, it is important to note that in the current study we found evidence that adolescents did consider long-term consequences of risk-taking behaviour. For example, they were able to think about and articulate the long-term consequences of unprotected sex and early pregnancy as evidenced by these remarks:

> Not all protection's 100 per cent protective basically, and there's always a chance of viruses and STDs and stuff like that in the future. (Girl, year 10)

> It (teen pregnancy) can ruin your education. (Boy, year seven)

> If you get a girl pregnant at our age well your life's kind of wrecked. (Boy, year 10)

> If she gets pregnant you are stuck with a baby, there's the long-term consequences. (Boy, year seven)

These comments refer to the perceived penalties of risk-taking in terms of personal consequences that may act to discourage risky behaviour.

Further comments on the potentially adverse personal consequences of risk-taking included remarks on tobacco and drug consumption:

> You get tar in your lungs and horrible teeth and yellow fingers [from smoking]. (Girl, year seven)
>
> If you have never taken them [drugs] before, you can get all hyper and die. (Boy, year seven)

In addition, young people demonstrated an appreciation of the potential complexities of the consequences of risk:

> There's two kinds of risks for taking drugs, [health risks] and being caught by the police and being charged and getting a record. (Boy, year 10)
>
> You might end up spending all your money [on cigarettes] and not being able to do anything else. (Girl, year seven)

However, the variability and unpredictability of the consequences of risk forces an analysis on incomplete information and there was an implicit acknowledgement of this. For example, the positive and negative aspects of drinking alcohol were clearly articulated:

> Like people say alcohol's a risk, I suppose if you have a really bad night you sit and think, 'Oh God, what have I done, that was totally bad' then that is a risk but if you sit there and you're totally high and like well, you just want that night to last forever 'cos it's been brilliant, then you're not bothered. (Girl, year 10)

The reward provided by risk-taking, therefore, appears to be an important determinant of its continuation. In this study, the personal rewards identified by young people included provision of a positive mood:

> You get a buzz. (Boy, year 10)
>
> It's exciting, you get a rush. (Boy, year 10)

and enhancement of status within the peer group:

> Your mates think you are a daredevil. (Boy, year 10)

There is a suggestion in the data from this experiment and from an earlier quantitative study by the same authors (Gillen *et al.*, 2001) of sex differences in the perceptions of risk. For example, boys appear to perceive less risk from activities that are physically exciting and potentially enhance their status in the group, while girls seem to perceive less risks from behaviours that potentially result in social affiliation such as smoking or drinking with friends. However, since this study examined perceptions of risk and not risk involvement, it is not possible to examine the link between sex differences in the perceptions of risk and involvement in risk-taking behaviour and further work is needed on this topic. Nevertheless, it is likely that the type of reward envisaged determines the type of risk behaviour undertaken. Further evidence for this view is provided by young people's comments on the differential consequences of unprotected sex for boys and girls:

> If a lass has sex with loads of lads then she's a slag, but if the lad does he's like a hero, a stud. (Girl, year 10)

> A girl's got to live with a brat inside her for nine months ... the boys just walk away. (Girl, year 10)

This finding suggests that health interventions should be differentially targeted for boys and girls, a point we will return to in the final section of this chapter. A fuller discussion is beyond the scope of this chapter and the authors plan further research on this issue.

Previous research has addressed the issue of reward as an incentive to risk-taking behaviour. Siegel *et al.* (1994) used the Risk Involvement and Perception Scale (RIPS) to test older adolescents' perceptions of the benefits and consequences of a wide range of behavioural health risks including smoking, drinking alcohol and unprotected sex. They found that where participants reported involvement in risk-taking behaviours, they also reported the perception of benefits from such behaviours. Perceived risks were negatively and less strongly related to reported involvement. Furthermore, the researchers report that analysis of their participants' involvement in risk-taking yielded six distinct clusters; alcohol use, illegal drug use, sexual activity, stereotypical male behaviours, imprudent behaviours and socially acceptable behaviours. A later study by Parsons *et al.* (1997) on the same constellation of behaviours suggests that, at least among 17–20 year olds, the perceived benefits of risk-taking behaviours are a better predictor of behaviour *change* than perceived risks are. However, both perceived benefits and perceived risks are key determinants of behavioural *intentions*. So a cost benefit analysis may well drive intentions to take risks, but a change in behaviour towards risk-taking depends on the predicted benefits. Further research is needed to test this prediction for younger adolescent groups and to explore age related changes in risk-taking; for example, such changes have been noted by Kandel (1998).

Identification with key risk-taking figures also promotes risk-taking. For example, Gibbons *et al.* (1995) found that positive perceptions about prototypes associated with risk-taking behaviour predicted participation in the behaviour of smoking and early sexual intercourse for both Danish and American youth. Therefore, identification with members of a clique or gang will encourage young people to mimic the risk-taking behaviours prevalent in the group. This is in accordance with the finding that suppportive social ties are not necessarily beneficial for health (Berkman *et al.*, 2000). In the current study, the peer group proved a powerful determinant of perceptions of risk-taking behaviour since it too provided social rewards in terms of affiliation and acceptance. Mostly risk-taking occurred with groups of friends, as these comments illustrate:

> You do it [take risks] to fit in and be grown up. (Boy, year 10)
>
> You take risks 'cos you want to join their gang. (Boy, year seven)
>
> There's no point in doing it [taking a risk] by yourself 'cos there's no one to see you do it. (Boy, year 10)
>
> Smoking's worth it, you just wanna fit in with everybody else. (Girl, year 10)

However, participants in the current study made fine distinctions about appropriate behaviour with different groups of friends and risk-taking appeared to be defined by the particular social group the adolescent was with:

> It [the risks you take] depends on your mates, you have riff raff mates, bully mates, good mates and those that tag along. You do different stuff with them. (Boy, year 10)

This finding suggests that individual psychosocial resources (Maggs *et al.*, 1997) play a role in determining risk-taking behaviour. With some groups of friends it may be easier to refuse to become involved in risk-taking than with other groups and the influence of the peer group on risk-taking behaviour appears to be more subtle than previously suggested. As the last extract illustrates, an adolescent may well display elasticity of risk-taking behaviour depending on the situation he or she is in and the potential social costs or benefits of taking (and not taking) a particular risk in that situation. In addition, avoiding risk may well be beyond a young person's control, for example, in the case of risks associated with the physical and social environment. A rather poignant extract supports this; when we asked in once focus group what the young people understood as a risk we got this response:

> Living in my street. (Boy, year seven)

The effect of the home environment has been introduced as a factor in risk-taking behaviour. Results from the current study show the perceived influence of parental behaviour on avoiding risk, illustrated by the following comments:

> They are just protective of you aren't they? So they try and stop you doing stuff. (Girl, year 10)
>
> You get the talk about the birds and bees and that. (Boy, year 10)
>
> My mam and dad think everything's a risk. It's their job, they don't get paid for it, so you have to be grateful. (Girl, year 10)

However, adolescents also indicated their perception that parental models of behaviour potentially promote health-threatening behaviours in young people:

> I reckon in a couple of years time little kids will be taking drugs. They see their dads taking drugs all the time. (Boy, year seven)
>
> Some of the mams are drug dealers and the kids see them. (Girl, year seven)

The potentially adverse effect of parents as negative role models noted by adolescents in this study has also been reported in prior research. Glendinning *et al.* (1997) found the home environment to be a predictor of risk-taking behaviour. They found that unsupportive parenting was associated with an increased likelihood of smoking, and that this association was stronger than the effect of the socio economic status of the family. Also, NeumarkSztainer *et al.* (1997) examined psychosocial correlates of health threatening behaviours among adolescents of different ages. They found that a disposition towards risk-taking was associated with participation in health threatening behaviours in the family.

It is possible that a good school environment could ameliorate the negative effects of a poor family situation. McBride *et al.* (1995)

found that school environment (both physical and psychological) is an important factor in commitment to social activities. Such commitment is associated with a decrease in the likelihood of taking part in risk-taking behaviours. These researchers found that the school environment determined social commitment and hence decreased the likelihood of risk-taking. However, the authors of this study argue that commitment to a particular social group within the school environment might actually increase risk-taking behaviour in an individual; as earlier comments from adolescents have demonstrated, risk-taking can be undertaken as a means of fitting in with a group. This argument finds support in Berkman *et al's* (2000) claim that not all social ties are beneficial and also in results from this study ('smoking's worth it, you just wanna fit in with everybody else', Girl, year 10).

Many young people are either excluded from school for misdemeanours or play truant regularly; some attendees at the young people's club in this study fell into these categories. For young people like these, it is important that a beneficial school environment is provided early enough to prevent or weaken factors that encourage risk-taking behaviours that may result in exclusion from school (with all the attendant risks) for the child.

Berkman *et al.* (2000) provide an interesting model demonstrating the pervasive effect of social networks on physical and mental health. The model refers to social structural conditions such as culture and socio-economic features, including the norms and values of particular groups, as well as social networks and psychosocial mechanisms. Therefore, on this model, structural factors such as unemployment and poverty as well as higher level factors such as parental and peer behaviours will powerfully shape an individual's risk-taking style. According to Berkman *et al.*, these factors lead to health behavioural pathways (for example, smoking, drinking) and psychological pathways (self-efficacy, self-esteem). Preliminary results from the current study provide tentative support for this model. However, the characteristics of adolescents' individual social ties, such as the frequency of contact, and the complexity, duration and reciprocity involved, as identified by Berkman *et al.* in their model were not directly investigated in this study and further research on this topic should be rewarding.

Finally, societal rules appeared to act as a catalyst for risk-taking, as these comments demonstrate:

> If there wasn't as many rules about things, I dare say that not so many people would do them [take risks]. (Girl, year 10)

> Like all girl's magazines [say] sex under 16 is illegal, it's printed all over the place, you look at it and like, print on a piece of paper isn't going to stop me from having sex if you (sic) really want to. (Girl, year 10)
>
> If there wasn't a law on it we wouldn't think about it [risk taking]. (Girl, year 10)
>
> Why do we take risks? Because we're not supposed to. (Girl, year 10)

There are at least two potential reasons for these perceptions. First, perhaps rules simply give young people an opportunity to rebel against them, thus helping adolescents to refine their own identity as different to that of the rule makers. Second, perhaps the illicitness of taking a prohibited risk provides a major physical charge for adolescents ('you get the buzz type feeling when you know you are doing something wrong', Boy, year 10) providing excitement and a sense of rebellion, both of which may be perceived as benefits by young people.

Conclusions

In conclusion, results from this study indicate that adolescents show a complex and subtle framing of risk-taking involving several thematic strands. These strands include the perceived personal and social consequences of risk-taking (both positive and negative), parents' behaviour (both as risk encouraging and risk discouraging factors) and societal rules that seem to act as a spur to risk-taking.

Perceptions about risk-taking appear to depend on the utility of outcomes for the individual, and perceptions about these often unpredictable outcomes appear to determine whether a risk is worthwhile for an individual to take. Results identified by prior research, including cost benefit analysis of risk-taking (Moore and Gullone, 1996), psychosocial factors (Maggs *et al.*, 1997) and the effect of the home environment on risk-taking (NeumarkSztainer *et al.*, 1997) are largely supported. However, the finding that young people do not consider long-term consequences of risk-taking (Moore *et al.*, 1997) is not supported.

In terms of developing more effective health intervention strategies for young people, the current study suggests that it is important to consider the following points. Since perceptions of risk seem to depend on an analysis of the potential rewards and penalties of taking that risk, facilitating a change from risk-taking behaviour to a safer lifestyle may be addressed in psychological and social terms by reducing the perceived benefits of the activity, relative to its perceived costs or increasing the perceived costs, relative to its perceived benefits. (There is support in the data for this suggestion with regard to the differential consequences of unprotected sex for girls and boys; girls acknowledge the potentially more serious consequences for them of unprotected sex.) For example, interventions to promote condom use by boys might usefully stress the potential costs to them of not using a condom during sex (e.g. disease; potential loss of face within the peer group should his partner become pregnant) in contrast to the potential benefits (e.g. transitory pleasure). The challenge is to make healthier lifestyles more attractive to young people and the authors acknowledge the difficulties associated with this challenge.

In policy terms, one potentially useful strategy would be to make educational establishments such as schools and colleges risk-reducing environments, by inducing a culture where few social or personal rewards are seen to accrue, for example, from smoking. Such environments have the potential to lessen the effect of perceived risk encouraging parental behaviours. Again, we acknowledge that this is not easy to achieve. Finally, the powerful effect of pervasive structural and social factors may mean that young people have little chance of changing to safer life choices.

Suggestions for further research

Cautious backing is given for Berkman *et al.* (2000) model of social networks and health but more research is needed on this topic and further work is needed to rigorously test the model in the context of risk-taking behaviour.

Other potentially fruitful areas for further research include investigating the connection between perceptions of risk and involvement in risk-taking activities, in particular the relationship between perceptions of the long-term consequences of risk-taking and involvement in risk-taking. An investigation of sex differences in risk-taking behaviour, particularly the idea that boys seek risks that enhance status within the group and girls seek risks that enhance social affiliation is also important.

Summary

Problems associated with risk-taking in adolescence have become key social issues and are the subject of government policy in many Western countries. However, initiatives aimed at reducing risk-taking in adolescence in the UK have enjoyed only limited success and one reason for this is that such initiatives may not be addressing issues pertinent to adolescents. The study reported here utilised focus group methodology with small groups of adolescents aged 11–12 years and 14–15 years to explore adolescent perceptions of risk-taking. Results indicated that adolescents demonstrated a complex framing of risk based around perceptions of the potential rewards and penalties associated with risk-taking. These included Personal and Social Consequences of risk-taking. Parents' Behaviours and Social Rules were also perceived as important determinants of risk-taking. Some recommendations for strategies to reduce risk-taking are made.

References

Berkman, L., Glass, T., Brissette, I. and Seeman, T. (2000) 'From social integration to health: Durkheim in the new millenium'. *Social Science and Medicine*, Vol. 51, pp. 843–57.

Department of Health (1999) *Saving Lives: Our Healthier Nation. The Stationery Office, CM4386.*

Gibbons, F. X., Helweglarsen, M. and Gerrard, M. (1995) 'Prevalence estimates and adolescent risk behaviour: cross cultural differences in social influence'. *Journal of Applied Psychology*, Vol. 80, No. 1, pp. 107–21.

Gillen, K., Guy, A. and Banim, M. (2001) Adolescent perceptions of risk: the key to tackling social problems?, paper presented at the British Psychological Society Social Psychology Conference, University of Surrey.

Glendinning, A., Shucksmith, J. and Hendry, J. (1997) 'Family life and smoking in adolescence'. *Social Science and Medicine*, Vol. 44, No. 1, pp. 93–101.

Hayes, N. (1997) 'Theory led thematic analysis: social identification in small companies' in Hayes, N. (ed.) *Doing Qualitative Analysis in Psychology*. Hove: Psychology Press.

Jessor, R. (ed.) (1998) *New Perspectives on Adolescent Risk Behaviour*. Cambridge: Cambridge University Press.

Jessor, R. L. and Jessor, S. (1977) *Problem Behaviour and Psychosocial Development: A Longitudinal Study of Youth*. New York: Academic Press.

Kandel, D. B. (1998) 'Persistent themes and new perspectives on adolescent substance abuse: a lifespan perspective' in Jessor, R. (ed.) *New Perspectives on Adolescent Risk Behaviour*. Cambridge: Cambridge University Press.

Maggs, J. L., Frome, P. M., Eccles, J. S. and Barber, B. L. (1997) 'Psychosocial resources, adolescent risk behaviour and young adult adjustment: is risk-taking more dangerous for some than for others?' *Journal of Adolescence*, Vol. 20, No. 1, pp. 103–19.

Massarik, F. (1981) 'The interviewing process re-examined' in Reason, P. and Rowan, J. (eds) *Human Inquiry: A Sourcebook of New Paradigm Research*. Chichester: Wiley.

McBride, C. M., Curry, S. J., Cheadle, A., Andermand, C., Wagner, E. H., Diehr, P. and Psaty, B. (1995) 'School level application of a social bonding model to adolescent risk-taking behaviour'. *Journal of School Health*, Vol. 65, No. 2, pp. 63–8.

Moore, S. and Gullone, E. (1996) 'Predicting adolescent risk behaviour using a personalised cost-benefit analysis'. *Journal of Youth and Adolescence*, Vol. 25, No. 3, pp. 343–59.

Moore, S., Gullone, E. and Kostanski, M. (1997) 'An examination of adolescent risk-taking using a story completion task'. *Journal of Adolescence*, Vol. 20, No. 4, pp. 369–79.
NeumarkSztainer, D., Story, M., French, S. A. and Resnick, M. D. (1997) 'Psychosocial correlates of health compromising behaviours among adolescents'. *Health Education Research*, Vol. 12, No. 1, pp. 37–52.
Parsons, J. T., Siegel, A. W. and Cousins, J. H. (1997) 'Late adolescent risk-taking: effects of perceived benefits and perceived risks on behavioural intentions and behavioural change'. *Journal of Adolescence*, Vol. 20, No. 4, pp. 381–92.
Siegel, A. W., Cousins, J. H., Rubovits, D. S., Parsons, J. T., Laverty, B. and Crowley, C. L. (1994) 'Adolescent perceptions of the benefits and risks of their own risk-taking'. *Journal of Emotional and Behavioural Disorders*, Vol. 2, No. 2, pp. 89–98.
Tees Health Authority (1997) *Report of the Director of Public Health.*

4

Risky Identities: Young Women, Street Prostitution and 'Doing Motherhood'

Eileen Green

Introduction

Women and children are routinely warned to guard against risk, to keep themselves safe and to be cautious of strangers, but what if making a living depends upon taking risks with strangers in unsafe spaces? What if the risks of not having enough money to provide for your children and feed your drug habit, appear to outweigh those of selling sex to strange men in run down, urban areas, frequented by punters, pimps and prostitutes? Focusing upon the experience of prostituted mothers, in this chapter I examine the ways in which young women working in street prostitution manage what they perceive to be 'normal, everyday risks'. In their accounts of 'doing family', the voices of these young women present a challenge to traditionally conceived boundaries between 'work', 'family' and 'home'. More generally, researching mothers working in prostitution helps us to see that women working in the sex industry may be among the most highly stigmatised and reviled of groups, but they are also 'ordinary women' preoccupied with being 'good' mothers. By highlighting the importance of listening to young women's everyday, narratives of risk, and risk-taking behaviour, we find accounts, which are interwoven with narratives of motherhood and 'family'. In order to understand such accounts, they must be grounded in the specific social and economic contexts in which they are embedded: local spaces and places where risk-taking is perceived as part of the 'normal everyday'. This is not to minimise the dangers involved, or the personal anxieties, which this group of young women must manage, for example, between the often-conflicting identities of good mother and streetwise prostitute. Such anxieties form part of the narratives, figuring strongly in the ways in which they define the boundaries between different selves.

This chapter explores the role and importance of motherhood in the lives and identities of a group of young women working in prostitution in the North East of England. In particular, it highlights the complexity of young people's risk narratives, which are interwoven, with the 'voices' of different and (often contradictory) identities. The first section briefly outlines the empirical study from which the qualitative interview data is drawn, the next section reviews some of the literature on young mothers and risk, as a back drop to the third section which focuses upon young mothers working in prostitution. The final sections explore the inter-related themes of multiple identity and risk management; in particular, the risks and benefits attached to crossing the boundaries between the identities of 'risky bodies' and mothers who care. The chapter concludes with a discussion of the complexities of performing motherhood as both stability and risk for young mothers in prostitution.

Empowering young parents

Drawing upon data from a DETR funded project which researched the place and experience of parenting in the lives of young people (14–24 years),[1] I address the barriers which young mothers,[2] existing on the margins of social in/exclusion perceive as preventing them from accessing the support services to which they are entitled. To capture the experiences of some of the most marginalised groups, and in particular, those who were widely perceived as 'a problem' and who rarely accessed statutory support services, a pilot study was designed. This included face-to-face interviews and participant observation with a group of young mothers accessed through a drop-in centre/cafe catering for young people involved in street prostitution.[3] In this way, the project attempted to create a space to listen to the voices of those young people, and to enable a clearer understanding of their lived experiences. One of the researchers did volunteer work at the drop-in centre over a period of 10 months, during which time she engaged in participant observation and conducted a series of in-depth interviews. At a broader level, through partnership initiatives, the project aimed to influence local social policy, in ways which would enable statutory bodies to deliver more appropriate services for the most excluded groups of young parents. As O'Neill (1994) argues:

> We need to stop treating these children and young people as 'social junk', as 'criminals', and to deliver child-centred responses across the spectrum of agencies and services with which young people have contact.

Risk and young motherhood

Motherhood within Western society has often been idealised as the greatest physical and emotional achievement in women's lives, with the implication that all women are waiting or wanting to be mothers (Phoenix, 1991). In contrast, feminists have provided more critical accounts of motherhood, suggesting that motherhood may be a common experience for women but that this experience is extremely diverse (Smart and Neale, 1999). Also, as Silva (1996) has commented, men and women can 'mother', motherhood is female but mothering need not be. At a societal level however, 'motherhood' has become a social institution, which is premised upon a specific type of (white, middle class) motherhood. This stems from a range of moral, legal and welfare discourses drawn from the nineteenth century, which helped to create the ideal of 'normative motherhood', which included a clear distinction between respectable, married mothers and single, deviant mothers (Smart and Neale, 1999). 'Good' mothers were respectable married women, unlike single or lone mothers, who carried the labels of bad or inadequate mothers (Phoenix, 1991). Many of the women interviewed in my study felt the weight of the moral censure attached to being not only lone, but also young mothers. Maybe young single motherhood has become so demonised, that despite the overtones of societal respect and regard for motherhood per se, it has become a risky identity for young women. A major conclusion drawn by academics and social commentators alike is that it is usually poverty not youth which explains young mothers' difficulties. For example, Silva (1996) points out that the state benefit dependency rate of lone mothers in poverty is greater in the UK than any other European country and a number of recent Government reports have identified teenage parenthood as a problem within the UK.[4] These statistics remind us that teenage births are much higher in economically and socially deprived areas and among vulnerable groups, for example, those living in Local Authority care and those who are excluded from school. This socio-economic profile is also characteristic of the specific geographical area in my study, which constitutes an economically and socially deprived urban centre in the North East of England. Teenage mothers are seen, in the moral panic stance, as having assumed an adult role before they are physically and emotionally mature, and teenage motherhood is seen as both dangerous and poverty inducing.

Moral panics about the family are not new; however, towards the end of the twentieth century they came increasingly to focus on the 'problem' of young motherhood. Under New Labour, teenage mothers and single parent households are discursively created as factors that destabilise the institution of the family. In addition, powerful family value discourses have demonised teenage mothers as part of a wider anxiety about the development of an underclass. Interest in teenage mothers as a research object is fuelled by social policy concerns, which link *young* motherhood with a range of risk factors for children. This has led to young mothers being subject to a level of scrutiny by a variety of agencies, a scrutiny, which they often experience as intrusive surveillance. It is also a surveillance most keenly experienced by mothers working in street prostitution, who are among those young people most in need of support services, for themselves and for their children. They are also one of the least likely groups to access such services, partly due to fears about their children being taken into care.

Young mothers working in prostitution

Arguably, the most scrutinised young mothers are those who, due to family breakdown, end up in local authority care (children's homes) and then 'drift' into prostitution. These young women's entry into prostitution is due to economic need, emotional neediness and vulnerability, which is more often than not, related to peer pressure. The young mothers in my study display multiple risk factor characteristics, like extreme poverty, drug addiction and health problems, but most of all; they are perceived as 'liminal' creatures that transgress all the boundaries of respectability and normality.

Who are young prostitutes?

O'Neill's (1997) ground breaking work with women working in prostitution in the UK, asserts that young prostitutes are women and men from a variety of backgrounds, whilst confirming that the majority of women are working class and have become prostitutes to escape poverty. We also need to understand that the drift into prostitution is usually a response to particular circumstances. Peer association, especially with other young people in local authority care (Melrose *et al.*, 1999), coercion from 'pimps' and moving into prostitution to support one's own or another's drug habit, appear to be the main routes in.[5] However, like young mothers, young women in prostitution cannot be lumped together as an undifferentiated set of 'risky bodies'. Instead, we need to understand the lived experience of women working in prostitution, which includes a focus on difference and multiple identities, as well as commonalities.

Are they the mothers most at risk?

If young mothers and their children are considered to be at risk from a range of factors associated with economic deprivation, young mothers working in prostitution, and their children, must be seen as even more vulnerable, particularly given that many of the young women began such work before their sixteenth birthday (Department of Health, 2000; Coy, 2003). Such children are at risk of a range of deprivations, precisely to the extent that their mothers are at risk. It is important to be clear here, that there is no automatic connection between being the child of a prostitute and any negative outcomes. It is also important to recognise that despite representations of them as whores, 'bad girls' and polluted bodies (Shildrick, 1997) that are a threat to 'normal' femininity (O'Neill, 1994), prostitutes are 'ordinary women'.

Turning to the situation of mothers working in prostitution, it is not the policy of local agencies to remove children of prostitutes from the care of their mothers, so long as no prostitution activity takes place in the home. However, many have a transient and nocturnal life style, and an association with class 'A' drugs, factors which lead to their children being placed on local authority 'at risk' registers. A situation which necessitates a higher level of official surveillance, of them and their children, than that experienced by the majority of young people. The stigmatisation of prostitutes, and in particular, the stigmatisation of prostitutes who are mothers, can have a huge impact on their mothering practices. They constitute a category of the most socially excluded mothers, in that they depart considerably from definitions of respectable motherhood.

Little is known about the everyday lives of young mothers in prostitution. In light of this, the project chose to adopt an approach, which listened to the voices of such young women, in an effort to understand their experiences. Working in prostitution leads young people to become enmeshed in local subcultures, subcultures that provide them with the required social networks of pimps and drug dealers, but which may also be networks of support and inclusion (O'Neill, 2001). To understand their position, we, therefore, need to understand those social and economic contexts, including the risk factors involved.

Mothers or whores?

Prostitutes are obviously defined in terms of sexual activity, or more accurately in terms of the provision of sexual services. As such, those who are mothers embody a contradiction. Assertive sexuality and motherhood are seen as incompatible, the more sexual and perhaps more importantly, the more sexually available a woman is, the less motherly she is perceived to be. It is the tension between what is popularly termed the whore and the Madonna, which most offends public moralities. Public perceptions of prostitutes' sexual, non-respectable status, impact upon their role as mothers, not least in the form of a representation of them as 'polluted bodies', a representation which denies them the respect reserved for 'good mothers'. However, although the public perception of young prostitutes would seem to mitigate against them being seen as motherly, the participant observation data collected at the drop-in centre for prostitutes, left me in no doubt that many of them are 'doing' motherhood. It is motherhood through providing; earning money to pay bills and keep a home together for their children. They are also managing what they perceive to be the 'normal' risks of street prostitution, in a similar way to other young people who inhabit such risky places and spaces.

I need the money, but is he safe?

It would be over simplistic to see prostitutes as passive victims. As I will attempt to demonstrate in the data from the pilot study interviews presented below, street prostitutes engage in a complex process of risk assessment each time a potential client or 'punter' approaches them. The kinds of factors that influence whether or not a prostitute will get into a car with a client are not just those relating to her perceptions of him in terms of personal safety. That risk will be weighed against other risk factors. Information collected over a lengthy period of regular volunteer work at the drop-in centre revealed that the women who used the centre were regularly assaulted and raped by punters but such 'routine' violence was balanced against a series of other risk factors. The risk of going home with insufficient money to pay-off personal debts and overdue bills, which may have provided the impetus for going out on the streets in the first place, often outweighed the risk attached to violence from potential clients. For those who lived with male partners, there was also the risk of going home without the anticipated level of cash and getting beaten up by a 'boyfriend'/pimp (Jarvinen, 1993). Unprotected sex is a further risk factor, but once again, the extra money that prostitutes can earn from clients who demand this, will form part of their complex risk management calculations.

Managing complex identities: from prostitute to 'good' mother

The management of complex identities, further demonstrated in a number of chapters within this collection appears to be an accepted part of everyday life for many young people, despite the attendant risks. Whilst the risks to self and family associated with working in prostitution are severe, for some of the young women, their dual identity as mothers made the situation even more risky. Like other young mothers, these young women are concerned with presenting themselves as 'good', respectable mothers. Prostitution is 'just a job', which they do to earn money, often to buy things for their children or to keep the home together. Much of the data presented below demonstrates that like some of the young mothers interviewed in Action Risk (Mitchell and Green, 2002), issues of respectability were reflected upon individually, focusing in upon the 'self'. The following quote from a young woman who entered prostitution via networks associated with a local children's home, illustrates her perceptions of the incompatibility between prostitution and motherhood:

Interviewer: And then it was through being in care that you got involved with, on the game?

Lucy: Yeah

Interviewer: And how do you feel about all that now?

Lucy: Well I wish I had never done it, I wish I never even knew anything about it. Before I moved into that kid's home I thought prostitutes were, do you know what I mean, it was just in America and things like that, I didn't know that it was in (town). It's a sad life and then I see all them young lasses down there it's terrible.

Interviewer: And what does your mum say about it?

Lucy   : She just tries to, well she doesn't know I've started working again, she'd go mad and try and take the baby away from me.

There are a number of different narratives going on here. In the first instance, Lucy is distancing herself from the reality and stigma of prostitution (Church, 1997), and second, there is also an expressed anxiety about the impact upon her status and rights as a mother, which her re-entry to street work might have. She also cites her own mother as 'guardian' of respectable motherhood, which excludes this young woman's identity and work as a prostitute, and prioritises the identity of mother.

This narrative also links back to contradictions between media and official discourse representations of young mothers and the ways in which they construct their own identities. For many young women, especially those who experience multiple social exclusion, becoming a mother may be a route to respectability (Chapter 11 and Mitchell and Green, 2002).

Managing risk via motherhood

Just as discovering that they are pregnant can be a point of reflection and change for many women, so can it be a key moment for women working in prostitution to review their situation and consider exiting prostitution, not least because of the perceived risk to their unborn child.

Pregnancy can be a point where women are put under tremendous pressure to give up all drugs simply because they are pregnant. Indeed, members of the public can feel entitled to criticise visibly pregnant women who are perceived to be endangering their health, for example, by smoking. A public censure, which would be even more critically directed at prostitutes who are pregnant, and/or are mothers. Prostituted mothers embody concepts of both 'polluted sexuality' and 'maternal risk'; existing in the public mind as 'liminal figures',[6] who transgress the boundaries between 'safe', 'respectable' women and 'loose', 'risky', 'dirty' bodies (Seymour, 1998).

For women working in prostitution, the services and support to which they become entitled once pregnant, can at the same time be self-negating of their identity as working women. If they have a problem with drugs, it can also be a point at which they re-consider their addiction. As pregnant women, they are routinely fast tracked for treatment programmes. Furthermore, the fact that those who are mothers, or about to become mothers, may lose care and control of their children, can be a major factor in women deciding to move out of exploitative relationships and remove themselves from groups using drugs. Paradoxically, impending motherhood can become another risk factor for them to balance, or, depending upon their social and economic context, it can provide a means to achieve a different type and level of risk management.

Becoming a mother then, can impact on the lives of prostituted women in two ways; first, they are positioned within powerful public discourses which emphasise the nurturing and caring role of mothers. These discourses may provide them with an impetus for re-considering self-destructive behaviour. Second, being the bearer of a child, with all the connotations of innocence and defencelessness associated with children, will entitle them to priority treatment from a range of statutory and voluntary organisations. For example, being fast tracked for drug rehabilitation programmes means they do not have to join a lengthy waiting list. Similarly, they are prioritised for housing. Help that was just as needed before they became pregnant will now be made available to them not on their own behalf, but on behalf of the unborn life. It could be argued that this reinforces selflessness, rather than building their self-esteem, in that they are encouraged to save their own lives, but not for themselves. However, in the short term it can provide women with an impetus for and sufficient support to, achieve a way out of prostitution. Being realistic, it does save some women's lives.

Early on in her interview, Lucy spontaneously provided an example of her pregnancy providing the opportunity to save her own life:

> I didn't try and get pregnant but when I found out I was pregnant I thought well I'll be able to get myself sorted out now you know, because I've got a baby.

Later in the interview when asked about alternative scenarios:

> Interviewer: Right and what do you think would have happened if you hadn't fell pregnant with (daughter)?

She said:

> I think I'd still be on it now.
> Interviewer: Yeah?
> Lucy: Because it's hard to get off it if you haven't got anything to get off it for.
> Interviewer: So you really feel the baby was the real incentive you needed?
> Lucy: Yeah, definitely.
> Interviewer: Why do you feel you wouldn't have been able to do it for yourself?
> Lucy: Don't know, because it's too hard, it's far too hard to get off.

Risky bodies or mothers who care?
Negotiating the boundaries

As much of the feminist literature on prostitution concludes, prostitution is double-edged and full of contradictions (O'Connell Davidson, 1996; O'Neill, 1997). Young mothers working in prostitution would appear to embody many of these contradictions and they are well aware that their bodies are, economically, often their most valuable asset, which can be bought and sold as commodities. However, they are also maternal bodies that are required to nurture their children, keeping them safe. The participant observation aspects of our study demonstrate that many of the young women who access the drop-in cafe are closely engaged in the complex construction of such multiple identities, which are often fluid and transitory. Rather than presenting as passive victims, many present as 'active selves' engaged in constructing their own biographies, or what Giddens (1991) has referred to as a 'reflexive project'. Several were clearly proud of their independence, an independence earned through arduous and dangerous street work. The following quote is from an interview with Ellen, a young woman who became a mother at the age of 15. Ellen entered prostitution at the age of 13 when she ran away from a children's home and in this section of the interview, describes her entry into prostitution as a positive choice she made in preference to returning to the children's home or becoming homeless. She has lived independently since the age of 13 and expresses pride in her ability to have done so and in so doing challenges the stereotype of prostitutes as one-dimensional victims:

> I'm glad I did it, because now I don't owe nobody, I can't turn round and say thanks for doing this for me because I did it myself. You never did nothing to help me, nobody ever did, I've always helped myself and I always will.

It is clear that, for most women (and men) economic need (to finance basic living, drug dependence etc.) is the trigger for entry into prostitution. The next quote from the interview with Lucy clearly demonstrates the economic imperative for prostitution. Earnings are spent on normal everyday items that mothers need:

> Well, I could manage on my social if I didn't smoke or if I didn't buy nice toiletries and nice things like that, like the Pampers nappies. If I bought her the cheap nappies and cheap wet wipes and everything

I could manage but I like to buy her Pampers nappies because they are better, you don't have to change her as much with the Pampers nappies. Like clothes and that, if I didn't have to buy her clothes all time I'd be able to manage.

Everyday 'family life': holding it all together

Despite their vilification as 'polluted, dangerous bodies' that are a threat to 'normal' femininity, many prostitutes, precisely through their prostitution activity are, in fact, 'doing motherhood'. This situation provides a stark example of the increasing fluidity of what constitutes 'family' in late modernity (Berthoud *et al.*, 1999), and includes mothers who are increasingly important as wage earners. One of the interviewees described her work as a prostitute as necessary to support herself, her male partner and their two children. Her partner here can legitimately be described as living off immoral earnings and, consequently be classed as a 'pimp'. This particular woman appears to have a stable, long-term and supportive relationship with the father of her children, he is part of what she experiences as 'family'. They were both heroin addicts and, at the time of writing, were both on a methadone programme.

The woman clearly worked as a prostitute to keep her family together. Although dangerous, prostitution is not an illegal activity for which one can be imprisoned. In contrast, her partner regularly accessed income through burglary and theft, activities for which he *could* be imprisoned. She took the view that his imprisonment would deprive the family of his presence and (economic and social) support, making her life with two small children very difficult. Bourdieu's concept of 'habitus' (see Crawshaw, Chapter 13) is useful here, to explore the habitual, acculturated nature of risk behaviours.[7] Rather than risking the absence of her male partner and de-stabilising her family unit, this young woman 'chose' to continue working in prostitution, precisely because it keeps the family together. In common with many mothers, that was her main priority.

Earning money for celebratory family moments

Although the public perception of prostitutes as 'other', risky, polluted bodies, mitigates against them being seen as ordinary women or 'good' mothers, observation at the drop-in cafe demonstrated that many of them were using their earnings to maintain their family at a number of different levels (economically, socially and emotionally). This included earning money to pay regular household bills and keep a home together for their children, as well as finding the extra funds necessary for special occasions like family celebrations, Christmas and children's birthdays. Lucy, for example, was not a regular user of the cafe; she only went in for coffee when she was working on the streets, which she did periodically, when her regular bills fell due.

The following extract from Judy's interview also demonstrates prostituted mothers' use of earnings to provide for their children. Judy had recently exited prostitution at the time of the interview because she was six months pregnant with her second child:

> I was (doing street work), but about two weeks ... a week ago I stopped it because it's getting too much for me again, with this pregnancy.

As the following extract confirms she also exited temporarily a few months before her first child was born:

> Yeah, when I was having X, well a couple of months before, I used to go out and work on a night-time, but it got too much for me when I was having X. I started going out again after having X. It's just money really.

Earning money to buy her child nice things took precedence and was necessary to supplement her income support. In her view, the need to provide for her child legitimised her work as a prostitute:

> After I had (son) I knew myself that I was out there for my son, like for clothes or food whatever. But there are a lot of people down there who have got children who are using drugs and that's what I didn't like about it really. I knew I was spending my money on (son) and everybody was saying 'what are you doing? What are you working for' and I used to tell them it was for my son and they used to say, 'you don't need the money you can go on the Social', but it's not enough when you think about it. I've been working since I was younger and it's just a lot different because now I go down there, like Christmas is coming up. I'm hoping to save for his presents and be able to afford nice things for him.

It is interesting to note, in relation to the previous discussion about the establishment of multiple selves or identities, that this interviewee employed a distinction between herself and drug users to establish her distance from them as stigmatised 'others'. It was also her perception, that this distinction would be emblemic in protecting her from the dangers involved in her work:

> There's all kinds of things that happen to you like, not myself, uh there's diseases going round and people getting battered. But that's a different situation because I think that's in the drugs part. Like myself, I don't get involved with drugs; I just keep myself to myself, down there.

She felt that this protection was associated with explaining to potential customers why she was working:

> I say to them (customers), look you can take it or leave it because I'm not like everybody else, I'm out here for my children, I'm not out here for the drugs.

This interview data demonstrates several narratives. A young woman drawing a series of critical boundaries between herself and other prostitutes and more specifically those who are drug users. Also in her active engagement with public discourses on motherhood, she attempts to extend the protection, popularly accepted as due to children, to herself. By presenting herself predominantly as a caring mother, she attempts to deflect the popular vilification of prostitutes and call on powerful discourses of motherhood in order to justify being treated well. This is clearly not a foolproof way of ensuring her safety, however, as a strategy it appeared, up to the point of the interview, to have worked.

'Doing family': parenthood as stability for mothers in prostitution

It could be argued that what these young women are describing, is what has been called 'doing family'. In their book *'Family Fragments?'*, Smart and Neale (1999) draw attention to the changes in family formation which have taken place in Britain and in addition, to the ways in which legislation on the family in the last decade, has failed to acknowledge such developments. Recent work on the sociology of the family has drawn attention to the increase in women mothering alone (McIntosh, 1996; Silva, 1996), arguably in ways not dissimilar to those described by these young prostitutes. What most contemporary sociologists of the family agree upon is that the 'family' can now no longer be defined in terms of blood ties, or co-residence.

The above debates are helpful in attempting to de-construct the kinds of 'family' evoked by the parenting experiences described in the pilot interviews. At the time of interviewing, three of the interviewees had no contact with the fathers of their children. The other two were unable to co-habit with the children's fathers and also live with their children, because of exclusion orders related to the father's violent behaviour towards themselves and potentially their children.

Conclusion: managing 'normal' risks

Prostitutes, without doubt, routinely occupy non-respectable spaces and places. Drawing upon Lupton:

> Prostitutes, for example, disturb such boundaries as that distinguishing between private and public by inhabiting public spaces to invite strangers to perform acts with them that are deemed to be appropriate only in private relationships. Their presence on the streets is constantly challenged by police and other authorities, who attempt to 'clean up' the streets and make these spaces 'respectable' by removing them. (1999, p. 146)

Prostitutes are not respectable because they do what women are not supposed to do; they hang around street corners attempting to catch the eye of passing men. This breaks all the taboos about how 'normal' women should behave, taboos which apply even more strongly to mothers, who are culturally charged with responsibility for respectability. Mothers working in prostitution routinely assess the critical boundaries between unsafe and 'safer' situations/behaviour for themselves, children and other 'family'. Many report experiencing a feeling of tremendous amount of guilt in relation to their children. In respect of this, Lucy said:

> Like you don't know whose car you're getting into, you don't know them or anything, you just think what if someone kills me, what's the baby going to think when she gets older. Your mum got killed by a punter while she was out on the game; it's not very nice is it?

Another mother at the drop-in cafe described how during an encounter when she was being violently assaulted and threatened with a knife by a 'punter', her first thought was she would be killed and miss her child's forthcoming birthday party, confirming that the mother voice is always present.

Prostitution is a high-risk occupation (Whittaker and Hart, 1996) and these risks are increasingly managed on a personal basis. Research observation and discussions with other multi-agency workers at the drop-in cafe; confirm that violent assaults are reported every week. As does the following extract from Ellen's interview:

Interviewer: *So you just definitely want to get out of the work?*
Ellen: Yeah I mean the money's good but it isn't worth it. I feel sorry for like some of the lasses that work down there. I mean the lass that come in the clinic and that you can tell she hadn't fallen off the settee. It's terrible and like there's lasses getting raped and that by some fella in a Jeep. I got picked up on Wednesday by some fella in a Jeep, but he wasn't bendy and he didn't look like the man so I thought I'd chance it but I shouldn't of really chanced it but he was alright, he turned out all right, he was dead nice.

Women working in prostitution are the recipients of 'routine' violence from 'punters', 'boyfriends/pimps', drug dealers and gangs of youths on the streets who clearly consider women working in prostitution to be 'fair game' for verbal harassment and violent assaults.

Concluding comments

In conclusion, this chapter has explored the 'everyday' worlds of young mothers working as street prostitutes, focusing upon the importance of motherhood in their accounts of managing risk. These young women are constantly negotiating the boundaries between risky and safe activities and spaces (physical, economic and emotional). Narratives of 'family', for example, using their earnings to pay for children's toys are intertwined with those of managing violence from customers, or 'punters' and violent pimps or partners. In this way, the critical boundaries between 'work', 'family' and 'home' are challenged. Prostitutes breach the perceived dichotomy between these spheres, by engaging in intimate acts (which belong in the private sphere) in exchange for money, a contractual agreement belonging to the public sphere. Barbara voices these dichotomies; she is juggling 'selves' or identities in an effort to manage risk and keep herself and her 'family' safe and with her. The poignancy about the following quote is related to both the romanticised, chocolate box view of the family that it evokes, and the fact that she is well aware that it is probably unachievable:

> My ideal world is a nice house, a nice husband or a nice boyfriend who goes out to work em a part time job and my kids. All my kids together, just a nice, little, normal happy family.

The same woman says of a violent male partner who is currently barred from living with her and her children via an exclusion order:

> He's a brilliant dad. He is a really good Dad; he'd spend 24 hours a day with her if he could. We've discussed if we have to finish, if the Social Services say that me and him have to finish through the kids, like I won't be able to have the baby, we will finish. We're not stupid we have discussed things. We have been serious about it, but we want them to give us a chance to work together to do it. Two parents is better than one.

As argued earlier in the chapter, the young women's narratives confirm that they are not passive victims, but rather that they actively engage with both public discourses of 'good mothering' that impact upon their sense of self and identity as mothers, and with discourses of 'fallen women', or 'dirty', street prostitutes. The respectable mothers discourses are utilised to legitimise their identities as mothers and to distance themselves from the more stigmatising aspects of street work, especially drug taking which is routinely linked with prostitution. Despite their anxieties and guilt about any impact that the stigma attached to prostitution might have upon their children, all of those interviewed spoke of the material benefits that their earnings enabled for the children. The desire to provide for their children and other family members where necessary outweighed the risk of criminalisation. Likewise, assessing the risk of violence from potential clients was an everyday occurrence, which they accepted as just 'part of the job'.

Appendix

Table A4.1 Sample of young mothers working in prostitution

Name*	Age	Number of children	Family background and current situation
Lucy	20	1 child (8 months)	Recruited into prostitution from a children's home aged 14. Just finished methadone programme after using class A drugs. Living alone but male partner/pimp who had just been released from prison, staying often. Just returned to street prostitution one night a week to earn extra money.
Judy	21	1 child (1 year) and 6 months into second pregnancy	Married but estranged from husband. Current pregnancy by another man who had denied paternity and deserted her. Recruited into prostitution aged 16 from children's home. Had largely exited prostitution but worked the streets occasionally when she needed the money. At time of interview living at mother's house with her child, her brother and sister and their children.
Ellen	18	1 (3 years)	Entered prostitution aged 13 to support herself after running away from a children's home. Stated that her child had no father. Has a long-term relationship with older man whom she keeps a distance from. Living in her own tenancy with child at time of interview. Has contact with step mother who is approximately the same age as her and was separated from violent father.
Barbara	19	2 children (2 years and 1 year). 7 months pregnant at time of interview	Stated that she had never worked in prostitution despite being accessed at the drop-in centre and observed working on the street. Homeless with children in care at time of interview.
Natalie	21	2 children (4 years and 4 months)	Entered prostitution after leaving home aged 16 after birth of eldest child. Living back with parents and her own children at time of interview. Baby on child protection register. Addicted to heroin but reducing steadily via methadone. Living away from child's father (a heroin user and pimp) to help her break habit.

Note: * All names have been changed to ensure confidentiality of participants.

Notes

1. The full project report: 'Empowering Young Parents', Green *et al.* (2001) is available from the Centre for Social and Policy Research, University of Teesside, Middlesbrough TS1 3BA email B.Cox@tees.ac.uk
2. See Table A4.1 for a profile of interviewees.
3. Dr Patricia Bell (the senior researcher on the project) carried out the interviews and participant observation at the drop-in centre. Although this centre is open to young men working as prostitutes, during the lifetime of the study, exclusively young women accessed it. This is probably due to the fact that male prostitution in the area is believed to be organised through bars and clubs and is not visible on the streets.
4. Department of Health/Social Exclusion Unit (1999) *Teenage Pregnancy*. Cm. 4342, London: Stationery Office.
5. The organisation of prostitution obviously varies a great deal. Our study focused exclusively on street prostitution, the bottom end of the market, where sexual servicing was exchanged for as little as £10, not coincidentally the price of a bag of heroin at the time.
6. Lupton, D. (1999) *Risk*. London: Routledge.
7. The 'habitus' is a set of dispositions and bodily techniques and ways of behaving that is passed down the generations and linked to membership of particular subcultures. Many of these dispositions or behaviours operate at the unconscious, embodied level in our everyday lives.

References

Berthoud, R., McKay, S. and Rowlingson, K. (1999) 'Becoming a single mother' in McRae, S. (ed.) *Changing Britain, Families and Households in the 1990s*. Oxford: Oxford University Press.

Church, J. (1997) 'Ownership and the body' in Tietjens Meyers, D. (ed.) *Feminists Re-think the Self*. Oxford: Westview Press.

Coy, M. (2003) 'Between the Self and the other: young women's experiences of the links between care and prostitution', paper presented to the *British Sociological Association Annual Conference*, University of York, April 2003.

Department of Health (2000) *Safeguarding Children Involved in Prostitution: Supplementary Guidance on Working Together to Safeguard Children*. London: HMSO.

Giddens, A. (1991) *Modernity and Self Identity*. Cambridge: Polity Press.

Jarvinen, M. (1993) *Of Vice and Women: Shades of Prostitution*. Oslo: Scandinavian University Press.

Lupton, D. (1999) *Risk*. London: Routledge.

McIntosh, M. (1996) 'Social anxieties about lone motherhood and ideologies of the family, two sides of the same coin' in Silva, E. (ed.) *Good Enough Mothering? Feminist Perspectives on Lone Motherhood*. London: Routledge.

Mitchell, W. and Green, E. (2002) 'I don't know what I'd do without our Mam'; motherhood, identity and support networks'. *The Sociological Review*, Vol. 50, No. 1, pp. 1–22.

O'Connell Davidson, J. (1996) 'Prostitution and the contours of control' in Holland, J. and Weeks, J. (eds) *Sexual Cultures*. London: Macmillan.

O'Neill, M. (1994) 'Prostitution and the state: towards a feminist practice' in Lupton, C. and Gillespie, T. (eds) *Working with Violence*. London: Macmillan.

O'Neill, M. (1997) 'Prostitute women now' in Scrambler, G. and Scrambler, A. (eds) *Re-thinking Prostitution: Purchasing Sex in Britain in the 1990s*. London: Routledge.

O'Neill, M. (2001) *Prostitution and Feminism, Towards a Politics of Feeling*. Cambridge: Polity.

Phoenix, P. (1991) *Young Mothers*. Cambridge: Polity Press.

Seymour, W. (1998) *Re-making the Body: Rehabilitation and Change*. London and New York: Routledge.

Shildrick, M. (1997) *Leaky Bodies and Boundaries: Feminism, Postmodernism and (Bio) Ethics*. London: Routledge.

Silva, E. B. (1996) *Good Enough Mothering? Feminist Perspectives on Lone Mothering*. London: Routledge.

Smart, C. and Neale, B. (1999) *Family Fragments?* Cambridge: Polity Press.

Whittaker, D. and Hart, G. (1996) 'Research note: managing risks, the social organisation of indoor sex work', *Sociology of Health and Illness*, Vol. 18, No. 3, pp. 399–414.

5
The Labour Market Inclusion and Exclusion of Young People in Rural Labour Markets in Scotland

Fred Cartmel

Introduction

This chapter investigates the processes operating in rural areas that contribute to the labour market integration and social exclusion of young people. I will contend that the 'risk' of unemployment for young people is based upon local social conditions and lack of contact with informal networks rather than global and individual factors that has been posited by Beck in 'Risk Society'. Recent sociological literature claims that old social cleavages have disappeared and that society has entered a new epoch where individuals have to create their own biographical trajectories (Giddens, 1991; Beck, 1992). The sociological ideas posited are not far removed from the Government philosophy and their policy approaches to dealing with unemployment among young people, which entails improving their 'employability'.[1] In this chapter I will analyse the extent in which older sociological theories pertaining to social divisions have become defunct and new concepts relating to 'risk' are relevant in modern Scotland, in particular considering the role of social networks in alleviating the risk of long-term unemployment in rural areas.

Throughout the last decade 'risk society' (Beck, 1992) has increasingly become an availed concept within the sociological literature for explaining social change within advanced industrial capitalism. The major differentiation between 'risk society' and the old industrial model of society is emphasis placed upon the individual to create their own biographical trajectories. Indeed, Beck has emphasised how 'risk' in society has sidelined class analysis to the periphery of sociological analysis or made redundant all together. Beck portrays this new epoch as 'capitalism without classes'. Beck goes onto argue that in 'risk society' individuals are being set free from constraints of the old order and encountering a new set of threats that impact on their daily lives. Beck (1992) argues that Risk Society (Giddens, 1991, 'high modernity') has replaced industrial society leading to a completely new set of risks and opportunities, as the introduction to this volume outlines.

Beck's work emphasises the increased capacity individuals have to create their own biographies regardless of class or other social location. Risk is heralded as a global phenomenon that cannot be analysed through investigation in local conditions or old social divisions. Although, these new sets of global risks (e.g. environmental disasters and nuclear war) are not evenly distributed across populations there is different vulnerability to risk, which is not based on social class.

There are numerous dissenters to the notion of social changes leading society into the new epoch of 'risk society'. Levitas (2000) disputes that the first condition of the risk society, the utopian nature of the existing society, arguing that this has never been met in Britain. The author contends that relative and absolute poverty has increased since 1979, welfare protections have been removed and the National Health Service is at near collapse. Therefore, material differences in income and the services that the disadvantaged rely upon for basic health care are no different to 20 years ago. This is especially true among young unemployed people, as changes in welfare benefit regulations have led to them being financially poorer that 10 years ago, more likely to face benefit sanctions and subject to increased surveillance of their job search activities.

The move to risk society is contended to have changed the relationship between the individual and society, which has shifted:

> The old social categories of modernity, such as class, have lost much of their salience, and individualization has become of greater significance'. (Caplan, 2000, p. 6)

Culpitt (1999) contended that the concept of risk posited in Risk Society is not neutral but based upon 'fabricated uncertainty', due to Beck's failure to engage with previous anthropological theories. In anthropological theory, Douglas (1992) defined risk as a neutral concept that took into account the 'probability of losses and gains' (p. 2). Douglas argues that social institutions that impinge upon individuals create risk. Beck (1992) argues that risks are global. The move from localised 'risks' to global risk has implications for micro-level empirical research of unemployment.

Quantitative studies have continually highlighted the importance of educational qualifications for alleviating the risk of unemployment (Bynner and Parsons, 2002). Links between lower social class and poor educational attainment have been shown to exist for a number of years. Therefore, risk of unemployment is substantially higher in the lower strata of society. Although, quantitative research highlights the importance of educational qualifications, the structure of rural labour markets reduces the need for educational qualifications due to the low skilled employment available, which recruits from a pool of similarly qualified young people. Therefore, employers use different mechanisms for selecting recruits which are based upon different risk assessment criteria. The main assessment used by rural employers is based upon local knowledge regarding the recruits or their families standing within the community. Leading to decisions being made about individuals that are based upon historical ideas about their family that are transmitted on to the young person, who cannot alter the past.

Pathways into the labour market

Shucksmith and Chapman (1998) ascertain that identifying pathways into employment and uncovering exclusionary practices that prevent individuals from gaining access to the labour market has become the focus of sociological research. Research on the transition of young people from education into employment has highlighted numerous structural factors that smooth the pathway into the labour market. In Scotland, Furlong (1993) argued that young people from working-class backgrounds had poorer life chances than other classes and were more susceptible to periods of unemployment. Roberts (1968) contented that local opportunity structures had a strong impact on young people's transition from school to work. Furlong and Cartmel (1997) demonstrated that structural factors are major determinants for predicting young people's transitional outcomes throughout Britain.

Previous quantitative studies of youth unemployment have highlighted the importance of educational qualifications on the employment chances of young people (Furlong, 1992; Bynner and Parsons, 2002). Furlong (1992) argued that level of educational qualifications was the main predictor of employment prospects for young people in Scotland. The author went on to argue that educational achievement was closely linked to social class, therefore young people from working-class backgrounds were more likely to face unemployment than youth from other social classes. Participation on Government training schemes (Youth Training Scheme (YTS), Youth Training etc.) was also stated to be the main indicator of future spells of unemployment (see Main and Shelley, 1990). The participation of young people in training schemes can be predicted through the unemployment rates within given localities (Roberts, 1995). There have been studies that have suggested that some employers used YTS to 'screen' potential young employees, as to the skills they acquired from schemes (Raffe, 1985).

Therefore, consideration of how structural factors in distinctive local labour markets impact upon young people's individual subjective orientations must be integrated into analysis of pathways into either integration or exclusion. Young people living in areas of high unemployment encounter structural barriers that for young people in labour markets where unemployment is lower do not have to negotiate. Similarly, young people living in a rural labour market may face problems related to accessibility to employment, training and education that their counterparts in urban labour markets do not. Therefore, young people in urban and rural labour markets have different experiences when negotiating the pathway into employment. Indeed, young people residing within the four rural labour markets all faced different problems and 'risks' when attempting to access the labour market.

Rural youth research in Britain has mainly concentrated upon young people's transition from school into employment, their occupational aspirations and participation in youth cultures (Macdonald, 1991; Wallace *et al.*, 1991; Furlong and Cartmel, 1995). The lack of sociological investigations into the experiences of rural youth is attributable to their invisibility. Young people residing in rural areas are not perceived as a threat to the established social order by policy makers, media and others which has led to a lack of investigations into their experiences. The sociological studies undertaken into rural youth have noted that the problems young people encounter are related to their rural location. Research conducted into young people's labour market experiences in rural areas, shows that rural youth have less accessibility to transport, training and have problems getting a 'sustainable career in the context of a highly seasonal labour market' (Dench, 1985 quoted in Wallace *et al.*, 1991; Stern and Turbin, 1987). The seasonal labour markets in rural areas have specific problems that will be addressed later in this chapter.

Family and friends networks provide young people with social capital that assists them in the integration process. The alleged 'individualisation' of pathways into the labour market has not diminished the influence of family background variables on the transition process (Furlong and Cartmel, 1997). Social capital can be defined as the set of informal values and norms shared by members of a group. The sharing of values and norms permits cooperation among members of a group (Fukuyama, 1999). The basis of social capital is trust, if members are honest and reliable then the group will trust one another. The problems that incomers face is the lack of trust given by locals, therefore, it is difficult for incomers to become integrated into the social networks within a locality. Fukuyama (1999) argues that the norms that produce social capital include: 'telling the truth, meeting obligations, and reciprocity' (p. 17). These norms overlap with the values that Weber found critical in developing Western capitalism. The family is central in the social capital accumulation, as parents are more likely to trust their siblings than trust strangers, hence, the reason that most businesses began as family concerns.

Qualitative data

The results from qualitative interviews with employers and young people in four rural areas cast doubt about the importance of educational qualifications on gaining employment. Rural labour markets are characterised by limited employment and educational opportunities, compared to their urban counterparts. Indeed, the concept of a rural labour market has been challenged by academics, as they argue that due to the nature of rural areas it is difficult to define in light of the low numbers of employment opportunities available.

The four contrasting areas used in our study encompass different labour markets: an ex-industrial area, traditional rural, urban fringe and seasonal labour market. The main differences in the labour markets related to the unemployment rates, access to educational establishments, main types of employment and travelling distances to urban areas. The ex-industrial area has the highest unemployment rate at 18.9 per cent (January 1997) with the nearest further educational establishment situated 10 miles away, with the closest urban area being 45 minutes travelling distance. The type of employment in the area has fluctuated since the demise of the coalfields, regeneration grants have led to new companies relocating to the area, with the majority offering low skilled employment. The two largest employers are in the textile industry based in a town with a population of 9500 people.

Unemployment rates in the seasonal area fluctuate from 8.8 per cent in January to 4.9 per cent in July 1997. There is no further educational establishment within the area. The nearest being in a central belt conurbation that is two hours drive away, this leads to young people leaving the area to attend further and higher education courses. Tourism related jobs provide the main employment opportunities in the area, which are predominantly seasonal and the majority part-time. There is also seasonal employment in local fish farms where employee numbers increase during October, November and December. The local town, Westport, population 8800 is the centre of commerce in the area and provides ferry links to islands on the West Coast of Scotland.

In the urban fringe, unemployment stands at 7.2 per cent in January 1997, an educational establishment is based in the urban area (population 32,212) one hour's drive from the furthest extreme. The main employment opportunities are in the urban areas, with local opportunities in forestry, tourism and small businesses.

The traditional area has an educational establishment in the local town of Southland, which has a population of 32,000 and an unemployment rate of 7.6 per cent (January 1997). The local town provides the majority of the employment opportunities and smaller local settlements have employment opportunities in old traditional industries. One small settlement has a creamery, which transports workers in from Southland due to lack of local residents available to take up employment. The traditional area had the highest percentage of workers employed in agriculture throughout Scotland.

The quantitative data used is from a European Union unemployment study that draws on a sample of 18 to 24 year olds who were both unemployed at the time of selection and who had been out of work for at least three months during the previous year. Distribution of the postal questionnaire was six months after original contact (for description of sample rates see Cartmel and Furlong, 2000). The sample was intended to reflect the national unemployment picture, but is skewed towards males with 527 (64 per cent) male respondents and 290 (36 per cent) female respondents. The sample covers the age range 18 to 24, with a mean age of 20.7. The young people in the sample have different labour market status when completing the questionnaire: employed, unemployed, in education/training and some had withdrawn from the labour market.

With the sample being drawn from those who have recently experienced unemployment, the qualification profile of the group is somewhat below that of the age range in general, as would be expected. Almost one in four males (24 per cent) and more than one in 10 females

(11 per cent) had no educational qualifications. However, the sample does include some relatively highly qualified young people: almost one in five females (18 per cent) and one in 10 males (8 per cent) had university degrees. Among the males, those from rural areas had a stronger overall academic profile, while among the females differences were minimal. Overall, over 55 per cent of young people who had attended training schemes were unemployed after completing the training scheme, while 28 per cent found employment. The young people in urban areas were more likely to find employment (59 per cent) compared to those (41 per cent) in rural areas.

Processes of integration and exclusion in the four contrasting rural labour markets were investigated through 80 in-depth interviews. The main findings were that structural factors existed that affected integration and exclusion in the four contrasting rural labour markets. The two most important factors for young people getting into employment are accessibility and social networks. The characteristic saying among young people in the rural areas was 'it's who you know, not what you know in this area'. The majority of young people who had become integrated into the labour market stated they had secured employment through friends or family. Employers contended that their preference when recruiting was young people with previous work experience, which many young people gained from part-time employment through social network recommendations. The informal network as a 'ladder' was evident in all the labour markets, with the majority of young people stating in the interviews that they had found employment through friends or family.

The excluded, drifters and the integrated

The qualitative interviews were divided into three typologies of young people: the excluded, drifters and the integrated. The categories are close to the work of Bynner *et al.* (1997) who identified three broad bands in a study of the Birth Cohort Study (BCS) 1970 cohort. The three groups were 'getting on, getting by and getting nowhere'. The three categories were based upon the labour market history of the young people. Those with substantial periods of employment are categorised as integrated and at low risk of future unemployment. The majority of young people in the integrated group within each labour market had accessed employment through friends of family at one point in time and many commented that they would never have found employment without the assistance of family networks. The drifters were individuals who had sporadic periods in the labour market and were at a higher risk of future unemployment. The excluded were respondents who had experienced long periods of unemployment and were at high risk of future unemployment.

The qualitative evidence suggests that educational qualifications are not as important for young people's integration in the rural labour market due to the low skilled work available in the locality. Our findings reinforce earlier investigations (Boyle, 1990 referenced in Wallace *et al.*, 1991) who found that educational qualifications were unimportant. Rural employers tended to prefer young people with practical skills and provided on the job training. The low educational qualifications of young people appear not to hinder their progress into the rural labour market. Transport accessibility and social networks are the largest denominators for young people becoming integrated into the labour market.

Previous research has highlighted that local informal networks are influential in assisting the unemployed to gain employment in labour markets. Indeed, Jahoda *et al.* (1972) argued that one detrimental effect of unemployment was losing contact with the social networks that provide information about local employment opportunities. Social networks provide important job information for the unemployed (Morris, 1984; Daniel, 1990). Coffield *et al.* (1986) ascertained that inclusion into the community provided access to 'family and neighborhood networks for hearing about jobs' (p. 141). Inclusion into the local community is important for young people for providing access to local job opportunities. In rural areas, inclusion into the community can also provide access to transport for travelling to employment in other areas. The feeling of inclusion in a local community can be detrimental to the unemployed, as moving away from the area to find employment is seen as a hardship (Harris, 1987). The ex-industrial community was close-knit with very few young people moving away for either work or education. The ex-industrial community was also very deprived and this could have a bearing on the reasons why young people did not want to move away from the area. As Jordan *et al.* (1992) found on a deprived housing estate in Exeter that 'for all the problems, the community provided them with a culture with which they were familiar ... where they got support and a sense of membership' (p. 7). The importance of local family/friendship networks and 'community life' can lead to young people ignoring employment opportunities outside their subjective boundaries. The community culture of the ex-industrial area was insular with respondents reluctant to consider employment outside their own locally subjectively erected boundaries. Although, unemployed Marie described the advantages of living in the ex-industrial area:

> Well you ken everyone. What I think here is more a comfortable atmosphere, you can go out and you know, you can let your weans play out and you can trust them here. It's a close-knit community and everybody looks out for one another here, not the likes of Glasgow. (Marie, ex-industrial)

Marie extolled the close-knit community where she resided as being safe for children. Marie stated that Glasgow was a place to be avoided, as she perceived it as dangerous and risky. Later in the interview Marie discusses her only excursion to Glasgow as frightening with nobody speaking to her and the fact that she did not know anyone. The close-knit community can impede young people's horizons and create fear about the 'other' external world being risky and dangerous.

The concept of place takes prominence in the life world hysteria; as young people reside in the same locality they increasingly have their own hobbies, work, social contacts and so on. Therefore, although this chapter is attempting to homogenise the experiences of young people across places, the employment prospects and life situations of all young people must be regarded as particular to them. The sphere of consciousness surrounding each young person is different, as the social world in which he or she resides is now becoming more and more different. Compared to Marie's negative experience of anywhere outside her close-knit local community, positive orientations to anywhere outside their local area were exhibited by the young people in the seasonal area. The explanation for these young people embracing other cultures is due to the absence of further educational establishments within the area. Therefore, high proportions of young people migrate from the area to attend college or university and everyone in the locality knows someone who has lived in either Glasgow or Edinburgh. A second reason for a more outward subjective orientation is that the seasonal area also attracted a high number of tourists who interact with the local population. Although migration for further education can reduce risk of unemployment when returning to the area, there remain risks with moving to gain educational qualifications. Jack moved to Glasgow to undertake a further education course but failed due to spending too many hours in the numerous bars in Glasgow and also failed to secure a permanent job on return to the area.

The role of the family in providing social support and information about employment opportunities could be argued to have become more pivotal for young people than for previous generations due to their extended periods of dependency upon the family. Throughout the European Union, the average age that the majority of young people enter employment has increased from 18 in 1987 to 20 in 1995. Young people are remaining in the family home longer with 65 per cent of 20–24 year olds residing at home in 1987 compared to 68 per cent in 1995 across the European Union. Young people are now becoming more dependent upon their families, with the young unemployed more reliant upon family members to provide information about employment. There were young people who were fatalistic stating that family networks were 'the only way that I've been able to get a job' (John, 21, ex-industrial). Another respondent who gained employment through his father stated that 'if it wasn't for him I would not have got a chance' (Mike, 22, traditional).

The role of the family was particularly important to certain young people with one stating that:

> It was my dad that helped me get into ******* when I worked there. (Mary, 21, ex-industrial)

The strength of family ties was important for young people who were seeking employment, but friends also played a part in providing young people with access to employment.

The role of social networks in providing information about local employment opportunities is only one of the functions that networks provide, as they perform various functions in a community. Wellman *et al.* (1988) studying East Yorkers constructed four different typologies of networks operating in the area; havens, band-aids, ladders and levers. The 'ladder' networks assisted people to change their situation (i.e. getting into employment etc.). Networks not only provide assistance to the unemployed to find work, but also provide advantages for local employers. Employment opportunities can be captured by a kin network (i.e. miners, fishermen, dock workers' etc.). The monopoly of employment opportunities being secured by family networks is positive for the kinship networks, but negative for young people who reside outside the network. When existing composition of a workforce is for a particular sector of community, subsequent recruitment can come from the same base, therefore certain areas are neglected. The strong mining communities in the 1970s recruited from small employment bases, ignoring individuals who lived outside the employment base. The advantages for employers recruiting from a small employment base come through the threat of censure from colleagues, who are also neighbours and friends. Stable employment bases can lead to individuals becoming disadvantaged, as:

> The process of chain employment or grapevine recruitment will serve to exclude those not socially connected to existing employers from the source of employment. Indirect discrimination may be as powerful a constraint or disadvantage as direct discrimination. (Grieco, 1987, p. 43)

The social reproduction of disadvantage onto young people can come from their parents' social standing in the community. Exclusion can manifest itself through intergenerational reproduction through family stigmatisation in the labour market. Young people whose parents have little social standing in the community can be excluded through mechanisms over which they have no control. The 'ladder' network is important for securing employment but also for providing information about jobs that will become vacant in the future. Granovetter (1983) describes weak ties as the connections that are maintained with socially distant individuals (i.e. acquaintances) compared with strong ties (i.e. friends and family). The weak ties are important for gaining access to information and goods and services that are not available through close friends and family.

> I get to know through like places I've worked before they'll tell me such and such a place is looking for someone, they'll phone up for me and then I'll go and see them myself and that's that. (Peter, 23, ex-industrial)

The quote illustrates the advantages for young people of accruing social capital through work experience.

The strength of the social ties in networks has been argued to be of significant importance. Granovetter (1983) argues that weak ties provide better connections for gaining employment as they link individuals to people who are dissimilar and operating in different social milieus. The strength of weak ties is the introduction to people who respondents would not normally encounter through their family networks. One example of a weak tie is Gillian who stated that:

> It was one of my pals I never seen for a while and I didn't think she would actually go into the factory and I asked her if there were any jobs and that and she says well phone up and give my name and say

that I told you to phone, so I phoned and eventually I got a job out of it. (Gillian, 20, ex-industrial)

The friends can provide references for young people or provide the information about employment that is coming available.

It was through my friend I got that one in *****, cos she worked for them before and she had said go in and mention my name and tell them you're looking for this and that, I got that job through her and there's another one I got a couple of years ago I got it through a friend as well. (Susan, 22, traditional)

This young person could be regarded a drifter, although she talks about getting employment, all the jobs were seasonal and she remained unemployed in the winter months.

My brother-in-law's father, he found out from my mate that I was looking for work and he just phoned me up and offered me a job so that was great. The fish farm I found out through a friend that they were looking for people, so I phoned and I got taken on, the fishing boat was through a friend. (Malcolm, 22, seasonal)

Malcolm spent short periods of time unemployed and decided to start his own business, although he faced many problems due to not being connected to the local informal networks. The type of work that Malcolm was involved in meant reliance on local contacts to provide information about openings. The local social networks are useful for young people in providing information about housing:

It tends to be one of those word of mouth things again, being a small area a lot of people know people's parents or they know when, you know, if someone's moving out they tend to recommend somebody else that they know is wanting to move, sometimes it tends to be who you know. (Alex, 21, seasonal)

Social networks are argued to be more emotionally supportive for women than men and this affects their psychological distress during unemployment (Russell, 1999). Female social networks are not as useful for finding employment as male social networks. This could be explained through women not having social contacts that have the power to hire or fire. Another more plausible explanation could be that

women do not see their social networks as useful for providing information about employment. The use of informal networks for gaining
employment can exclude certain social groups in the population including ethnic minorities.

Excluded

The young people who were excluded from the local labour market had
little connection with the social networks in the area or had friends who
were also unemployed, which prevented them from gaining access to
the local labour market. The excluded are a group of young people who
have experienced either a long duration or numerous periods of unemployment and have not succeeded in getting engaged with the labour
market. One respondent commented that:

> Its hard to get a job – if you've done something wrong in one job,
> whereas in Glasgow you could walk in and out of jobs and ... not like
> here you can't. (Sharon, 19, seasonal area)

The problem that this girl faces is the stigmatisation from employers
after making one mistake in her last employment. The lack of work
experience was another structural barrier that many young people faced
with many stating that they could not find employment due to not
having a job in the past.

> I find it hard to get a job because I do not have extensive experience
> in work and because most employers locally say that I am overquali-
> fied, too old or will be leaving shortly. In addition, I find that since
> my parents do not have extensive local connections and are not
> wealthy, I am at a disadvantage in getting a job also there is not an
> awful lot of jobs locally anyway. (Glenda, 20, ex-industrial)

The above extract highlights the necessity of young people residing in
rural areas to be involved in social networks to secure employment.
Although, returning graduates are seeking employment in the national
labour market, which does not rely that heavily upon social networks.
There were several graduates who had moved home due to the high cost
of living away and whilst seeking work in the national labour market
were seeking fill in employment in the local labour market.

The failure to gain integration into the labour market created identity
problems for several of the respondents. Prolonged unemployment is

associated with lack of self-confidence and low self-esteem, which is often caused through no positive activities and because of the absence of a work role. Jake discussed his problems while being unemployed:

> Boredom, you see hundreds of people just walking about the streets during the day and at night and it's just boredom, there's nothing to do. (Jake, ex-industrial)

The area where Jake lived had a high concentration of unemployed people, which has been argued minimises the stigmatisation of unemployment. The negative consequences of unemployment were worse for males than for females due to many young women adopting alternative social roles to maintain their social identity. The negative social roles associated with females varied between the areas. In the ex-industrial area single parents were accepted, whereas, in the seasonal area lone parents were stigmatised. One young woman talked about the reaction of local community when taking her daughter to nursery:

> I took her to playgroup last week and all the other mothers were looking down their noses, pulling their kids away from her 'cos I was a single parent and they weren't. (Kim, seasonal)

The stigmatisation of Kim by other parents forced her to consider migrating from the area and moving into a city, which meant leaving behind her family and friends.

The risk of prolonged unemployment increases when individuals do not have access to local informal networks, but there are also dangers associated with gaining employment through family and friends. When the young people acquired jobs through this route there was more likely to be coercion to conform in the workplace from the person making the recommendation. Ann, after a long period of unemployment gained a job in a shop her best friend had rented. Ann talked about there being extra pressure to work harder, as she felt beholden to her friend for providing her with the opportunity to work. Ann finally left the shop for other employment and stated:

> ... I don't think that you should work with friends because when we don't speak, it kinda turned nasty at the end, I just don't think it should ... (Ann, urban fringe)

Ann stated that living in a small village and falling out with her friend had caused problems, as there were no other young people of her age within the local area. The respondents generally stated the risks associated with gaining employment through informal networks to be minimal, but in certain cases exploitation undoubtedly took place.

Discussion

The importance of social networks in alleviating the risk of prolonged unemployment in rural labour markets cannot be under estimated, although it is difficult to assess any difference with urban labour markets. Integration into informal networks was through different mechanisms operating within the areas. Long family ties within the area were important for gaining the employment from local employers who knew members of the extended family. Incomers faced problems through having very few local connections.

Cliff, an incomer when asked why his family had moved to the village replied:

> It sure as hell wasn't at my behest, I'll say that much ... there's nothing but kids and coffin dodgers out here, I tell you, there's nothing for you. (Cliff, urban fringe)

Cliff argued that there were few employment opportunities and he had not wanted to or become integrated into the area. There is an element of mistrust about incomers, as very few people trust someone who was not born and bred in the area or indeed had previous connections with the locality. Strangers or incomers were treated with little trust due to not being known locally. The way that many incomers become accepted into the community is through 'fitting' into the local rural area of life, or putting something in to fit into the way of life (see Jones, 1999). Incomers face particular problems, as William states, recreation in a new locality of social networks among kin and friends is something of an 'art' (Williams, 1981).

There has been little research highlighting the different mechanisms operating in rural and urban labour markets, but a small amount of evidence suggests that social support in rural labour markets is stronger than in urban areas (Harding and Sewel, 1992). Coles (1988) stressed the importance of local knowledge for young people gaining employment in their rural labour market. Grieco (1987) contends that networks play an important role in the filling of vacancies in both local and national labour markets. Young people who migrate from the area can provide information about employment opportunities to friends and relatives back home. Research into people moving to Corby from Scotland found that individuals contributed information about employment opportunities but more importantly provided accommodation for migrants moving into the area (Greico, 1987). Although, our research did not investigate young people who had moved to other areas, there was a small amount of evidence that young people moved to where their family or friends had found employment.

The social capital gained in rural areas through networks is phenomenally high with young people integrated into a network more likely to gain employment than those outside the networks. The accumulation of social capital is important for young people to fend off the threat of social exclusion. Young people accrue social capital from their educational experiences, family background and so on but the accumulation of social capital in rural areas might be more diverse with employers not requiring the high level of qualifications that are required by urban employers. Indeed, employers in our sample stated that work experience was an important criterion for recruiting workers. Atkinson *et al.* (1996) investigated the reason why employers failed to recruit the unemployed. They found that (43 per cent) this was due to lack of work experience. The Training and Employment Research Unit (1997) found that less than 6 per cent of employers regarded qualifications as important. This emphasises the need for young people to accumulate social capital through social networks to gain a 'ladder' into employment.

Conclusion

Informal networks provide a valuable source of information for young people living in rural communities on employment opportunities. Within the four contrasting labour markets differences do exist, with the informal network in the ex-industrial community providing a 'haven' for young people but not providing a network which constitutes a 'ladder'. The integrated, relied heavily upon social networks to provide access to employment opportunities. Conversely, the excluded appear to have difficulties breaking into the informal networks that would provide information on opportunities in the local labour market. The drifters are a group of young people who are situated upon the fringes of the labour market and rely on informal networks to continue their struggle against exclusion. The structural factors affecting young people's integration into the labour market include family stigmatisation, which can thwart a young person's chances of getting any employment and increase the risk of exclusion. Therefore, risk of unemployment associated with global influences and poor educational qualifications are minimal in rural areas compared with structural influences like connections to informal networks that provide information about employment. Although, as the majority of workers in rural areas operate within the volatile low skilled sector of the labour market, information provided to potential jobseekers is related to work in this sector, which is in itself precarious. One solution for minimising the risk of unemployment for young people in rural areas is to provide quality employment and better quality training.

Acknowledgements

I would like to thank Andy Furlong for comments on early drafts of this chapter. This chapter is based upon work funded by the Joseph Rowntree Foundation, European Commission DG 12 and DG22 under the TSER SOE2-CT96-3025 and YfE: EEC916-10-EET-0128-00.

Note

1. Employability is a concept used in the development and implementation of active labour market policies, yet has no one agreed meaning but rests upon the premise that an individual is deficit in certain skills. (See Hillage and Pollard, 1998 for a definition of one meaning.)

References

Atkinson, J., Giles, L. and Meager, N. (1996) *Employers, Recruitment and the Unemployed*. Brighton: Institute of Employment Studies.
Beck, U. (1992) *Risk Society. Towards a New Modernity*. London: Sage.
Bynner, J. and Parsons, S. (2002) 'Social exclusion and the transition from school to work: the case of young people not in education, or training (NEET)'. *Journal of Vocational Behavior*, Vol. 60, pp. 289–309.
Bynner, J., Ferri, E. and Shepherd, P. (1997) *Twenty-Something in the 1990s: Getting On, Getting By, Getting Nowhere*. Aldershot: Ashgate.
Caplan, P. (2000) *Risk Revisited*. London: Pluto Press.
Cartmel, F. and Furlong, A. (2000) *Youth Unemployment in Rural Areas*. York: York Publishing.
Coffield, F., Borrill, C. and Marshall, S. (1986) *Growing up on the Margins: Young Adults in the North East*. Milton Keynes: Open University Press.
Coles, B. (1988) (ed.) *Young Careers*. Milton Keynes: Open University Press.
Culpitt, I. (1999) *Social Policy and Risk*. Sage: London.
Daniel, W. W. (1990) *The Unemployed Flow*. London: Policy Studies Institute.
Douglas, M. (1992) *Risk and Blame: Essays in Cultural Theory*. London: Routledge.
Fukuyama, F. (1999) *The Great Disruption*. London: Profile Books.

Furlong, A. (1992) *Growing up in a Classless Society*. Edinburgh: Edinburgh University Press.

Furlong, A. (1993) 'The Youth Transition, unemployment and labour market disadvantage. Gambling on YTS'. *Youth and Policy*, Vol. 41, pp. 24–35.

Furlong, A. and Cartmel, F. (1995) 'Aspirations and opportunity structures: thirteen year olds in areas with restricted opportunities'. *Journal of Guidance and Counseling*, Vol. 23, pp. 361–75.

Furlong, A. and Cartmel, F. (1997) *Young People and Social Change: Individualism and Risk in the Age of High Modernity*. Buckingham: Open University Press.

Giddens, A. (1991) *Modernity and Self Identity. Self and Society in the Late Modern Age*. Oxford: Polity.

Granovetter, M. (1983) 'The strength of weak ties: a network theory revisited' in R. Collins (ed.) *Sociological Theory* (Vol. 1). San Francisco: Jassy Bass, pp. 201–33.

Greico, M. (1987) *Keeping it in the Family: Social Networks and Employment Chance*. London: Tavistock.

Harding, L. and Sewel, J. (1992) 'Psychological health and employment status in an island community'. *Journal of Occupational Psychology*, Vol. 65, pp. 269–76.

Harris, C. C. (1987) *Redundancy and Recession in South Wales*. Oxford: Basil Blackwell.

Hillage, J. and Pollard, E. (1998) *Employability: Developing a Framework for Policy Analysis*, RR 85, Department of Education and Employment, Sanctuary Buildings, Great Smith Street, London WC2N 6HT.

Jahoda, M., Lazerfeld, P. and Zeisel, H. (1972) *Marienthal: The Sociography of an Unemployed Community*. London: Tavistock Publications.

Jones, G. (1999) 'The same people in the same places?'. *Sociology*, Vol. 33, pp. 1–22.

Jordan, B., James, S., Kay, H. and Redley, M. (1992) *Trapped in Poverty? Labour-Market Decisions in Low Income Households*. London: Routledge.

Levitas, R. (2000) 'Discourses of risk and utopia' in Adam, B., Beck, U. and Van Loon, J. (eds) *The Risk Society and Beyond*. London: Sage.

Macdonald, R. (1991) 'Youth, class and locality in rural England'. *Youth and Policy*, Vol. 33, pp. 17–26.

Main, B. G. M. and Shelly, M. A. (1990) 'The effectiveness of Youth Training Scheme as a manpower policy'. *Economica*, Vol. 57, pp. 495–514.

Morris, L. (1984) 'Patterns of social activity and post redundancy labour market experience'. *Sociology*, Vol. 18, pp. 339–52.

Raffe, D. (1985) 'Degrees of informality: methods of placement among Scottish school leavers'. *British Journal of Guidance and Counseling*, Vol. 13, No. 3, pp. 292–307.

Roberts, K. (1968) 'The entry into employment: an approach to a general theory'. *Sociological Review*, Vol. 16, pp. 165–84.

Roberts, K. (1995) *Youth and Employment in Modern Britain*. Oxford: Oxford University Press.

Russell, H. (1999) 'Friends in low places: gender, unemployment and sociability'. *Work, Employment and Society*, Vol. 13, pp. 205–24.

Shucksmith, M. and Chapman, P. (1998) 'Rural development and social exclusion'. *Sociologia Ruralis*, Vol. 38, pp. 225–42.

Stern, J. and Turbin, J. (1987) *Youth Employment and Unemployment in Rural England*. London: Development Commission, Tavistock Institute.

TERU (Training and Employment Research Unit) (1997) Report to Scottish Enterprise. Unpublished.

Wallace, C., Dunkerley, D. and Cheal, B. (1991) 'Young people in rural South West England'. *Youth and Policy*, No. 33, pp. 10–16.

Wellman, B., Carrington, P. and Hall, A. (1988) 'Networks as personal communities' in B. Wellman and S. Berkowitz (eds) *Social Structures: A Network Approach.* Cambridge: Cambridge University Press.

Williams, R. G. A. (1981) 'The art of migration: the preservation of kinship and friendship by Londoners during a history of movement'. *Sociological Review*, Vol. 29, pp. 621–47.

Part II
Space, Place and Leisure

Part II

Space, Place and Everyday

6
From Policy to Place: Theoretical Explorations of Gender–Leisure Relations in Everyday Life

Cara Aitchison

Introduction

Leisure is a significant site of identity construction and contestation for youths. Constructing identities in and through leisure often involves risk, adventure and the testing of boundaries. Recently, however, leisure sites and activities have become the focus of a society preoccupied with minimising risk, increasing safety and dominated by what Furedi (2002) has described as a 'Culture of Fear' that has resulted in increased anxiety and reduced engagement in activities deemed to be 'risky' or where leisure participants may be seen as 'at risk'. The subject field of leisure studies has offered critiques of the ways in which public policy has attempted to regulate both risk and leisure for young people. These critiques have drawn on structuralist accounts of leisure and have recently been supplemented and complemented by post-structural critiques developed within a range of social science disciplines and subject fields including gender studies and social and cultural geography.

This chapter evaluates the subject field of leisure studies as an increasingly complex and contested site of social and cultural critique. In addition to looking at leisure studies, readers are invited to direct their gaze through the lenses of gender studies and social and cultural geographies to explore relationships between gender, place and identities constructed in and through leisure. In doing so, the chapter outlines ways in which leisure studies has responded to theories of leisure relations developed within gender studies and geography whilst also evaluating leisure studies' contribution to theories of gender and spatial relations. Drawing on geography, as an underpinning or 'parent' discipline to the subject field of leisure studies, the chapter highlights contrasting and, at times, competing discourses of gender and leisure whilst also seeking to tease out the extent to which 'risk' is accommodated within these discourses.

These competing discourses are simplified within this chapter under the two broadly defined labels of structural and post-structural. These contrasting discourses have developed at different rates in different subject areas; often resulting in the development of discursive tensions when one theoretical perspective, epistemology or claim to 'ways of knowing' about social and cultural relations is seen to conflict with another. The chapter reviews: the development of a policy-focused structuralist orthodoxy in leisure studies; the response by feminist leisure scholars to add the personal to these political critiques; the rise of more recent post-structuralist perspectives in social and cultural geographies; and the challenge of seeing a way through this false dichotomy of structure and culture by rendering visible, what is termed here, the social-cultural nexus of gender–leisure relations (Aitchison, 2000, 2003).

This chapter engages with recent theoretical developments in gender studies and social and cultural geographies where dialogue between the social and the cultural, the structural and the symbolic, the material and the discursive has begun to illustrate the usefulness of exploring the spaces between such binary or dualistic constructs. By introducing the concept of the social–cultural nexus, the chapter seeks to synthesise social and cultural theories from gender studies and social and cultural geographies and to apply such thinking to discussions of gender–leisure relations in everyday life. The aim, then, is not to introduce any new empirical data but to provide an integrated theoretical exploration of the material and symbolic reality of gender and place as mediators of leisure relations. In other words, youth, risk and leisure are not objective realities that exist independently of the gender and spatial relations at work (and play) within society.

The concept of the social–cultural nexus acknowledges the contribution of structuralist discourses in informing our understanding of formal leisure relations. Structuralist discourses are those that focus on the big picture or the grand narratives of capitalism, patriarchy, racism or ableism in explaining social and cultural relations. Simultaneously, the social–cultural nexus embraces post-structural theory to engage with analyses of the productive consumption of leisure in everyday life, where leisure is seen as a significant site of gendered identity formation. Post-structural theory focuses on the micro-level of the everyday where difference and diversity may be visible *within* class, gender, race and (dis)ability categorisations in addition to being identifiable *between* such categories. The concept of the social–cultural nexus therefore builds on the much earlier work of sociologists such as Goffman (1963), cultural theorists such as R. Williams (1961) and the writings of sociocultural theorists belonging to the Frankfurt School to address the spaces revealed between the contrasting structuralist critiques evident within orthodox leisure studies and the post-structuralist writings of contemporary social and cultural geographies.

Although there is insufficient scope within the chapter to present a detailed exposition of post-structural theory, it is important to indicate that the chapter relates more closely to political theories of post-structuralism as expounded by Foucault (1977) than it does to the linguistic theories of post-structuralism developed by French psychoanalytic theorists. In doing so, acknowledgement is made of the irony of drawing on a Foucauldian critique, which largely ignored gender–power relations and ignoring linguistic critiques, which did acknowledge the interrelationships between discursive and gendered power. However, the accommodation of a Foucauldian exposé of cultural power relations does render more visible the power and place of leisure as a mediator of both hegemonic social relations and transgressive cultural agency in constructing identity in everyday life.

The chapter is structured in three main sections. The first section outlines the development of leisure research and its dominant focus, within the UK, on issues of public policy. The second section charts the response, by mostly socialist feminist leisure scholars, to the dominant structuralist discourse of leisure studies outlined in the first section of the chapter. This second section introduces the personal into the political analyses of previous leisure studies literature by chronicling the development of feminist research within leisure studies from the first studies of women and leisure in the 1980s through to present day research. The third section provides an overview of recent theoretical developments in social and cultural geographies where post-structural analyses have provided a meeting ground for critiques of gender, leisure and place. These analyses of cultural production and consumption have accommodated critiques of gender, sexuality and identity that were previously marginalised within orthodox leisure studies. Moreover, this recent research has contributed to new theorisations of risk within leisure. Whereas the sociology of leisure has largely turned its back on what it has defined as 'dark' leisure or 'deviant' leisure, and leisure management has become preoccupied with 'managed' risk in leisure, social and cultural geographies have explored risk as an everyday, and frequently sought after, aspect of contemporary leisure, particularly young people's leisure. The chapter concludes by stressing the interrelationality of leisure studies, gender studies and social and cultural geographies in our attempts to create more sophisticated analyses of the place of leisure and leisure places in constructing gender identities. The place of risk and risky places are central to such future integrated analyses of youth, risk and leisure.

Leisure research: public policy and the marginalisation of the personal

This section of the chapter attempts to outline dominant paradigms and discourses within the subject field of leisure studies. In the next section the discussion introduces a series of challenges to these dominant discourses in the form of emergent feminist resistances to what Spender (1981) has referred to as the 'patriarchal paradigm' (Aitchison, 2001a).

As disciplines and subject fields mature so the extent to which academics reflect upon the discursive developments within these fields and disciplines tends to increase. Leisure studies evolved from a number of different lines of academic enquiry that experienced rapid expansion in the 1960s and early 1970s. These included, but were not confined to, the geography and planning of outdoor recreation, the sociology of work and physical education and human movement studies. Although gender critiques now form important areas of research in all of these fields, feminist research was in its infancy in the 1960s and early 1970s and did not make its way into the emerging field of leisure studies until a decade later. Within the UK, the new subject field of leisure studies came to be dominated by the academic orthodoxy of the times, structuralist and Marxist analyses of class relations and the impact of economic inequity on leisure participation and provision. Within North American leisure studies the influence of psychology was more predominant than that of sociology. On both sides of the Atlantic, however, there was a shared neglect of feminist and cultural critiques and it seems quite likely that had leisure studies emerged 20 years earlier or 20 years later then its academic canon would undoubtedly have been different.

Coalter (1997, p. 255) has surmised these differences succinctly by suggesting that leisure research in the UK and North America is 'characterised by different epistemological, methodological, and theoretical perspectives'. He sees UK research as forming a collective body of knowledge termed 'leisure studies', whilst North American research has defined the field of 'leisure sciences'. Although this polarisation is clearly a generalisation, Coalter's definitions are symbolised in more than just the titles of academic leisure journals in the UK (*Leisure Studies*) and North America (*Leisure Sciences*):

> The predominantly sociological leisure studies has adopted a *society in leisure* approach, exploring how broader sociocultural structures are reflected in leisure and largely ignoring issues of individual meaning. The predominantly sociopsychological leisure sciences, with its stress on positivist methodology, has often produced analyses of *leisure without society* and failed to address issues of the social and cultural meanings associated with leisure. (Coalter, 1997, p. 255)

Although Coalter refers to UK leisure studies as having addressed 'issues of social and cultural meaning', the emphasis within UK leisure studies has been skewed strongly towards social critique rather than cultural analysis. Interestingly, Coalter talks about how the UK 'society in leisure approach' has explored 'sociocultural structures' although the very reference to structures implies a *structuralist* rather than cultural critique. The relationship between the structures of industrial capitalism and the provision of leisure can be seen in the form of the 'Rational Recreation' movement and 'Muscular Christianity' of the modernist public policy of the late nineteenth and early twentieth centuries where attempts were made to regulate the leisure activities and behaviour of working people. Leisure pursuits perceived to have a high degree of risk such as drinking, large festivals and public gatherings and 'dangerous' sports and games were outlawed in an attempt to reduce the risk to the developing economic and social order. Although the pretext given for such regulation is frequently individual and public safety a Foucauldian analysis would point to the ways in which such practices serve to regulate the body and produce conformity.

Whereas 1970s leisure studies had close links with one of the UK's first Cultural Studies departments in the form of the recently closed Centre for Contemporary Cultural Studies at Birmingham University, by the late 1980s there had appeared a large gulf between leisure studies and cultural studies. Leisure studies, as a subject field intent on providing both academic critique and practical application, had engaged with the new managerialism evident in Thatcherite public policy whilst cultural studies appeared to remain more true to its critical origins, spanning social science and aspects of the humanities. But, as Rojek (1995, p. 1) has emphasised, the importance of cultural analysis to our understanding of leisure in late modernity cannot be overstated: 'one cannot separate leisure from the rest of life and claim that it has unique laws ... the object of leisure is subsumed by the subject of culture'.

Within leisure studies, however, traditional welfarist approaches to leisure provision, underpinned by structuralist ideology, have continued to dominate academic policy and non-commercial sector management agendas (Henry, 1997; Coalter, 1998). Similarly, in the related field of tourism studies, academic critiques have been influenced strongly by economics, planning studies and policy studies where structuralist critiques remain dominant. The study of leisure and tourism as *products*, rather than *processes*, therefore continues to dominate the literature (Law, 1994).

Within these structuralist critiques the policy-driven agenda of eman-cipatory politics or social inclusion has formed an enduring theme in leisure studies scholarship and debate for over two decades. From the 1980s *Sport for All* campaigns, developed in response to the English urban riots of 1981, to the 1990s *Tourism for All* and *Countryside for All* initiatives, leisure-related policies have been seen as playing a central role in alleviating social inequality and economic inequity. These poli-cies, developed largely as welfarist responses to the limitations of a free market economy, have resulted in formal and facility-based leisure, and the academic analysis of such policies has been underpinned by struc-turalist theory and socialist ideology. Unsurprisingly, leisure studies has continued to be developed as part of what Coalter (1997) identified as the dominant equal opportunities discourse of *society in leisure* whereas social and cultural geographies have embraced post-structural theory in their socio-cultural analyses of what Sibley (1995) has termed *Geographies of Exclusion*. The structuralist approaches, with their macro-analyses, have therefore found it difficult to embody the individual or even the sub-cultural in theorisations of leisure provision and participa-tion or productive consumption (de Certeau, 1984). Moreover, the dom-inant focus on public policy by mainstream leisure studies has served to perpetuate Spender's notion of a 'patriarchal paradigm' where, with a few notable exceptions, critical studies of the family and leisure or youth and leisure are largely absent (Shaw, 1992; Kay, 1996; Roberts, 1999).

In North American leisure studies (leisure sciences), a focus on socio-psychological approaches to leisure research should have facilitated more extensive critical studies of youth, risk and leisure or gendered leisure behaviour. There is now an extensive literature on serious leisure (Stebbins, 1992), volunteering and leisure (Stebbins, 1992) and women and leisure (Henderson *et al.*, 1996) but still limited North American research investigating youth, risk and leisure or gendered leisure. One notable exception is Grossman who has worked within leisure studies to publicise his work on transgendered youth, risk and leisure in an attempt to bring about both theoretical and social transformation (Grossman *et al.*, 2002).

North American leisure sciences research has been driven by methodological concerns rather than a commitment to theoretical, ideological or social transformation. Burton (1996, p. 19) has criticised this reification of methodology as producing 'an obsession with method that is divorced from substance', whilst Hemingway (1995, p. 36) has critiqued leisure science's 'tendency to reduce enquiry to technique'. Whereas UK leisure studies remains dominated by structuralism and North American leisure sciences by positivism, neither UK nor North American leisure scholars have engaged fully with post-structuralism. In contrast with this assertion, Mommaas (1997, p. 251) claims that UK and European leisure studies *have* witnessed a 'shift from American-based scientism and functionalism to Gramscian neo-Marxism, French poststructuralism, semiotics and psychoanalysis'. There is some evidence to support this view from non-UK-based European leisure research, particularly that emanating from the Netherlands, which has sought to engage with post-structural and postmodern theory. In addition, there is now an emergent and rich seam of Antipodean research that incorporates post-structural analyses of gender and leisure (Wearing, 1998; Fullagar, 2000, 2002). Both Wearing (1998) and Fullagar (2002) have also critiqued the ways in which leisure and health policy, respectively, have served to 'govern' the site of the gendered body in attempts to reduce risk.

The potential of gender research to transform the canon of leisure studies is acknowledged by Coalter (1997) who notes that:

> Within leisure sciences, a major challenge to the positivist/ individualistic paradigm has come from feminist researchers, with their assertion of the need to understand 'situated meaning' and the role played by structure and ideology in creating contexts and meanings.... From a leisure studies perspective, it is interesting to note that feminist writers appear to be the most consistently international in orientation. (Coalter, 1997, p. 263)

However, even feminist researchers in both the UK and North America have argued that a lack of theoretical sophistication in leisure studies research extends to feminist and gender research of leisure (Henderson, 1994; Kinnaird and Hall, 1994; Swain, 1995; Shaw, 1997). Moreover, at a time when gender research in cultural studies, gender studies and social and cultural geographies was struggling to come to terms with the disruption of deconstruction, diversity and the arrival of postmodernism in the 1980s, leisure studies was still generating liberal and socialist feminist analyses of a kind which were increasingly viewed as overly essentialist, homogenising and outmoded in these other social science disciplines and subject fields. Whereas the arrival of post-structuralism and postmodernism had brought about a de-differentiation of the category 'women', and an increased focus on gender research rather than feminist research, leisure research, according to Mommaas (1997, p. 251), had 'related itself rather ambivalently to postmodern thinking' and postmodernist interjections have been 'made by people from outside the conventional domain of leisure research and remain on a rather general level of analysis'.

Thus, leisure research undertaken from a post-structural perspective has been more visible outwith, rather than within, leisure studies. For example, in social and cultural geographies we have seen the *Mapping of Desire* (Bell and Valentine, 1995), the theorisation of *BodySpace* (Duncan, 1996), *Images of the Street* as refracted through leisure and tourism (Fyfe, 1998) and analyses of the inter-relations between *Shopping, Place and Identity* (Miller *et al.*, 1998). In sociology, we have witnessed increasing interest in *Food, Health and Identity* (Caplan, 1997), *Body Cultures* (Bale and Philo, 1998), *Touring Cultures* (Rojek and Urry, 1997), *Culture of Fear* (Furedi, 2002) and in gender studies and cultural studies we are aware of the significance of *Barbie Culture* (Rogers, 1998), *Nike Culture* (Goldman and Papson, 1998) and *Internet Culture* (Porter, 1997). In all of these disciplines and subject fields, leisure, culture, sport and tourism have been theorised as central sites and processes of identity construction, contestation, negotiation *and* risk.

Engagement with post-structural theory has enabled analysis of both structural and symbolic power through the direction of our attention to what Adkins (1998, p. 47), writing at the interface of sociology and gender studies, refers to as the 'social/non-social nexus' or what, for the purpose of this chapter, could be termed the *social–cultural nexus* of gender–leisure relations. Critical engagement with structuralist theory, for example, in the form of Gidden's (1984) structuration theory, Beck's (1992), Bauman's (2000) and Lasch's (1990) theorising of modernity and Furedi's (2002) combative exposé of society's construction of moral panics, fear and paranoid parenting, has facilitated extensive debate of the meaning, prevalence and significance of risk in social, cultural and leisure relations. In contrast, leisure studies has been reluctant to embrace these discussions of risk and only now, through leisure management discourse, has the subject field of leisure studies begun to consider the significance of the social construction of managed risk in relation to leisure and sport pursuits, adventure education and independent travel. Leisure studies, therefore, has yet to play host to a nuanced debate about risk and leisure or to the inter-relationships between gender, risk and leisure.

Feminist research: the addition of the personal to the political

Green *et al.* (1990, p. 131), in their sociological study of women and leisure, acknowledged the significance of spatial determinants of women's leisure and, by association, the relevance of geographical critique by stressing that a 'significant aspect of the social control of women's leisure is the regulation of their access to public places, and their behaviour in such places'. During the 1980s a growing body of feminist research within leisure studies pointed to inequalities in leisure opportunities between men and women, with the majority of this research focusing upon informal leisure, recreation and sport (Deem, 1986; Wimbush, 1986; Green *et al.*, 1987; Wimbush and Talbot, 1988). Although this research was developed largely within the orthodox structuralist discourse of leisure studies and leisure policy it served to add the personal to these political critiques. The addition of the personal can be seen as a significant prerequisite for post-structural analyses, or even the adaptation of symbolic interactionist critiques, where agency forms a central component in transformative social relations.

Within feminist leisure studies, the publication of *Women and Leisure: A State of the Art Review* by Talbot (1979) represented the first piece of published research on women and leisure and it acted as a catalyst for feminist research to be undertaken within the subject field over the next decade. Whilst Stanley (1980) called for a 'radical feminist alternative' to the study of leisure, the ensuing research all tended to adopt a liberal or socialist philosophy (Deem, 1986; Wimbush, 1986; Green *et al.*, 1987). A series of publications based on research case studies was then produced during the 1980s. These case studies were specific to particular groups of women, particular types of leisure participation and to clearly defined geographical locations. Whilst each case study served to highlight and clarify a further aspect of the feminist agenda, the research did not explicitly address spatial issues and none of the research was undertaken from a geographical perspective. Moreover, although risk was not identified or named as such in these accounts, it is clear that the notion of risk, in the form of threats of violence and/or unwarranted attention from men, formed a central and thematic concern within all of these research projects.

However, these research projects, mostly informed by a socialist feminist standpoint and underpinned by sociology and its concomitant interest in class relations, did serve to introduce broader critiques to the politics of leisure. For example, Woodward *et al.* (1988), introducing gender, sexuality and the family, stated that their survey:

> ...had indicated that some of the most significant influences on women's leisure were their social class, level of household and personal income, employment status, age group, marital status and stage in the family life cycle. (Woodward *et al.*, 1988, p. 99)

From the mid-1980s efforts were made to increase women's participation in leisure through the provision of 'women only' sport, leisure and recreation opportunities by local authorities, the Sports Council and the private sector (Sports Council, 1993). In other words, change was instigated through public policy rather than through acts of transgression or performativity (Butler, 1990). Many of these public policies sought to provide designated spaces and places for women in the form of specific times when women could use leisure facilities and services. These policies, often founded on largely unarticulated notions of managed risk, had mixed success and one major criticism was that they failed to recognise women as a diverse or heterogeneous group capable of being empowered to manage their own leisure and, by association, their own risk.

The feminist leisure research projects, undertaken in the UK in the 1980s, all highlighted ways in which women attempted to subvert male dominated control of leisure. Dixey and Talbot's (1982) study of women and bingo in Leeds served to highlight the existence of gendered leisure space, the male domination of public leisure space, and the response by women of carving out a spatial sanctuary in the form of the bingo hall. This was the first study to look at women's occupation of public leisure space as previous studies had focused upon women's leisure around the home and family and the different meanings and motivations for women participating in leisure compared to men. Deem's (1986) study of women and leisure in Milton Keynes emphasised further these gender differences but also built on Dixey and Talbot's work by stressing the differences *between* women in relation to their access to leisure and control of public leisure space. Thus Deem's work focused on the difficulties which working-class women, or women with young children, may experience in gaining access to leisure; difficulties which middle-class women may not experience to the same degree. This heterogeneity among women was further emphasised by a study of leisure participation by women with pre-school age children undertaken by Wimbush (1986) in two distinct areas of Edinburgh. Wimbush's study denoted clearly the inter-relationships of social class, space and risk, with working-class women's leisure largely confined to their inner-city homes and indoor community space while middle-class women were better able to enjoy outdoor recreation in safe leisure in suburban fringe of the city.

The largest and most frequently cited piece of feminist leisure research undertaken in the UK was that conducted in Sheffield by Green *et al.* in the form of an ESRC and Sports Council-sponsored research project to investigate *Leisure and Gender: A Study of Women's Leisure Experiences* which was published in 1987 and later formed the basis of a comprehensive text on the subject of women's leisure (Green *et al.*, 1990). All of the studies outlined above contain a wealth of insight into the construction of gendered leisure space; both indoor and outdoor, public and private, although spatiality remains largely untheorised as a result of the dominant emphasis on social class issues. This is in strict contrast to feminist geographical research from the same period where the relationships between gender, risk and leisure were clearly articulated in what Valentine (1989) described as the 'geography of fear' (Aitchison, 1999). The socialist feminist analyses developed in leisure studies also had the unwitting effect of largely invisibilising sexuality from the analysis of the data. It is the inter-relationship between spatiality and sexuality that has been reintroduced so visibly by the 'new' cultural geographers and their research outlined in the next section of this chapter.

Social and cultural geographies: (re)placing gender–leisure relations

What has come to be known as 'the cultural turn' of the 1980s and 1990s redirected the gaze of social and cultural geographers from social structures to cultural symbols and from the macro-analyses of global power relations to the micro-analyses of everyday life (Aitchison, 1999). Within these emerging critiques of everyday life, the inter-relationships between youth, risk and leisure have been rendered increasingly visible through a focus on the social and cultural relations played out in informal leisure arenas of spaces ranging in scale from the body, to the bedroom, to the street, to global backpacking and youth travel. In contrast, with the exception of limited contemporary studies of gender and leisure, leisure studies has remained more focused on 'the big picture' of structural power, with this perspective continuing to be informed by public policy and a vision of leisure participation and provision mediated through the formalised leisure facility and facilitator in the form of the leisure centre and leisure manager. Here, the focus is upon minimising risk for leisure participants by viewing leisure within a health and safety context rather than exploring or even celebrating informed engagements with risk witnessed in extreme sports, street culture, music and other forms of productive consumption.

Although the economic importance of leisure has long been recognised within both geography and leisure studies, the social and cultural significance of leisure is only now beginning to be acknowledged within the rapidly evolving discourses of post-positivist and post-structuralist social and cultural geographies. These recent epistemological developments have forced the sub-discipline of social and cultural geographies to recognise the place of leisure and leisure places in informing discourses of spatiality (Skelton and Valentine, 1997; Aitchison *et al.*, 2000). Vice versa, leisure studies has begun to re-establish its relationship with geography by acknowledging the contribution of recent social and cultural geographies to spatialised analyses of the productive consumption of leisure. Such a synthesis of clearly differentiated discourses has not been easy. Following significant academic congruencies in the 1960s and 1970s, largely centred around a mutual valuing of structuralist critiques of inequality in production and consumption, geography and leisure studies departed from their shared script as the 1980s approached. With the increasing adoption of post-structuralist perspectives by many social and cultural geographers, leisure studies' structuralist orthodoxy appeared an insignificant anachronism to geography's new wave of researchers.

Previously, the relationship between geography and leisure research had been well established (Carlson, 1980; Barbier, 1984; Mowl and Turner, 1995). Indeed, the first issue of *Leisure Studies*, published in 1982, included an article by Coppock titled 'Geographical contributions to the study of leisure' in which he chronicled the increasing involvement of geographers in the field of recreation and tourism since the 1930s. The article paid particular attention to methodological developments in the spatial analysis of recreation and tourism during the 1970s, the decade preceding publication. Following Coppock's article, however, the discipline of geography underwent radical and transformative developments both resulting from and contributing to a number of new and competing philosophies within the social sciences. These recent social and cultural geographies have made significant contributions to the study of gender, youth, risk and leisure but, unlike leisure studies, have been less concerned with identifying policy and practice as *leisure, tourism, sport* and *the arts*, and more concerned with situating leisure within the commercial, everyday and informal contexts of cultural consumption, risk and identity formation (Shields, 1991; Shurmer-Smith and Hannam, 1994; Bell and Valentine, 1995, 1997; Miles, 1997; Skelton and Valentine, 1997; Fyfe, 1998; Skeggs, 1999).

The geographical discourses from the 1970s and 1980s, when combined with leisure and tourism studies discourses from the 1990s, highlight the role of structural relations in shaping spatial and leisure relations. This focus is in contrast to the emphasis on cultural relations displayed by the new cultural geographies of the 1990s where, for example, Deforges (1998) has provided an account of youth travel and engagement with risk in his chapter titled 'Checking out the planet'. Both Rojek and Urry (1997) and Sheilds (1991) have stressed the importance of cultural spaces in constructing leisure patterns and cultural relations. S. Williams (1998, p. 172), too, has asserted that, '[T]he construction and subsequent consumption of tourist places is essentially a socio-cultural process'. This process has previously been conceived of as being mediated through a 'leisure industry', where commodification and consumption are controlled increasingly by professional and commercial interests (Adorno, 1993). In contrast, writers such as de Certeau (1984) have stressed the importance of *everyday life* as a form of productive consumption where 'consumers', instead of being 'cultural dupes', are themselves constantly involved in remaking culture. This scope for agency allows us to see leisure as a continually evolving landscape with space for resistance, contestation, disruption and transgression of dominant discourses and wider hegemonic social, cultural and leisure relations (Aitchison, 2001b).

The social–cultural nexus: integrating policy and place in gender–leisure studies

Future explorations of gender, leisure and place would undoubtedly benefit from a theoretical framework that encompasses structural *and* cultural critiques. In addition, the adoption of such an epistemological approach offers scope to recognise the significance of the interface or nexus of the structural and cultural. Moreover, recent social and cultural geographies of gender and sexuality have referred to the importance of the betweeness of space as a place where iterative, productive and performative reworkings of power relations take place outside the public gaze.

Geography's *cultural turn* has given rise to such post-structural analyses of power where, as Cooper (1994) has emphasised, power is seen (or not seen) as 'productive, relational and everywhere'. This emphasis on cultural construction rather than material determinacy can also be viewed as building on Elshtain's (1981) critique of socio-structural theories as 'narratives of closure'. Post-structural analyses guide the critical eye from structures to cultures by revealing underpinning discourses and networks of power beneath society's social structures. This focus on the micro-analysis of cultural foundations of power emphasises the need for critical commentaries to be contextually, temporally and locally specific and to negate theories of power as a holistic, global and systemic phenomena (Hartsock, 1990). With no systemic power, however, there can be no overall system of domination and oppression: only specific and localised contexts of subordination, resistance and transformation exist.

In providing a critical commentary of gender, leisure and place, one of the questions for this chapter to consider is the extent to which systemic power, in the form of patriarchy or capitalism, exerts influence over gender–leisure relations and/or the extent to which localised, contextualised and pluralised power relations serve to shape inter-relationships between gender, leisure and place. In attempting to answer such a question, any analysis of contemporary gender–leisure relations needs to be contextualised within relevant social and cultural milieu and within the structural contexts that have contributed to the making of these social and cultural contexts. The concept of the social–cultural nexus accommodates the reworking of logocentric structures by problematising historical facts and truths as series of social and cultural constructions that offer neither total nor static explanations of social and cultural relations. The totalising explanations offered by the meta-narratives of structural theories have been critiqued in post-structuralist writings as 'narratives of closure' because of their emphasis on power as repressive and dominating, rather than productive and relational. By the same token, the social–cultural nexus acknowledges that structural relations embodying systemic power do exist and that it is often the interface between the social and the cultural that serves to inscribe and reinscribe power relations.

To conclude, a conceptual framework such as the social–cultural nexus, which recognises the signification of productive and relational power, the regimes of structural power, *and* the inter-relations between these productive and determined relations, offers scope to develop a socio-cultural critique of hegemonic social relations and transgressive cultural agency of gender–leisure relations in everyday life. Such a critical perspective offers an accommodation between the structuralist accounts of leisure studies and the post-structuralist accounts of social and cultural geography. In doing so, it is possible to reveal the structuralist legacy of public policies intent on managing risk within and through leisure and the post-structural engagement with risk in leisure sites and processes revealed within contemporary social and cultural geography.

References

Adkins (1998) 'Feminist theory and economic change' in Jackson, S. and Jones, J. (eds) *Contemporary Feminist Theories*. Edinburgh: Edinburgh University Press.

Adorno, T. (1993) *Dialectics*. London: Routledge.

Aitchison, C. (1999) 'New cultural geographies: the spatiality of leisure, gender and sexuality'. *Leisure Studies*, Vol. 18, No.1, pp. 19–39.

Aitchison, C. (2000) 'Poststructural feminist theories of representing others: a response to the "crisis" in leisure studies' discourse'. *Leisure Studies*, Vol. 19, No. 3, pp. 127–44

Aitchison, C. (2001a) 'Gender and leisure research: the codification of knowledge'. *Leisure Sciences*, Vol. 23, No. 1, pp. 1–19.

Aitchison, C. (2001b) 'Theorising other discourses of tourism, gender and culture: can the subaltern speak (in tourism)?' *Tourist Studies*, Vol. 1, No. 2, pp. 133–47.

Aitchison, C. (2003) *Gender and Leisure: Social and Cultural Perspectives*. London: Routledge.

Aitchison, C., MacLeod, N. and Shaw, S. (2000) *Leisure and Tourism Landscapes: Social and Cultural Geographies*. London: Routledge.

Bale, J. and Philo, C. (eds) (1998) *Body Cultures: Essays on Sport, Space and Identity by Henning Eichberg*. London: Routledge.

Barbier, B. (1984) 'Geography of tourism and leisure'. *Geojournal*, Vol. 9, No. 1, pp. 5–10.

Bauman, Z. (2000) *Liquid Modernity*. London: Polity Press.

Beck, U. (1992) *Risk Society*. Beverley Hills, California: Sage.

Bell, D. and Valentine, G. (eds) (1995) *Mapping Desire: Geographies of Sexualities*. London: Routledge.

Bell, D. and Valentine, G. (1997) *Consuming Places: We Are Where We Eat*. London: Routledge.

Burton, T. L. (1996) 'Safety nets and security blankets: false dichotomies'. *Leisure Studies*, Vol. 15, No. 1, pp. 17–19.

Butler, J. (1990) *Gender Trouble: Feminism and the Subversion of Identity*. London: Routledge.

Caplan, P. (ed.) (1997) *Food, Health and Identity*. London: Routledge.

Carlson, A. W. (1980) 'Geographical research on international and domestic tourism'. *Journal of Cultural Geography*, Vol. 1, No. 1, pp. 149–60.

Coalter, F. (1997) 'Leisure sciences and leisure studies: different concept, same crisis?' *Leisure Sciences*, Vol. 19, No. 4, pp. 255–68.

Coalter, F. (1998) 'Leisure studies, leisure policy and social citizenship: the failure of welfare or the limits of welfare', *Leisure Studies*, Vol. 17, No. 1, pp. 21–36.

Cooper, D. (1994) 'Productive, relational and everywhere? Conceptualising power and resistance within Foucauldian feminism'. *Sociology*, Vol. 28, pp. 435–54.

De Certeau, M. (1984) *The Practice of Everyday Life*. Berkeley: University of California Press.

Deforges, L. (1998) 'Checking out the planet: global representations, local identities and youth travel', in Skelton, T. and Valentine, G. (eds) *Cool Places: Geographies of Youth Cultures*. London: Routledge.

Deem, R. (1986) *All Work and No Play: The Sociology of Women and Leisure*. Milton Keynes: Open University Press.

Dixey, R. and Talbot, M. (1982) *Women, Leisure and Bingo*. Leeds: Trinity and All Saints College.

Duncan, N. (ed.) (1996) *BodySpace: Destabilising Geographies of Gender and Sexuality*. London: Routledge.

Elshtain, J. B. (1981) *Public Man, Private Woman*. Princeton, New Jersey, USA: Princeton University Press.

Foucault, M. (1977) *Discipline and Punish: The Birth of the Prison*. Harmondsworth: Peregrine.

Fullagar, S. (2000) 'Desiring nature: identity and becoming in narratives of travel'. *Cultural Values*, Vol. 4, No. 1, pp. 58–76.

Fullagar, S. (2002) 'Governing the healthy body: discourses of leisure and lifestyle within Australian Health Policy'. *Health: An Interdisciplinary Journal of the Social Study of Health, Illness and Medicine*, Vol. 6, No. 1, pp. 69–84.

Furedi, F. (2002) *Culture of Fear: Risk Taking and the Morality of Low Expectation*. London: Continuum.

Fyfe, N. R. (1998) *Images of The Street: Planning, Identity and Control in Public Space*. London: Routledge.

Goffman, E. (1963) *Stigma*. London: Penguin.

Goldman, M. F. and Papson, S. (1998) *Nike Culture: The Sign of the Swoosh*. London: Sage.

Green, E., Hebron, S. and Woodward, D. (1987) *Leisure and Gender: A Study of Sheffield Women's Leisure Experiences*. London: The Sports Council/Economic and Social Research Council.

Green, E., Hebron, S. and Woodward, D. (1990) *Women's Leisure, What Leisure?* London: Macmillan.

Grossman, A., O'Connell, T. and D'Augelli, A. (2002) 'Transgender youth: challenging traditional "girl–boy" activities – implications of an exploratory study for new directions in research' in Lawrence, L. and Parker, S. (eds), *Leisure Studies: Trends in Theory and Research*. Eastbourne: Leisure Studies Association, pp. 83–104.

Hartsock, N. (1990) 'Foucault on power', in Nicholson, L. (ed.) *Feminism/Postmodernism*. London: Routledge, pp. 157–75.

Hemingway, J. (1995) 'Leisure studies and interpretative social inquiry'. *Leisure Studies*, Vol. 14, No. 1, pp. 32–47.

Henderson, K. (1994) 'Perspectives on analysing gender, women and leisure', *Journal of Leisure Research*, Vol. 26, No. 2, pp. 119–37.

Henderson, K. A., Bialeschki, D., Shaw, S. and Freysinger, V. (1996) *Both Gains and Gaps: Feminist Perspectives on Women's Leisure*. Pennsylvania, USA: Venture Publishing.

Henry, I. (1997) *The Politics of Leisure Policy*. London: Macmillan.

Kay, T. (1996) 'Women's work and women's worth: the leisure implications of women's changing employment patterns'. *Leisure Studies*, Vol. 15, No. 1, pp. 49–64.

Kinnaird, V. and Hall, D. (1994) *Tourism: A Gender Analysis*. Chichester: Wiley.

Lasch, S. (1990) *Sociology of Postmodernism*. London: Routledge.

Law, C. M. (1994) *Urban Tourism: Attracting Visitors to Large Cities*. London: Mansell.

Miles, M. (1997) *Art Space and the City: Public Art and Urban Futures*. London: Routledge.

Miller, D., Jackson, P., Thrift, N., Holbrook, B. and Rowlands, M. (1998) *Shopping, Place and Identity*. London: Routledge.

Mommaas, H. (1997) 'European leisure studies at the crossroads? A history of leisure research in Europe'. *Leisure Sciences*, Vol. 19, No. 4, pp. 241–54.

Mowl, G. and Turner, J. (1995) 'Women, gender, leisure and place: towards a more "humanistic" geography of women's leisure'. *Leisure Studies*, Vol. 14, No. 2, pp. 102–16.

Porter, D. (ed.) (1997) *Internet Culture*. Routledge: London.

Roberts, K. (1999) *Leisure in Contemporary Society*. Walingford, Oxon: CABI Publishing.

Rogers, M. F. (1998) *Barbie Culture*. London: Sage.

Rojek, C. (1995) *Decentring Leisure: Rethinking Leisure Theory*. Sage: London.

Rojek, C. and Urry, J. (eds) (1997) *Touring Cultures: Transformations of Travel and Theory*. London: Routledge.

Shaw, S. (1992) 'Dereifying family leisure: an examination of women's and men's everyday experiences and perceptions of family time'. *Leisure Sciences*, Vol. 14, No. 3, pp. 271–86.

Shaw, S. (1997) 'Cultural determination, diversity and coalition in leisure research: a commentary on Coalter and Mommaas', *Leisure Sciences*, Vol. 19, No. 4, pp. 277–80.

Shields, R. (1991) *Places on the Margin: Alternative Geographies of Modernity*. Routledge: London.

Shurmer-Smith, P. and Hannam, K. (1994) *Worlds of Desire, Realms of Power: A Cultural Geography*. Arnold: London.

Sibley, D. (1995) *Geographies of Exclusion*. London: Routledge.

Skeggs, B. (1999) 'Matter out of place: visibility and sexualities in leisure spaces'. *Leisure Studies*, Vol. 18, No. 3, pp. 213–32.

Skelton, T. and Valentine, G. (eds) (1997) *Cool Places: Geographies of Youth Cultures*. London: Routledge.

Spender, D. (ed.) (1981) *Men's Studies Modified: The Impact of Feminism on the Academic Disciplines*. Oxford: Pergamon Press.

Sports Council (1993) *Women and Sport: Policy and Frameworks for Action*. Sports Council: London.

Stanley, L. (1980) *The Problem of Women and Leisure: An Ideological Construct and a Radical Feminist Alternative*. London: Sports Council/Social Science Research Council.

Stebbins, R. (1992) *Amateurs, Professionals and Serious Leisure*. Montreal: McGill/Queen's University Press.

Swain, M. B. (1995) 'Gender in Tourism'. *Annals of Tourism Research*, Vol. 22, No. 2, pp. 247–66.

Talbot, M. (1979) *Women and Leisure*. London: Sports Council/Social Science Research Council.

Urry, J. (1990) *The Tourist Gaze*. London: Sage.

Valentine, G. (1989) 'A geography of fear'. *Area*, Vol. 21, No. 4, pp. 385–90.

Wearing, B. (1998) *Leisure and Feminist Theory*. London: Sage.

Williams, R. (1961) *Culture and Society, 1750–1950*. London: Penguin.

Williams, S. (1998) *Tourism Geography*. London: Routledge.

Wimbush, E. (1986) *Women, Leisure and Well-being*, Final Report to Health Promotion Research Trust, Edinburgh: Centre for Leisure Research, Moray House College of Education.

Wimbush, E. and Talbot, M. (eds) (1988) *Relative Freedoms: Women and Leisure*. Milton Keynes: Open University Press.

Woodward, D., Green, E. and Hebron, S. (1988) 'Research note: the Sheffield study of gender and leisure: its methodological approach'. *Leisure Studies*, Vol. 7, No. 1, pp. 95–101.

7
Youth, Leisure Travel and Fear of Crime: An Australian Study

John Tulloch

This chapter is based on a study of fear of crime among three generations of respondents (teenagers, parents of teenagers, older people) in Australia at the turn of the twentieth century. The primary focus of the research fieldwork was qualitative, drawing on methodologies like the long interview and the focus group which had been little used in fear of crime research, especially in Australia. The main study, directed by Deborah Lupton, in fact incorporated an innovative quantitative/qualitative methodology (via interviews with 148 participants in different urban and rural areas in New South Wales and Tasmania). But even in this part of the study, the major methodological thrust was qualitative, providing more in-depth insights into how people construct their fear of crime as *situated* everyday experience. Two qualitative case studies, directed by myself, ran parallel to the main study, focusing on 'areas of concern' that had become apparent early in the main study interviewing process: fear of crime and public transport; and fear of crime and the media.

Overall, both the main study and case studies avoided the conventional 'rational/irrational' fear approach in the literature to emphasise 'lay knowledge', producing (especially via long interview and focus group methods) many socially situated tales (themselves deeply embedded in issues of age, generation, gender, sexual preference, ethnicity, class and physical location) to give us access to 'lay criminological' knowledges. In this chapter, my main emphasis will be qualitative case studies, and on the teenage cohort in our research, in particular their concerns about leisure-time travel after dark. It will try to give a sense both of the individual richness and the systematic similarities and differences among young people in their perceptions of leisure-time train travel. In the conclusion I will return briefly to the more generalised 'fear of crime' pattern against which these case studies need to be considered.

Teenagers on trains

> It's getting worse with teenage kids who will nick female's bags because they need the money because they can't get a job ... . They pin a lot of the crimes on teenagers making generalised comments that all teenagers are like that, when there's teenagers that are scared of teenagers.

> Other teenagers are the worst. They're getting worse. (Blue Mountains teenage focus group)

Young people are the most likely victims of crime. While older people may fear teenagers and young men generally, and feel that much of the crime and the visible vandalism stems from them, teenagers themselves are acutely aware of *both* the general stigma *and* the reality of teenage aggression to other teenagers.

Teenagers (especially girls) often fear to travel by train at night but, unlike older people, still tend to travel anyway. They are more mobile as a result of age. But also, given the shortage of major leisure facilities outside the centre of Sydney, young people regularly travel by train to the City (for example, from the Blue Mountains) for concerts, live television recordings and sports events; and they frequently travel back late at night. This means that many devise strategies for making themselves feel safer at night. *Girls* in particular spoke of these strategies:

- avoiding eye contact with males in the carriage;
- keeping alert at all times in the train, on the platform, in the street at night;
- discouraging conversation with people who sit next to them;
- surveying the carriage by looking at the reflection of the people around them in the darkened train windows;
- travelling usually in groups;
- sitting in the 'Blue Light' compartment (which in New South Wales trains indicates the proximity of the guard's cabin).

At the same time, teenagers were acutely aware of deficiencies in the strategies that had been adopted by the State Rail Authority. Virtually all the teenagers we spoke with felt that there was far too little visibility of people who were supposedly there to help them such as guards and police. 'If they've got a uniform its visual, it says okay there are cops on here.'

Whether or not these criticisms were always fair is not the whole point (though when we interviewed train guards, we did find a number who locked themselves in their cabin at night). Rather, these were the views that circulated by word of mouth because, individually and collectively, that is what enough teenagers encountered for them, as an age group, *not* to feel comfortable in trains at night.

Teenagers said that things had 'got much worse' recently, and they could usually offer 'lay' theories about the reasons: particularly unemployment and drugs. But, unlike older people who also spoke of unemployment and drugs as a cause for youthful crime, young people were also able to make cultural distinctions *within* their age group: for example, about the relationship between risk, public transport and *particular* groups of young people.

- They're getting worse. I mean the more conservative teenagers are threatened more by the 'Homies'. Because the 'Homies', they mightn't even want to do anything, but they look it ... I really don't like 'Homies'.
- In my year they're the main bullies and so on.
- Yeah.
- It's because they're trying to copy this culture that crime is part of, because it's trendy.
- And to be more American.
- And you get like little girls that say like I want to go over to America and hang out with the 'Homies', and it's like they're little blond white girls – if they went there they'd get *killed*. And they don't realise what they're sort of joining when they get into that sort of thing ...
- 'Homies' seem to stand on stations a lot.
- Yeah. [laughter]
- They just seem to stand on stations. (Blue Mountains teenage focus group)

'Homies' or 'Homeboys' is the popular designation of young men and teenagers (often of unskilled or semi-skilled migrant background) who adopt the Los Angeles 'basketball' style-image. Most of the Blue Mountains teenagers said that the 'Homies' they encountered nearer to home were 'aping' the Sydney 'Homies' and were not really dangerous like them. But teenagers who lived, travelled and went to school in areas where 'real Homies' congregated could give a very different account.

North Shore GPS teenagers

Mark, who lived and went to private school in the socially privileged North Shore area of Sydney, encountered 'Homies' every day at Chatswood station. Like the Blue Mountains teenagers, he emphasised that 'Homies' congregated at train stations. The 'Gordon Homies', he said, hung around the North Shore suburban station of Gordon in their beaten-up cars. The 'Homies' at the North Shore Chatswood station were on the platform when he went to school in the morning, and they were still there when he got back after school in the afternoon. If he stayed at school for rugby training, and got back to Chatswood at 6 p.m. they were still there, and he felt they posed a real threat to him because there were far less people getting off the train then. Consequently he arranged to be picked up from school by his mother.

Mark would not go on the train in the evening under any circumstances by himself; and even in the company of six other boys recently he (and they) felt scared taking a train home after going to a pub in the evening. They travelled by car whenever possible, making sure there was always one person who didn't drink. And there were always a couple of them carrying mobile phones (he borrowed his parents' mobile for security).

Mark's account was the first of many we heard that seemed at first to us to have an almost obsessive fear in relation to train travel, parties and 'Homies'. Unlike other potentially troublesome groups of young men, the 'Homies', we were told, targeted trains as part of their petty criminal economy. They were all, said Mark, ethnic Australians ('Wogs'), and his mother who used to fear for him in relation to 'weirdos' now worried about Homeboys, and said she would prefer to pick him up at 4 a.m. than that he risk train travel. His younger brother was also fearful of travel, and both had experience of violent assault on friends while in their company.

Mark talked of a particular series of assaults outside a party at a house close to Chatswood railway station, and argued that the Homeboys picked out the white drill trousers and polo top gear of 'GPS' (private school) types as a sign of whom to bash. His description of attacks outside his school and at parties was graphic. He described the largest boy in his school being beaten by a group of 'Homies' and being covered with a big blood-covered towel; and on another occasion he was outraged by 'the worst things personally' at a party (friends being 'knocked half-unconscious, with split lips and eyes all bruised up, seeing a friend kicked in the head, and a girl who got slashed').

Mark argued that the police did nothing, and that the media didn't cover the real crime on the trains (which in one sense he approved of, because more reporting would give the Homeboys more prestige). Tougher penalties not more media coverage was what he believed was needed. His increase in fear had been fairly recent, stemming particularly from a very violent assault which put some of his friends in hospital (he was not attacked, he thinks, because he happened to be wearing more baggy clothes – closer to the Homeboys' own gear).

There was a clear race/ethnic and no doubt also a class component in Mark's perception of Homeboys, and his sense of anger and outrage was all the stronger because of that. He said that he and his friends' anger was sufficiently strong sometimes to want to kill Homeboys, but he recognised that things would escalate if they did.

> They chase you and beat the crap out of you; and if you stand there they do the same ... That's why people *hate* them so much. And I personally, after some parties where my friends have got their faces smashed in, just wanted to jump into a car with a gun and shoot them, because for them logic doesn't exist.

But despite his continual fear of the Homeboys, Mark felt his community was lucky compared with friends in the Annandale (inner-City West) area who were threatened by organised gangs. In contrast, the Homeboys, he said, were ethnic 'amateurs', bored, 'with a chip on their shoulders', and looking for someone to bash. So even for the North Shore Mark and his friends, as for the Blue Mountains teenagers, the 'worst' teenage-to-teenage risk actually lay elsewhere.

Some inner-city Sydney 'Others'

'Teenagers', as a stereotype, were often constructed as 'the Other' by interviewees who feared travelling on public transport. But, as we have seen, even teenagers themselves would say that it was other teenagers that they most feared on the train.

For this reason we decided to take a *self-designated* group of teenage 'Others' in Sydney, to hear from them their own experience of travel on public transport when going to leisure activities. These were teenagers from a gay refuge in inner city Glebe. They came from a wide range of class and ethnic backgrounds, with varying contact with their parents (some of whom were quite affluent). Yet in an important sense this group of teenagers were 'determined' by their *performativity* as self-chosen 'outsiders': one had been a street kid, another girl self-presented so strongly as a male that she was regularly thrown out of female toilets, another self-presented as a Queen, another, who called herself 'Mission Girl', was a boy even though the interviewer initially thought that by dress, hair and voice she was a 'feral lesbian'. An extract of discussion between 'Orchid', 'Minister', 'Sharon Stone', 'Dexter', 'Jake', 'Mission Girl' and 'Christy' (their self-chosen 'Other' names, adopted for the focus group interview and for other 'public' occasions) will illustrate both how this group of teenagers self-presented as 'Other' and some of the leisure-time travel problems that they encountered.

 - We went to the beach ... and it was about 1 o'clock ... Friday night, and there were all these little 'Homie' shits.
 - 'Homie' drunks, fuckwits ....
 - The 'Homie' culture's pretty pathetic in general.
 - Well anyway, they were looking at me and Dexter.
 - Cause they [the guys] were wearing dresses ... pretty-punce style.
 - Like Mission Girl hopped on the bus and they looked at 'her'. And I hopped on the bus behind Mission Girl.
 - I was wearing a gorgeous dress too.
 - So was I. (male respondent) And they looked at us and they go, 'Oh my God, it's a guy dressed up as a chick' ....
 - And there was like, we were at the front and there was the whole back of the bus packed with these drunken twits ...
 - 'Homies.'
 - Screaming and going off like fuckwits. And they started throwing ....
 - Think about it but. You two guys got on in dresses, and this one gets on with just a towel and a pair of boots ....
 - I had a huge dog collar ... I looked like the guy from *The Prodigy*.
 - He had a dog collar on and I looked like a 'Homie' male but I was really a female.

The performativity of visual style as between Mark and his friends – with their white pants and polo jumpers when going out in the evening – and Mission Girl, Minister and Dexter, on the bus back from Bronte Beach, could hardly have been greater. In both cases they encountered abuse as 'Other' from the Homeboys. But their responses to this were different. There was a constrained class-based anger among Mark's group – with references to the 'Wogs' who 'hang around all day doing nothing', while the GPS boys are 'properly' at school, and where even their leisure time is regimented and co-ordinated via 'rugby training' and 'polo' style clothes. The group of gay teenagers were much more 'post-modern', performative and anarchic in style, so that they described *their* leisure encounter with the 'Homies' as 'a great Bronte story'. They deliberately played and performed with their identity visually, drawing on popular cultural names and stereotypes to disturb and challenge all social categories of what they define as 'straight' society, *including* the 'Homies' and the group of surf boarders also on the bus, whom they described as 'shark-fuckers'.

In the focus group discussion, there was a lot of laughter as they told their story of the ride from Bronte Beach which ended with the bus breaking down and them all ('Homies' included) having to push; and more laughter when one of them described the abuse meted out to him by an older lady when he was 'minding his own business sitting having a smoke' at a Sydney station. The lady was offended in particular by his 'Goth' black painted fingernails; and, according to this boy, the 'cracked lady' (accompanied by a pair of 'Yuppies') followed him on and off the train, abusing him still.

But this is not to say that Homeboys and other males could not cause them fear and anxiety. If one listens to the interview tape carefully, one notices that some of their 'stories' were told in almost complete silence: such as the girl who was hassled by the 'Homies' – 'I *hate* Homies!' – because they thought she was a boy; or the story of a girl who was severely punched in the eyes on the train from Liverpool to Redfern by males (after a platform argument with her girlfriend) who thought she was a guy. This was in the 'Blue Light' carriage at night, and when no guard appeared, she pulled out a knife to protect herself, and ended up in the police station as a result. Equally grimly narrated was the story of one of the girls who would not catch buses at night anymore after a very recent experience when first 'some boys down the back... were all calling me like "slut" and "whore", and I was like stressed by it, sickened in myself, and then an older man came up to me and ... wanted me to go back to his house and "suck his dick" and buy him drugs.' After an abrasive interchange with this man, he shoved her down the stairs off the bus into the road. 'And that was fairly late at night in Balmain and there was quite a few people on the bus, but because nobody did anything, they just didn't dare, I haven't got any faith in people on the bus. I haven't caught a bus at night since then.'

For this Glebe gay group, trouble on public transport was recurrent, significantly perhaps because of their self-performance as 'Other'. Apart from the incidents already described, in this Glebe teenage group

- a girl was asked while waiting for a country train at Central Station, Sydney for a 'head job' for $20, then for $100 when she refused. The man followed her on to the train and harassed her till Hornsby, where she got off;
- a girl living on the streets near Central Station was accosted there by a guy who couldn't communicate except by gesture. He gave visual signs that he wanted money, then followed her through Centrepoint Tower shopping complex, Hyde Park toilets, and then back by train to the inner-city suburb of Enmore, where she hid in her neighbour's house until he was gone;
- a boy was asked if he was 'cool' by a guy on the train, who then started rubbing his crotch;
- a girl allowed a bum on the train that she felt sorry for to chat to her – then he asked to have sex with her;
- a boy kept meeting an Aboriginal boy who offered him money for sex;
- a number of the group had been 'rolled' on the train for money, clothes, shoes, cigarettes, jackets, knives, wallets – though, the group also said 'They don't bother us because we don't wear Nikes'; and the two 'Goths' said that wearing black and a pentagram around their neck could scare people and prevent them from robbing them.

The Glebe group compared themselves with the 'general' or 'straight' public in terms of travel threats. 'We're targeted because, you know, she has short hair, we wear black, Jake's a Queen, you know we have all these different things that people pick us out of a crowd and that targets us. Old people get robbed, suits get robbed, but they only get robbed whereas we get hassled.'

A Blue Mountains teenager group

By no means all teenagers emphasised either upper-middle class or 'Other' visibility when travelling in leisure time. Many teenagers in our Blue Mountains focus group deliberately 'dressed down' on the train in order not to attract attention. As Chris, a Blue Mountains teenager told us in a long interview, his strategy on the trains was 'not to draw attention to myself in any way, not to interfere in anyone's business, not to insult anyone. Not to show intimidation, but not to be cocky either.'

A number of girls in the Blue Mountains group, only too aware of the unfairness in the legal system of judges pointing to the way women dress as a 'cause' for assault, spoke of being cautious about dress on public transport at all times, and especially after parties and social gatherings. The Blue Mountains group were divided broadly along gender lines over their level of anxiety at train travel. One male did indicate some concern particularly about local Blue Mountains stations and their environs (e.g. the Katoomba station underpass, where there had been a recent bashing) and he would avoid night travel if he could because he felt 'much safer during the day'. This boy, in his big black ('literary', Oscar Wilde-style) brimmed hat and long coat was, however, much more visible as a 'loner' than another, much bigger boy in the group who deliberately dressed neutrally. In contrast to the other boy, he travelled regularly to Sydney by train at night by himself, and though occasionally hassled by 'Homies', he 'laughed it off'.

The Blue Mountains girls' major concern was about leisure travel at night. They varied in the extent to which they did this: one travelled quite a lot at night alone, others always travelled in groups. The issue was not seen as a debilitating worry by these teenage girls, but would come to the fore when they found themselves in uncomfortable situations. It is important here to emphasise the pervading effect of 'social incivilities' on these teenage girls who travelled at night: from men who stared at them in the carriage; from the man in the next seat who vibrated his knee close to yours; to seeing males masturbating in the train or in the next telephone booth on a station platform. As we have seen, teenage girls who neither performed as 'Other' nor were dressed to emphasise their class, commonly adopted a range of surveillance strategies if they were on the train after dark, while at the same time pretending not to be looking around, in case it drew attention to them or made them seem nervous.

The Blue Mountains boys, too, could encounter situations that scared them even when trying to keep out of trouble. One teenage boy, aware that his older brother had been beaten up and robbed after getting off the train at Wollongong (supposedly for 'looking' at two other teenagers on the train), tended to travel quietly, in company when he caught the train at night. Once he was travelling late with two friends (one male, one female) from a concert in Sydney when a tough-looking middle-aged man, 'scruffy clothes, some teeth missing, covered in tattoos and excited in a weird sort of way', approached them on the platform and began to talk. The man then sat with the three teenagers, saying he'd just been released from Long Bay Jail that day. When asked, he said he was imprisoned for murdering a man 'with a Bowie knife in the back' during a drunken brawl. He told them how tough life had been in jail, but he had now made it out of 'sixteen years in Hell'. While he went for a smoke, the teenage girl spoke to another man that she knew in the carriage, who confirmed that he had met men out of prison on their day of release on three occasions before, and 'they were a lot like this one'. After the man returned from his smoke, he sat with the teenagers again and unnerved them by continuously slamming an old-fashioned can opener into his case. He spoke with them about going to see if his parents still had property at Lithgow, then suddenly changed his mind and got off the train, thinking he had reached Parramatta. This incident has made Chris 'a bit more nervous' of travelling by himself on the train because he didn't know how he would 'have handled it if alone'.

However, the Blue Mountains teenagers talked of incidents like this as 'one-off', and were generally concerned about train travel at night 'only from Penrith on to Sydney' (i.e. through Sydney's Western Suburbs), though some of them worried over the lonely, sometimes long waits for trains at deserted, unmanned Blue Mountains stations. The locational map of fear was quite different for our inner city Sydney teenage 'Others', and was much more variably related to direct and systematic personal experience. For example, one boy who had worked sexually in Kings Cross and had been a street kid said he was not prepared to travel there even in the day because they 'hate him', but was happy to go West because of lots of friends at Paramatta and Bankstown. Another boy said he wouldn't travel to the Western Suburbs since he had 'come out' because of the prejudice there, but nor would he catch buses in the City at school time. The personally situated and differentiated nature of their City travel fear among this gay group in leisure time was very evident, even though as a group there was strong camaraderie and mutual recognition.

Agency, security and structure

The Blue Mountains teenagers strongly criticised security technology: help points that didn't work and surveillance cameras so fuzzy that they were no use to the police in identifying culprits after a Katoomba Station underpass mugging. Unlike the North Shore teenagers, who tried to use their parents' cars wherever possible, the Blue Mountains group were heavily reliant on trains to Sydney for their leisure-time activities, and these teenagers called for the 'greater physical pressure' of uniformed security as they were travelling back by train late at night; and for a technology that could be trusted to gain help and catch offenders (so that potential offenders would feel that they 'would actually be caught').

The group of gay Sydney teenagers also emphasised the importance of uniformed surveillance on the trains, arguing for security men in every carriage at night. This request for '24-hour security' was not surprising in a group with such a high record of harassment and theft against them on and around trains. Nevertheless, there was a distinct difference in the request for uniformed security between this and every other group we interviewed. *Only* this gay group of Sydney teenage 'Others' emphasised the difference between uniformed police and security guards. A number of them had had trouble with police interrogation. One girl said that she was 'as scared of cops as much as anything'. Police, she said, picked on a girl who looked like a boy and interrogated her. Another boy claimed he got beaten up, his ticket ripped up by a policeman, and dragged off the train at Lidcombe because he was a street kid, then he was fined for not having a ticket. Another teenager who was attacked at Paramatta station by someone who thought she was a prostitute told the police, but she said, she got no help. Another girl said men had dragged her halfway out of the train at Guildford, but no one had helped and she only got away when the train moved. Yet, they argued, in contrast they have all had had the experience of surveillance cameras on trains 'telling you to stop smoking'; whereas 'Men can fully harass you and then get violent as well and there's supposed to be cameras everywhere but no one comes and helps then.'

This gay group wanted more security guards on trains. Whereas police interrogated and scared you, with security guards 'they'll just tell you to put drinks away ... As long as you're not making trouble, that's all they care about.' And as for the much vaunted extra lights at stations (which the Blue Mountains teenagers liked because it lit up 'all those bushes and trees on the station'), this gay group found them 'too bright ... especially when you're tripping'.

But one boy in this gay-refuge group said, to some general agreement, 'If we really want to solve the problem we have to get back to the main source – the family, the media. People need to be educated that violence isn't the way.' These refuge teenagers knew enough about 'the structure' – not least through the activities of their 'rich-bitch' parents – to know that their 'Otherness' was only partly self-determined.

Levels of risk perception

The Sydney group of gay teenage 'Others' rated their likelihood of being subject to public transport harassment and violence as high (in contrast to the general public); and when asked whether 'compared to other things in your life at the moment, these concerns or worries are all that important to you?' a number of the group said they were, but as much because of the police as anyone else. The North Shore teenagers, represented by Mark, also felt they were at high risk from 'Homies' in very specific leisure-time sites, and wanted the police to do much more to these 'Wogs'. In contrast, the Blue Mountains teenagers rated the level of their concern about crime on public transport as 'minimal' compared with other things in their lives (most of these students were currently studying for their higher school certificate), even though they judged that there was a real risk to girls on the train at night.

In fact, only one girl in each of the Glebe and Blue Mountains groups was prepared to say that she travelled alone at night, come what may. The behavioural strategies of these two groups of teenage girls might vary from the self-ostending to the self-effacing (though one of the gay Sydney girls did say that she would dress like a 'Homie' boy in Auburn, in the Western Suburbs); but foundationally the issue of gender exploitation underpinned these cosmetic differences. All the sexual invitations (and ensuing violence) encountered by the gay Glebe group, lay waiting for the Blue Mountains girls just beyond the slightest of visual cues, which they avoided so scrupulously via their various train strategies. Their policy of surveying their train carriage companions not eye to eye but through a glass darkly might be a sad indictment of male/female relations. But it was soundly practical as fear-reducing behaviour.

Conclusion

My emphasis here has been primarily on just three of our teenage 'leisure-time travel' sets of interviewees, to give a sense of the continuities and differences among risk narratives via their 'lay criminological' knowledges. But we did, as mentioned, also conduct a larger qualitative/quantitative study; and I will conclude by drawing attention briefly to some of the quantitative findings to give my observations so far a more general context.

As in previous fear of crime studies, females saw themselves as at higher risk of crimes against the person, felt less safe walking the streets at night and did so less frequently. Underlying women's fear of attack (including on trains at night) was the perception that they were at greater risk of sexual assault; and it was perception of risk rather than gender itself which predicted worry about sexual assault. Age was also a highly salient predictor of perceived risk and worry about crime.

Middle-aged people saw themselves as most at risk of property crime and worried most about it. Younger people saw themselves as at greater risk of (and had a higher level of worry about) crime related to the person. Older people tended not go out alone in the streets or on trains at night, unless they felt safe. Young people, because of the greater likelihood of using public space for leisure activities, or for travelling to them, often went out alone even if they did not feel safe. Female teenagers were fearful of the 'unpredictable stranger', being frightened of sexual and physical assault from men of all ages. Because teenage girls were subject to endemic sexual harassment (especially on trains) ranging from looks, through touching to occasional actual assault, there was a spectrum of harassment which was *intelligibly* related to young women's fear of crime when travelling, which was too often misunderstood or ignored by professionals (City Rail, police etc.). Teenage girls adopted a wide range of surveillance and avoidance strategies when travelling, but by and large did not feel disempowered from travelling by these fears. Male teenagers departed from the overall norm of fearing the 'unpredictable stranger', in that they worked with an 'anthropology' of different sub-cultures of 'risk', which they could detail physically, behaviourally and culturally, and for which they devised specific fear management or avoidance strategies. Teenage boys feared above all the 'Homies', especially because these groups targeted trains and train stations which were an important part of teenagers' leisure circuit.

Overall, we concluded that: crime is typically perceived as nomadic (on the move) and as committed by the 'unpredictable stranger'. Respondents were more fearful of this figure when moving in public spaces than of crime in their own homes. The construction, therefore, of 'landscapes of fear' (the dark alley, the park at night, the train at night, the shopping mall after hours, the river or beach area) became part of people's risk perceptions, narratives and strategies, thus impinging on (but not generally preventing, except among the older group) their evening leisure-time activity. These generic 'landscapes of fear' – together with media-mythologised symbolic locations of danger in Sydney like Kings Cross ('prostitution'), Redfern ('drunken Aborigines'), Cabramatta ('Vietnamese drug gangs') and Mount Druitt/Western Suburbs ('Homies') – became symptomatic locations of an ambivalent late-modern notion of the city as a place of danger, as well as excitement and pleasure. For example, 80 per cent of our respondents strongly agreed or agreed that 'Big cities in Australia are more dangerous than they used to be', whereas 56 per cent strongly agreed or agreed that 'Small towns in Australia are more dangerous than they used to be'.

The case studies in this chapter have revealed a variety of local and situated strategies for avoiding or addressing fear aroused by uncertainty about one's safety during public leisure-time travelling. But a longer, policy-oriented study would need to elaborate these in the context of five 'generic' strategies nominated by respondents in our quantitative study to 'deal with' uncertainty and fear. Our respondents overall tended to speak of: (a) socio-economic solutions (addressing poverty and unemployment), (b) 'law and order' solutions (harsher penalties, legalising heroin, gun laws), (c) surveillance solutions (greater police and security guard presence in public spaces, CCTV in trains and shopping malls), (d) community solutions (more community spirit and 'ownership' of the system) and (e) activity solutions (more leisure activities and facilities for young and unemployed people). These were the broad social policy strategies recommended in the larger study, but what the locally focused qualitative studies revealed was how, in the absence of such policies, or in their interstices, different individuals, groups and sub-cultures wove their own personal versions of these strategies – and even the few case studies briefly mentioned here can illustrate several of these generic strategies being called for within one focus group or long interview conversation.

A general note

In 1999, before the official Ministerial launch of our fear of crime report, but after its findings had been made widely available to, and work-shopped with, various surveillance and community-oriented agencies, NSW State Rail put uniformed security guards on all suburban and inter-city trains after 7 p.m. We felt that some of the 'lay criminological' voices reported here had, one way of another, been heard.

8
Streetwise or Safe? Girls Negotiating Time and Space

Tamara Seabrook and Eileen Green

Introduction

Leisure has traditionally been portrayed as time free from the stress and strain of work and other obligations (Roberts, 1970; Parker, 1971). However, as contemporary theorisations of leisure demonstrate (Furlong and Cartmel, 1997) such representations fail to include the leisure experiences of young people excluded from regular employment and teenagers for whom 'the street' represents the centre of their leisure experiences. This chapter draws upon empirical data collected as part of a case study of young girls in Townville and aims to shed light on how different groups of girls living within the same locality negotiate time and space as part and parcel of their everyday leisure experience. The case study provided an opportunity to work with 20 girls, aged between 10 and 17 years old, who were loosely organised into two different groups. The first group regularly attended a girls group located within a local women's centre, whilst the second group of girls chose not to take part in centre-based activities, choosing instead to 'hang out' on the streets. A variety of qualitative research methods were negotiated with each group to enable an exploration of their ideas and perceptions about the links between their leisure time, space and risk. This chapter will present and interpret the findings from the case study, which adopted three specific methods: a photographic workshop, in-depth semi-structured interviews and an art/poetry workshop.

The use of photography as a means of communicating ideas about how the girls mapped their locality visually became an important part of the research, since many of the girls were uncomfortable with traditional text as a means of documentation. Using photography enabled the young women to *show* their locality as they saw and *experienced* it.

The researcher asked them to go into the community in friendship pairs and to photograph spaces that they considered to be either safe or dangerous. The photographs were developed on the same day and the girls wrote comments on the back of each of their photographs to explain why they had taken each image. Later on, in a poetry workshop many of the young girls drew upon the photography experience to write poems on how they felt about Townville.

In order to explore the theme of identity further, during art workshops at the women's centre, the girls were asked to make collages from various magazines and catalogues. They each made three collages, giving examples of: first, how they thought that they looked and what they wore. Second, how they would 'like' to look and what they would like to wear but perhaps felt that they could not. Finally, they made collages of clothes and 'looks', which they would never wear. After the workshop the girls deconstructed their collages discussing the meaning of each collage and writing short comments about them. During workshops the following week, the girls, in friendship pairs, took part in a semi-structured interview to discuss and explore issues of community space, leisure and identity. The workshops were an important part of the action approach of the project, facilitating discussion and building self-esteem and self-awareness. Exploring the inter-relationships of risk, particularly those associated with time and space revealed very different everyday experiences, depending upon whether the girls attended the girls group at the women's centre, or preferred to hang out on the streets. Leisure space and time is an important site for fostering and developing female identity and self-esteem; as Hey (1997) suggests, it is where diverse femininities and perceptions of what is 'normal woman hood' are played out.

Theorising time and space

Recent theorists within the fields of sociology, human geography and women's studies have increasingly begun to highlight the importance of varying use of space by different groups within communities, associated with such factors as sexuality, age, gender, disability and race (Soja, 1989; Skelton and Valentine, 1997; Aitchison, 1998; Crang, 1998). They have criticised the dichotomous characterisation of time and space (Rose, 1993; Massey, 1994) by drawing attention to the historical and ideological differentiations associated with the terms masculine and feminine, arguing that the use of time and space are not gender neutral. Feminist geographers have, in fact, argued that concepts such as time and space are implicitly gendered and power-ridden and also in geographical studies and discourse, the concept of time has been given priority over space. Time is represented as dominant, historical, positive and 'marching on' whilst space remains its passive, negative other; in stasis where nothing happens (Massey, 1994). Furthermore, Rose (1993) and Massey (1994) have criticised recent theorists of space for neglecting time, suggesting like Aitchison (Chapter 6), that time and space are both separate and yet inextricably interrelated. The use of time and access to space is important in understanding the often differential experiences between and within gender. Rather than exploring the functional experiences of leisure space–time as if it existed outside of experience, that is, as a force that can impinge upon women's freedom rendering them passive victims, it is important to consider leisure spaces and time as dynamic relations, that is, process. This allows us to understand the diverse experiences of young women. Also, by paying careful attention to ongoing leisure practices in terms of time, space and risk, we may come to understand more about the ways in which gender practices are created, reproduced and sustained.

Understandings of risk and danger

As argued throughout this volume, risk is an everyday experience for most young people in Townville and for the girls who took part in our case study, it was embedded in specific spaces and places within their locality. Our data demonstrates that the experience of local place and space is central to everyday life and impacts upon social relationships. In addition, space and place related experiences are deeply embedded within local traditions and knowledges. Accounts given by the girls in our research clearly demonstrate the importance of both time and locality in their lives showing how localities are subjectively inhabited, and affected by calculations concerning the relative risk, danger and safety associated with them. As Pile (1996) suggests, in urban landscapes people live out their daily lives within mental maps of their locality, rather than within the actual physical locality itself. The way that the young women involved in our research experienced and interpreted time and access to space was highly subjective, and often incongruous with how adults might perceive certain times and spaces. For example, most of the girls experienced their locality as very firmly divided into two halves. Their territory was marked by the very real boundary of a main road but acquired further significance through their subjective understandings of the nature of the 'other' area, which they were not part of. Hence, the 'other' space became inherently dangerous for them at all times.

Safe spaces are 'inside'

Most of the girls in the centre-based group thought that their locality was a dangerous place to live. They generally considered 'outside' public space to be dangerous, but portrayed 'inside' private spaces as safe. Indeed, when asked where they felt safe the girls always listed indoor spaces such as home, the Women's Centre, the Youth Club and the Police Station. These girls had an overwhelming and predominant fear of what might happen to them in outside spaces, especially in the evenings, which they considered to be their time for leisure. They linked this fear with the presence of 'dangerous men'. Dangerous men were often portrayed, as 'men out of control' who had dangerous desires as a result of drug taking, excessive alcohol consumption and uncontrollable sexual urges. They referred to these dangerous men as maniacs, perverts, nutters, stalkers, flashers, dirty men, mucky men, paedophiles, drunken men, smack heads and druggies. The girls repeatedly expressed fears of being kidnapped, raped, murdered, flashed at or grabbed. As these dangerous men were perceived to be unpredictable, this increased the young women's uncertainty and heightened their sense of risk. Outside space associated with the physical characteristics of darkness and enclosure featured predominately in their photographs. Poorly lit spaces, boarded up houses, alleys, a tunnel to the supermarket; parks and bushes were all perceived as potential hiding and entrapment spaces. In a similar way, photographs of bushes and alleys were represented as dangerous spaces where the girls might get kidnapped, grabbed, raped and so on.

It is important to recognise that many of these spaces were on routes between the girls' homes and other places they considered to be safe. Spaces and buildings were also perceived as dangerous when they were dirty, messy, littered with rubbish and drug needles, vandalised and covered with graffiti. These spaces were linked with the presence of unruly 'others' who occupied the streets and outside spaces in the evening, mainly due to a lack of organised leisure facilities.

The young women displayed anxiety about these spaces because they portrayed the results of out of control behaviour, which they perceived as dangerous, and a threat to their own safety and right to occupy such spaces. The researcher working with the girls that attended the women's centre became aware that their knowledge of these spaces as threatening or dangerous had evolved from local informal and formal communication networks. The girls' recounted reports of 'terrible happenings' in the locality were mostly gained through local gossip and adult women's social networks, for example, the stories of mothers, aunts and grandmothers or from the media. The girls frequently blurred media reports with their own imagined experiences, for example, a 12-year-old girl recounted an incident reported in the local paper thus:

> Someone got killed and cut up, And they (the papers) were 'erm, they were saying, there was an 'erm old man sleeping over there and if he walked by me he always, he gets you and he kills you and all that, that's what they were saying ... I won't go up there now.

Accessing and identifying with particular spaces

At worst, the girls felt incapacitated by their fears and anxieties, which sometimes involved not going out at all in the evening:

> I go to the park but I don't go on a night, but I go through the day. (13 years)
>
> I'll go to my nana's after school but most of the time just go in, 'cos you don't feel safe hanging around the streets. (13 years)

Many of the girls limited themselves to indoor activities, thereby reinforcing gender stereotypes and reducing their opportunities to develop skills needed in the 'outside' world (Pearce, 1996). When asked what they do and where they go in their leisure time, most of the girls said they 'stay in', listen to music, play board games, practice timetables, clean up, baby sit or dress up in each others bedrooms. They often talked about being bored and unhappy and this was reflected in their poetry. The following poem is written by one girl aged 11 in the poetry workshop:

> I live in Townville
> Rubbish, broken glass everywhere
> Lonely place to live in
> Except at home and at my friend's house
> You'll find Townville girls inside
> Red and yellow tracksuits
> Everyday is the same old day
> In the houses we play board games
> Dreaming of a different world to play in.

Other girls suggested that they did play out in the evening but always stayed close to home, as it was too risky to venture further afield. When asked where they played out the girls reported:

- In our houses and like next to our houses and that where we go. (12 years)
- On me own end [or]
- Round me own end. (11 years)

The girls also continually distinguished themselves from 'the other girls', who they characterised by the fact that they were non-attendees of the 'girls group'. Douglas (1986) suggests that risk and blame through the process of 'othering' can play an important role in terms of maintaining solidarity within groups. These other girls were seen to choose to hang out on the street, associate with boys, wear make up, short skirts, high shoes and generally were believed to be heavy drug and alcohol users. These girls were also seen to be making themselves sexually available by the sheer fact that they occupied outside space during the evening. They were referred to as bullies, slappers and tarts. Even though many of the girls attending the group did drink alcohol, have boyfriends and smoked cigarettes, they in contrast referred to themselves as good respectable girls. Respectability was an important issue to these young women and this was demonstrated in the collages created in the fashion workshops.

The fashion workshops were an activity which they had expressed interest in. As noted earlier, each of the 20 girls were asked to design three different collages reflecting, 'what they do wear', 'what they would like to wear' and 'what they would never wear'. They were also asked to put their comments on each collage reflecting their thoughts. To demonstrate the importance of respectability, an example of one young girl's designs will be given. In the first collage entitled 'what I wear', the young girl chose pictures of a young woman wearing casual jeans and t-shirt with a pair of trainers and wrote the words 'I would wear it because it is my type and my friends in Townville wear this type'. In the second collage entitled 'what I would like to wear', the young girl chose a dark red, buttoned-up silk suit with a black bra slightly showing through and wrote the words 'I would like to wear this because it is nice and comfortable and more respectable'.

In the final and third collage 'what I would never wear', the young woman chose a blue silk suit identical in style to the dark red suit, the only difference being that the suit jacket was open showing more bra and cleavage. She wrote 'I wouldn't wear a suit like this because it is tarty and shows your body'.

As Skeggs (1999) suggests, respectability is central to how women occupy space. Women who move out of safer spaces are often accused of negligence and irresponsibility, particularly by authorities who suggest that women who are attacked were in the 'wrong place at the wrong time'. Two girls when asked if they think that these 'other girls' feel safe on the streets replied:

- Yes they [girls on the streets] hang around with all these lads and tarts and everything. (14 years)
- Well they feel safe doing what they want to do dont they. (15 years)
- Well myself I wouldn't do what they do (laughter). (14 years)

Researching with the street girls

For the girls who did not attend the centre, public space, in the form of the street was also a key arena for acting out their daily routines and leisure experiences. In general they were more confident and did not perceive the locality as dangerous. They considered 'being outside' to be an everyday learning experience, more empowering than the centre-based club environment. They 'hung out' in the evening and felt that knowledge gained through this experience enabled them to have greater spatial mobility than other girls.

You learn where to go and where not to go … people make the danger themselves. (16 years)

The street is traditionally envisaged as a space which presents more risk for women, especially during the evening. A lack of facilities and opportunities for leisure often led to some young women occupying the street as a meeting place. The street however, can also become a site of conflict, as adults frequently view young people on the street as threatening.

- Our presence annoys people not what we do. (15 years)
- You can see them looking you up and down like … you know like they expect you to go home like good girls. (15 years)
- It's like the older people, 'aint it … like they're waiting for you to do sommat. (16 years)

These conflicts reflect inherent contradictions. Whilst several adults expressed a fear of young people gathered in groups on the streets, these girls felt unsafe on the streets and sought to manage this through staying in groups.

- You follow your friends. (15 years)
- There's always people that will stick up for you, you got like connections all over, haven't you really. You got like all friends spread all over so everyone knows somebody else. (15 years)

It can be argued that the street girls were perceived as not respectable and thus 'risky' by the very fact that they occupied outside spaces that were perceived to be dangerous. Any association with them or the spaces that they occupied would present the danger of a direct physical risk or being drawn into risk activities that may threaten the identity of the centre-based girls. Also, paradoxically the presence and perception of the street girls as 'other' worked to sustain the identity and solidarity of the centre-based girls. In some respects, risk was seen to be 'embodied' by certain groups of girls felt to be almost contagious by association.

The negotiation of risk and leisure space–time

This section will consider, the role that 'risk' plays in the life of the girls and how this comes to affect their use of time and space. For the girls involved in the research, risk is often presented as an organising principle of their daily experiences. That is, the girls suggest that they encounter and need to manage risk on a daily basis and this can come to determine their use of time and space within Townville, as well as determining their other daily experiences. The two main areas of the town that the girls viewed as being most risky, due to a perceived dangerous male presence, were known as 'the black path' and 'old man's square'. After talking to older residents of the town it came to light that both of these places had traditionally been male only spaces. Prior to the mid-1980s, before the local coal and steel sites were downsized and closed, 'The black path', was a path that male workers used to take to and from work. At that time it was known as the 'Black Pass', since male workers, dirty and black from working on the furnaces would trundle along it. Today, this area is an overgrown wasteland, whereas before there was a distinct pathway. Also prior to the mid-1980s, 'old mans square', was a small, well-kept, green area located in the centre of town, with wooden benches where working men of all generations would congregate, relax and chat to each other. Today, although still in the same location, the square is concreted over with bushes poking through. There are some worn, graffittied benches and in the evenings, young males mainly populate the square. It is interesting that both these spaces seem to have remained male preserves. The town's heavy industry and related employment declined long ago and the external constraints on these spaces have been removed, but the effects of the traditional order are still exerted. As Bourdieu suggests, this is a symbolic force:

> ...a form of power that is exerted on bodies, directly and as if by magic, without physical constraint...exerted invisibly and insidiously through insensible familiarization with a symbolically structured physical world and early, prolonged experience of interactions informed by the structures of domination. (2001, p. 38)

A force that is deeply embedded in the form of 'bodily emotions – shame, humiliation, timidity, anxiety, guilt – or passions and sentiments – love, admiration, respect'. There have been radical structural changes within the context of Townville, for example, in terms of the movement from heavy industry to service based employment. But contrary to Giddens' (1991) view that individuals become 'disembedded', for these young girls, negotiation of risk as an organising principle is deeply embedded in the traditional knowledges of their locality.

What the data suggests is that it is not whether certain times and spaces are inherently dangerous, or whether there actually is a dangerous male presence lurking outside. It is rather, as suggested by Burgess (1998) that what is *perceived* to be risky or dangerous is *real* in its consequences. Individuals who the girls felt represented either a direct physical risk to themselves, or presented the danger of drawing them into risk activities, may or may not populate spaces at certain times. What is important is that it is these social constructions that define/create their perceptions of space and time. Constructions, which become embedded within their own discourses and are influenced by both traditional knowledge of the locality and gendered contemporary relations in the peer group.

All of the girls expressed concern over the lack of safe leisure spaces 'outside' and suggested that boys monopolised those spaces that were available. As Pearce (1996) suggests, girls' access to specific spaces is limited. Girls are often found to use 'inside' spaces and this can be of detriment to their psychological and social well-being. They may become excluded from developing specific knowledges and skills necessary for accessing outside spaces. Furthermore, in terms of risk, the girls were continually prioritising and negotiating their leisure time and space. They suggested that they sometimes accessed the spaces that they perceived as dangerous in the evening, in order to have a smoke or drink, as it was unlikely that other female friends and family would catch them there. However, these girls adopted such risk management strategies as going in the company of other girls, usually with no less than three. Being caught smoking or drinking by an adult was seen as more risky than entering a space that they perceived would put them in danger of physical attack. When asked why they smoked, they suggested that it was because they were bored and it was wonderful as it got them out of the house. They acknowledged that if they had other things to do they probably would not smoke, as smoking became boring when there were other things to do. Unlike their perception of risky, drunken 'others', they did not see their own drinking of alcohol to be a risk to them or to anyone else; for them it was ordinary and not dangerous. They justified it by creating hierarchies of risk, comparing activities that they considered to be risky, illustrated in the following dialogue,

> Drinking, it used to be really bad on streets, didn't it? (15 years)
> Every night and every night, week ends, especially Friday and Saturdays. (16 years)
> Yea, some friends have been hit badly with drugs but they've got over it now. (15 years)
> There is people still with drugs but most people avoid them now. (16 years)
> Drinking's alright. (15 years)
> Drinking not drugs, god! (16 years)
> If there's loads of yous ... not just us two. (15 years)

Girl 1:   We just drink, we don't smoke or take drugs, that's really bad but drink isn't all that bad. (14 years)

Girl 2:   We have a good drink most of the time, it just depends how much money we can get or we raid from her dad's bureau. (14 years)

Interviewer: What about sex?

Girl 1:   No never. I want to try it but daren't ... I think I'll get pregnant or something. (14 years)

Girl 2:   Yeah especially with the lads round Townville you don't know what you'd get. (14 years)

Interviewer: Do you attend school regularly both of you or do you truant?

Girl 1: No I wouldn't truant, that's too risky. (14 years)

Some of the girls negotiated leisure time and space by befriending boys. Adopting boyish traits seemed to both enable them to retain their respectability and to gain male protection:

Girl 1: I play out with my boyfriends. (10 years)
Girl 2: Yeah, 'cause they're like. (11 years)
Girl 1: Boys look after you don't they? (10 years)
Girl 1: Like your boyfriends look after you 'cause if you get battered your boyfriend might get them back. (11 years)
Girl 2: Right we're like tomboys and we like to play with boys instead of girls 'cause girls are boring, like to play with Barbies and that ... (10 years)

Paradoxically, the latter two girls also talked about playing kiss chase and building dens on outside spaces where they felt it was safe to play out traditional female roles, playing mums and babies.

Concluding remarks

The data supports our argument that the girls encounter and manage risk on a daily basis. Constructions of time and space are not just related to the structural design of spaces but are also, and perhaps more importantly, premised upon emotions, fears and anxieties which are evoked by specific areas in the locality. Such felt emotions are deeply embedded in discourses of local knowledge, gender and power. An understanding of the subjective understandings, which impact upon young women's negotiation of their leisure time and use of space, is crucial for policy makers and those working directly with young people. Such information is also of key importance to policy makers and planners concerned with regenerating this and similarly disadvantaged communities. External decision making about the placing and design of facilities can be enhanced by research which explores young people's embodied local knowledge and experience as users of the area. Within the accounts presented by these girls, perceptions of risk are depicted as an organising principle of their daily routines and differing dispositions towards risk and come to dictate the young women's diverse use of time and space.

The data suggests that there was not only differentiation between genders but also within gender, through the issue of identity labelling, for example, of other people as 'insiders' or 'outsiders'.

Massey (1994) suggests it is not only that the interrelations between objects occur in space and time, but it is also these relationships themselves which create/define space and time. The girls perceived certain times and spaces as risky and thus their own position/place in time and space was continually under self-surveillance. For example, some of the girls who considered themselves to be streetwise found themselves to be part of the 'in' crowd, but they were also situated as 'out' by others, perceived as tarts or slappers. By being 'out' and by not conforming to traditional female roles and dress, they found themselves to be 'in' with the boys and visible to the male gaze. An awareness of the dynamics of subject positions, that are both multidimensional and fluid but also influenced by class and gender related historical discourses of place and space, challenges one-dimensional understandings of time and space. It also constructs young people as active agents of their own lives, in the words of one 11-year-old girl who took part in the art/poetry workshops:

> Townville
> Is like
> An empty
> Box
> But
> Our brains
> Are like
> Full boxes
> Full of
> Ideas

References

Aitchison, C. (1998) 'New cultural geographies: the spatiality of leisure, gender and sexuality'. *Leisure Studies*, Vol. 18, No. 1, pp. 19–39.

Bourdieu, P. (2001) *Masculine Domination*. Cambridge: Polity Press.

Burgess, J. (1998) ' "But is it worth taking the risk?" How women negotiate access to urban woodland: a case study' in Ainley, R. (ed.) *New Frontiers of Space, Bodies and Gender*. London: Routledge.

Crang, M. (1998) *Cultural Geography*. London: Routledge.

Douglas, M. (1986) *Risk Acceptability According to the Social Sciences*. London: Routledge.

Foucault, M. (1976) 'Power as knowledge' in Lemert, C. (ed.) (1999) *Social Theory: The Multicultural and Classic Readings*. USA: Westview Press.

Furlong, A. and Cartmel, F. (1997) *Young People and Social Change: Individualization and Risk in Late Modernity*. Buckingham: Open University Press.

Giddens, A. (1991) *Modernity and Self-Identity: Self and Society in the Late Modern Age*. Cambridge: Polity Press.

Hey, V. (1997) *The Company She Keeps: An Ethnography of Girl's Friendship*. Buckingham: Open University Press.

Massey, D. (1994) *Space, Place and Gender*. Cambridge: Polity Press.

Parker, S. (1971) *The Future of Work and Leisure*. London: Paladin.

Pearce, J. (1996) 'Urban youth cultures: gender and spatial forms'. *Youth and Policy*, Spring, No. 52. pp. 1–11.

Pile, S. (1996) *The Body and the City*. London: Routledge.

Roberts, K. (1970) *Leisure*. London: Longman.

Rose, G. (1993) *Feminism and Geography*. Cambridge: Polity Press.

Skeggs, B. (1999) 'Matter out of place: visibility and sexualities in leisure spaces'. *Leisure Studies*, Vol. 18, No. 3, pp. 213–32.

Skelton, T. and Valentine, G. (eds) (1997) *Cool Places: Geographies of Youth Cultures*. London: Routledge.

Soja, E. W. (1989) *Postmodern Geographies: The Reassertion of Space in Critical Social Theory*. London: Verso.

9

Sites of Contention: Young People, Community and Leisure Space

Anne Foreman

> Community formation, its maintenance and the importance placed on public and private spaces by residents and outside decision-makers shape people's perceptions about society, themselves and the social values they adopt.
>
> (Stilwell, 1993)

Theorists such as Beck (1992) and Giddens (1991) see risk as a key driver in current industrial societies, which accompanied by a growth in individualism, has weakened the effects of social structures and curtailed collective action. Furlong and Cartmel (1997) argue however that such structures continue to be influential. Young people are still significantly social beings and need to feel a sense of belonging or 'communion' with others, in order to develop our self-identities and manage the risks we encounter.

The importance of the concept of community is particularly evident in places in transition, such as Townville which forms the focus of this chapter (as detailed in the introduction to this volume). Here the concept of community acts as a fundamental social construct, instrumental to how residents seek to manage the risks they face. People, however, can at any one time establish a sense of community within a variety of settings, for example, the workplace, a town or the peer group, but will, in the light of individual circumstances, seek to promote or defend the community which best fits their experience and need. Far from being a unifying concept, community is often the site for a range of competing and conflicting interests, as this chapter highlights. Whilst adults in Townville attempt to protect themselves from the social and economic risks they face by adhering to their traditional concepts of community, young people look to their peer group for support to create new or different communities. These peer groups are perceived by both local adults and often by the Government, as an additional threat or risk that must be overcome. In Townville the struggle between these competing groups is revealed most clearly by adult attempts to control public leisure space. This 'battleground' therefore forms the focus of this chapter, as it considers the effect such conflict can have on the ability of both adults and young people to manage the risks they face and explores what opportunities for 'conflict resolution' exist.

The chapter begins by investigating how differing perceptions of community, and young people's place within it, have developed within Townville. It then explores how public leisure space has become both a metaphorical and an actual battleground between the generations as they seek to manage the everyday risks (for example, unemployment, financial insecurity, drugs and the fear of crime). The implications, of failing to resolve such tensions are highlighted, before consideration is given to the contribution community development approaches can make to addressing conflict within communities. It is claimed that these approaches have the potential to bring different members of a community together to address issues of mutual concern and challenge. The Community Design Initiative undertaken with young people and other members of the Townville community by the Action Risk team, provided an opportunity to test such approaches. The aims, methods and outcomes of the initiative are therefore described, before an assessment is made of their impact on conflict within the town. However, since the research was undertaken the policy environment has changed. The UK Labour Government has implemented a range of policies and initiatives seeking to renew neighbourhoods and encourage the active involvement of young people. The chapter concludes by considering these changes and their likely success in supporting communities such as Townville to address the risks they face.

Concepts of community

The concept of community was important to many Townville residents' sense of belonging and identity. Indeed living in an area with a strong community spirit continues to be an ideal that many people aspire to. However, as suggested earlier, community is not a singular concept. Hall and Williamson classified community as either categorical, normative or lived. Categorical communities referred to:

> Concrete units of population; groups of people (not always living in the same place) with something in common – shared interests

and attitudes – which makes it reasonable to think of them as if they were a single entity, separate from other, different communities. (1999, p. 304)

Normative communities, by contrast, refer to the invocation of nostalgia, community values, tradition and idealisation of intimate, collective and shared forms of values. Their final category, lived communities, describes the reality of the character of shared life as we actually experience it. Each of these versions of community can be found in Townville.

In the past Townville's sense of community appeared to cohere around the collective tradition and security many local people shared through employment in its steel and chemical plants. Although undermined when these industries relocated, that unity was something local leaders continued to try to salvage and perpetuate, in the hope that it could act as a buffer to the risks the town faced. Unsurprisingly, with little or no memory of a vibrant, working town and vulnerable to economic cycles beyond their control, Young people tended not to share older resident's nostalgic perspective. Instead they were pre-occupied with the realities and risks of the 'lived' community, something they experienced as full of competing and conflicting voices and demands, amongst which they were struggling to be heard. As research undertaken by Demos found, young people experiencing severe disadvantage do not 'recognise the conventional [dominant] definition of community, seeing it as sentimental and irrelevant – a source of interference and control' (Davies and Markham, 2000, p. 31). Although community can signify belonging and inclusion for some, it can also mean exclusion and marginalisation for others. Indeed, many would contend, that significant proportions of young people generally, feel peripheral to the decisions being taken both locally and nationally, which never the less affect their lives and their ability to manage the risks they face. Competing concepts of community are particularly apparent in places like Townville where the threats and risks posed by social and economic change have had a significant impact on both the area and on relationships between adults and young people. We will now consider how many young people in Townville responded to these uncertainties, and the concerns it can raise amongst adults.

Community, risk and the threat of the peer group

With the closure of Townville's steel and chemical works and the degraded environment they left behind acting as a barrier to new investors, young people's employment opportunities have been dramatically reduced, in effect, removing what used to be seen locally as a key stepping stone to the adult world and full membership of the Townville community. Their consequent lack of status, combined with an acute sensitivity to the environment in which they live, frequently contributes to young people's feelings of worthlessness and can result in the belief that poverty is an inevitable consequence of living in such a town; as one young man succinctly notes:

> If you're brought up in Townville you're on the dole.

Furthermore, as France (1998) identified when studying a comparable area in Sheffield, young people start to think that 'their community is responsible for their feelings of hopelessness and lack of opportunity' (p. 106). It is therefore not a place they want to be associated with; they feel they have no stake in it and no obvious reason to invest in community life in the way other residents think they should. Consequently, in areas like Townville those who have the opportunity to leave frequently do so. While those who do not, often form their own communities or peer group in the search for self-identity and protection. To these young people, deprived of the opportunity for full-time work and the benefits it brings, communities of choice are frequently of greater importance than the communities where they live and all too commonly encounter crime, drugs and decline; as one young Townville resident explained:

> All it is now in Townville is if you're past the age of ten your either on drugs or pinching cars.

Indeed, the peer group is vitally important to many young people because it provides them with what the workplace gave previous generations, a sense of identity and belonging, the opportunity to develop and experience 'relationships of trust, co-operation and reciprocity amongst individuals and groups outside the immediate family' (Aitken, 2001, p. 136) – the essential components of community life. Other residents however do not see the peer group as encouraging the social development of its members, but as a risk, setting itself up in opposition to the wider community and encouraging 'unchildlike' behaviour. As a group of Townville women explained:

> – On the night we can't go out after 7 o'clock, because of the big gangs standing on the corners which sort of stops you
> – Intimidate you

- You feel scared inside, you, they're probably not say anything and stuff, but you are scared ... that is why you sit locked in the house.

Unchildlike behaviour, defined by Aitken (2001) as 'any behaviour beyond the comprehension and control of adults' (p. 147), can manifest itself in a number of forms: 'hanging out' on the streets, drinking and expressive behaviour such as music, language, dress and so on. However, many of these activities are seen as risky by adults and at odds with the perception, commonly held in areas like Townville, of childhood as a time of innocence and naiveté – something to be protected alongside their conventional notion of community. They fail to understand that young people choose to gather in their own neighbourhoods and to move around in groups because that is how they feel safest – it is how they 'manage' the risks they experience within the town.

Moreover, in Townville the external pressures facing the community are further compounded by the perceived threat that young people represent:

- The extent of youth unemployment, which has stimulated the development of an alternative economy and criminal behaviour.
- The 'uncontrolled invasion of children's minds by market driven media images' (Aitken, 2001, p. 129) which encourage individualism over family and community values.
- Media and police campaigns that portray young people as deviant, barbaric and a threat to social order.
- An academic literature that highlights 'problem' youth but rarely reveals the essentially unproblematic nature of young people's activities.
- The momentum of the children's rights movement following the introduction of the United Nations Convention on the Rights of the Child (1989). A Convention that not only gives young people the opportunity for free expression and association, privacy, leisure and to have their views given due weight in all matters that affect them; but also 'dissolves' parental control once a child becomes 'self-governing'. This again underscores the image of an autonomous and unchild-like being, further adding to the bewilderment of the seemingly embattled adult community.

These pressures and others can help to undermine the foundations of social life, creating a sense of powerlessness and panic amongst adults. This, as Measor and Squires (2000) have found, 'impacts upon a community's ability to cope and shapes the broader outlooks and conditions the attitudes of older people towards younger people' (p. 206) who with their different perceptions of community and risk either can not or will not fulfil their expected role. As two girls aged 15 and 16 from Townville explained:

> – Our presence annoys people, not what we do. You can see them looking you up and down like ..., you know like they expect you to go home like good girls.
> – It's like the older people, ain't it ..., like they're waiting for you to do sommat.
> – ... the older ones forget what it's like to be young.

Public space: a site of conflict

The anger instilled by the apparent intransigence of young people and the visibility of a group other residents already perceive as threatening to them as individuals and as a risk to the sustainability of the community as a whole, ensures public leisure space becomes a site of conflict. Adults, many of whom have little contact with or responsibility for young people, witness their community decline and see young people gathering in public spaces and almost automatically consider them to be 'up to no good'. Brown (1995) concludes there are now

> persistent linkages in adult's perceptions between crime, young people and the disintegration of the community resulting in community practices that are exclusive of and oppressive of young people ... [They] want their own world to be made safe, and the 'tidying away' of young people off the streets appears to them one of the solutions. (p. 44)

This is an adult form of risk management, one very much at odds with the approaches adopted by young people outlined in the previous section. Ultimately, therefore as Malone (1999) asserts

> Public space is not neutral – geographies of power, resistance and control are mapped out in real and imaginary boundaries across the landscape. To transgress, as many young people do, is to disrupt these boundaries and to find one's self out of place. (p. 22)

This is illustrated by the experience of two boys aged 10 and 11 trying to find somewhere safe to play in Townville:

> They swear at you and say you've done things when you haven't. And they chase you. They don't want you to play near their houses.

However, adult attempts to gain some influence over their circumstances, by seeking to control public space and through it the threat young people have come to symbolise, have resulted in the streets and open areas becoming 'adult' spaces, leaving young people to occupy the fringes of the community. This not only adds to the mutual suspicion between young people and other residents, but also impedes young people's ability to gain the personal and social skills they need in order to manage the risks they face and contribute to the wider community.

As highlighted earlier, the peer group provides its members with a chance to develop the practical and social skills they need to play a full role in community life. This, however, requires access to 'transitional' space where young people can meet without undue surveillance or intervention by adults. A space that acts as an essential mediator of lived experiences, offering young people the opportunity to take risks, discuss their opinions, grow in self-confidence and develop a stronger sense of personal identity. Public spaces within the community with their familiar geography and people, should provide a safe environment from which young people can make the transition to other social worlds. However, as we have seen, adult fears exclude young people from, or at the very least try to control young people's activities within, what is supposedly 'public' space – a space which as members of the community young people have the right to use.

The impact and implications of spatial exclusion

Spatial and emotional exclusion from the community has been found to affect young people in a variety of ways, all of which have repercussions for the ability of the community to work together to address the risks it faces. Without access to transitional space and the opportunities it provides to develop their personal and community identity young people frequently experience a sense of 'placelessness'. This can have 'long-term consequences for their capacity to contribute now and in adult life to the reconstruction of their communities' (Malone, 1999, p. 19). In addition, the limited opportunities young people now have for day-to-day contact with adults from outside their immediate family circle, means they suffer from the erosion of relationships with adult members of the community, increasing the potential for individualistic, rather than community-centred responses to risk. For as Elshtain (1990) identifies, children and young people 'need particular intense relationships with adults to help them make distinctions and choices as adults ..., it is only through identifying with concrete others that a child can later identify with non-familial human beings and come to see herself as a member of a wider human community' (p. 60). Adult failure to appreciate the important role young peoples' peer group activities play further excludes young people, leaving them without a sense of ownership (defined by May (1997) as 'the power to make a difference to one's own life or to that of the community' (p. 27)) or responsibility for the town and the risks it faces. What then can be done in response to these divisions and exclusive practices?

Addressing conflict and exclusion

Several commentators (Cooper and Hawtin (1997) and Measor and Squires (2000)) have argued that community conflict and exclusion are best addressed using community development approaches. This is due to the fact that they adopt a holistic perspective that seeks to develop the whole community, rather than 'selectively focus' on young people and thereby perpetuate division. How would such approaches, 'based on the sharing of power, skills, knowledge, and experience' (Harris, 1994, p. 3), fare with regard to the contentious issues of public space and risk in Townville? Would they help the community to:

- understand that young people and adults share concerns about the same issues and risks but from different perspectives and should be working together?
- see how the generations often scapegoat each other rather than address the real roots of their problems?
- begin to address the fears surrounding young people?

The Community Design Initiative gave researchers and practitioners an opportunity to explore these questions.

The initiative was based on a partnership between action researchers and a local authority project attempting to find new uses for derelict land created by targeted demolition of surplus housing in the town. The council project sought to:

- work with as many community representatives and young people as possible to design the open spaces to meet their requirements, needs and future aspirations, and
- ensure that what ever was put on to the sites was sustainable.

While the researchers aimed to complement and support the project by:

- facilitating 'a more participatory context in which young people's ideas and concerns are listened to and acted upon, i.e. they are able to participate as valued citizens within the local community' (Bunton *et al.*, 1998)

- fostering 'feelings of community ownership and responsibility through direct community involvement in the re-developing of specific areas, particularly those which have a history of vandalism' (ibid.).

As local people had already begun to both demand that something positive be done with the new spaces and express concerns about young people 'hanging out' in the area, all generations quickly identified an opportunity to create some much needed leisure space and facilities for children and young people. As young residents explained:

> there's four swings between every kid in Townville.
>
> there's nothing to do

and older residents agreed:

> I mean I don't think there is much for the kids around here not at all, no parks or anything .... the kids are going to go out and vandalise things when they have nothing to play with.
>
> from the age of maybe eight years onwards there's nothing for them

Work focused on three spaces, all key sites of contention within the town, but which also presented opportunities to:

- bring the community together around a common issue;
- involve young people in a planning process in which they may encounter conflicting values, difficult decisions and the necessity of compromise;
- challenge the myths and misconceptions held by all parties.

Initial consultations with all sections of the community by the local authority led to an agreement to: locate a play area for young people on one site; a community centre and outdoor leisure facilities on the second; and a youth shelter, football and basket ball provision on the third. The Community Design Initiative then used a range of methods and tools including workshops, outreach, artwork, photography, mapping, model making, site visits, public meetings, a questionnaire survey, evaluation sheets, visits to other facilities and interviews to assist local people, including over 300 young people, to work together to select, design and create the new facilities.

The reasons young people gave for their involvement included 'I wanted to have my say', 'because I care about Townville's future',

'I was interested in what would happen' or as one young man explained:

> Well I had the opinion that if I didn't come along and make sure everyone else heard this opinion, that they're [adults] just going to make their own minds up and then nobody's [young people] going to use it [the new facilities]. And you know really we want what we want, and if we don't get it, we won't use it, because it isn't what we want.

Generally the adults who took part in the initiative recognised the importance of involving young people, one explaining:

> I'm anxious that the kids own this, what ever we're doing, the children need to be part and parcel of the planning because if we don't get them on board then I don't think they'll succeed, ... they need to be part of this building process.

Although some were not completely comfortable working with young people, as one man said when recalling a workshop event:

> It was very nosy, because they had ... about 15 youngsters in it, ... A lot [of adults] didn't go to the second meeting because of the noise, they seemed to be a lot of babble about

Some explained they would have preferred a segregated approach:

> I think at school they [young people] would all be in order. No disrespect to the meeting but some of them were talking over things and some people are trying to listen, but kids will do that. It'd be better idea to see them in the schools.

While others found their preconceptions were challenged by the experience:

> It's young people we've got a look at for the future, some of them are unruly fair enough, but they seemed a genuine lot at that meeting.

Yet, as one young man explained, during initial consultations by the local authority, before the researchers became involved, adults had not always been so willing to consider young people's views:

> When there's been young people attend in the past they've [adults] actually talked down to them and that isn't the way to get them more

involved ... [thinking] you don't really know what you're going on about because you're young, which is not true, they [young people] usually have a better grasp on life than some of the people.

However, the attitudes of some adults were not the only problems encountered or issues around which lessons where learned during the study:

• It was recognised that the failure to make the parameters of each project clear from the outset, for example, around the budgets available and the technical and legal requirements that would influence decision-making, had resulted in the re-emergence of old misgivings and questions such as:

When are they [the Council] going to start focusing on the people of Townville and what the people of Townville want?

• The need to appreciate young people's time frames, for example, although it had been explained that the project might take up to two years to complete, delays between the initial and final phases of the consultation did leave some young people feeling 'frustrated', 'angry' and affected their willingness to participate.
• The benefits of properly resourcing consultation with communities. As Lowndes *et al.* (2001) found 'local authority resources rarely matched their ambitions in this area' (p. 211). This was the case in Townville, where the lead officer explained: 'I haven't this huge team, I do consultations basically on a shoe string.' However, he agreed that working with Action Risk had enabled him to experiment, work with more young people and try out a wider range of approaches.
• Participants admitted they had particularly enjoyed the practical aspects of the project commenting:

Using the plans, well you can see it then, ... yes even though it's only lumps of cardboard and plaster and stuff, you're making a scene and you're creating something (adults).

Stuff like the visit to the play park, you know why wasn't that done earlier, a brilliant idea that, you know get them [young people] on the equipment to see what they liked (young man).

The one where the representatives from the play companies came and made their presentations, that was actually a good idea that, really, they couldn't have involved us any more, we made a decision (young man).

Overall, evaluation of the initiative revealed that it had: encouraged more young people to become involved in the regeneration process; begun to challenge how older residents viewed young people; and had given the community some hope for the future, with residents expressing their dreams of:

- A better Townville.
- People more optimistic about the future of Townville.
- More community spirit, closer community spirit.

While young people had particularly appreciated having a positive investment made in them and the community, explaining:

> We've a guarantee that we're going to get something that's going to be here and it's going to stay.
>
> If young people are involved in it and old people are involved in it it's theirs, they own it ... the kids are going to fall in love with it, you know, it's what we need and we haven't had something like that in ages.

Therefore, it appears that with their inclusive yet challenging agenda community development approaches do offer the different generations, with their differing perceptions of risk and community, the opportunity to share their experience and knowledge in ways that can benefit and strengthen a place like Townville. However, questions remain about the sustainability of such approaches, many of which, like the Community Design Initiative, are subject to the vagaries of government funding and policy making. It is therefore, important to ask whether such initiatives can find a place within the current policy responses to community, youth and risk?

The new policy context

A review of key policy documents reveals that the adult residents of Townville are not alone in their belief that traditional notions of community offer some defence against the risks they face. The UK Government too, with its acceptance of communitarian philosophy, views community as 'the foundation of human stability' in the 'epicentre of change' (Blair, 2000), and is equally afraid that the young will reject the currently dominant traditional concept of community. Indeed since early 2000, just as the researcher's role in the Community Design initiative was coming to an end, the Government implemented a range of policies and initiatives which sought not only to strengthen communities by increasing residents' involvement in local decision-making,[1] but most particularly to encourage the active involvement of children and young people.[2] As the former Minister for Children and Young People John Denham proclaimed in 2001:

> We want children and young people to feel they can influence the services they receive. We want to see them contributing to and bene-fiting from their local communities. We want them to feel heard and valued and to be able to make a difference. (CYPU, 2001b, p. 1)

However, the targeting of additional resources to involve young people has been accompanied by the development of increasingly rigorous systems for dealing with those who do not engage and can therefore be perceived as being a risk to society (community) and to themselves. The majority of recent Government youth focused initiatives[3] concentrate on identifying risk and preventative factors, thereby broadcasting the implicit message to young people that 'what they are, and what they are into, are not acceptable and need to be changed' (Davies and Marken, 2000, p. 32). Furthermore, the 'Building a Strategy for Children and Young People Consultation Document' (2001a), the fore runner of what will be the Government's central tenet on youth policy, does little to dispel such notions with references to 'identifying desirable outcomes' and communities choosing what actions to take 'for' their local children and young people.

It is therefore, unsurprising that commentators question the 'UK New Labour' Government's motives, suggesting that it promotes participation 'not because it will bring young people what they want, but because it will do them good or improve society' (Borland, 2001, p. 20); and that it is 'concentrating on improving children's future lives as adults, rather than their present well-being and social participation' (Prout, 2000). Why? Consciously or not it appears that the Government still believes young people to be 'too uninformed, unreliable and untrustworthy to carry responsibility' (Davies and Marken, 2000, pp. 30–1). Thus it seems that neither the Government or the adult residents of Townville, with their ardent belief in community and the benefits it can bring, can fully accept the contribution young people can make to managing, rather than adding to, the risks a community like Townville faces. Perhaps this is considered a greater risk, as it would entail accepting the validity of young people's alternative perspectives on risk and supporting the crucial role they can play in questioning their communities, rather than merely contributing to the existing order (Hall and Williamson, 1999).

It appears, however, that the main hope for a new policy direction with regard to young people and their role within communities rests with the European Commission. As rather than attempting to re-enforce traditional notions of community, the Commission is seeking to support young people to 'create new forms of social relations, different ways of expressing solidarity or of coping with differences and finding enrichment in them' (European Commission, 2001, p. 4) – or, when set within the context of the Action Risk study, of enabling them to find new ways of responding to risk.

Ultimately, instead of segregating 'youth issues' and involvement, a whole community approach to decision making should be adopted, as during the Community Design initiative. For if the current largely paternalistic approach persists, young people will continue to feel let down by policies and communities which rarely take into account their versions of 'reality' and 'truth' preferring, for example, to offer young people 'purposeful leisure', when all they want is somewhere welcoming and safe to spend time together – a space in which they can develop the practical skills needed to respond to the risks they and the wider community face.

Conclusion

This chapter has used empirical evidence gathered during Action Risk to demonstrate how the concept of community clearly influences local responses to risk. By examining this case study of Townville and the issues raised over the use of public leisure space, it has been possible to explore the reactions of a community experiencing a heightened state of risk awareness. As the chapter illustrates, feeling unable to influence the broader social and economic changes their community was experiencing, local adults projected their fears about the future on to young people whose behaviour they found difficult to understand. However, such 'turf wars' will do little to help the community address the risks it faces. Instead the scape goating of visible youth diminishes any opportunities for collective action and success. Yet, as Beck (1992) recognised, awareness and reflection on the concept of risk and risk management has the potential to empower. Action Risk provided the opportunity for reflection, while the Community Design element gave young and old a framework within which to work together and make decisions for their town. In doing so, the initiative began to facilitate change within the community, bringing it together around a common issue, challenging preconceptions and encouraging young people to feel more valued.

But can such activity be sustained in a socio-political environment that re-enforces the traditional notions of community and the role of the young? What chance will there be to engage young people in communal risk management if the traditional forms of public participation, which they are already disaffected from, persist? In Townville, however, there is the hope that the experience gained during the Action Risk study will help young people, in particular, to see themselves as influential and able to engage with the wider community to address the risks they face.

Notes

1. For example the Social Exclusion Unit, a range of regeneration initiatives, best value and the democratic renewal agenda.
2. Children's Fund, Connexions, the citizenship curriculum, Millennium volunteers and a draft national strategy for children and young people.
3. Connexions, Youth Offending Teams, Drug Action Teams, the Children's Fund and so on.

References

Aitken, S. (2001) *Geographies of Young People: The Morally Contested Spaces of Identity*. London: Rutledge.

Beck, U. (1992) *Risk Society: Towards a New Modernity*. London: Sage.

Blair, T. (2000) Speech to the Active Convention Awards, 2 March.

Borland, M. (2001) *Improving Consultation with Children and Young People in Relevant Aspects of Policy Making and Legislation in Scotland*. London: Stationary Office.

Brown, S. (1995) 'Crime and safety in whose community? Age, everyday life and problems for youth policy'. *Youth and Policy*, No. 48, pp. 27–45.

Bunton, R., Crawshaw, P., Dewhirst, W., Green, E. and Mitchell, W. (1998) *Strategies for Life Project – Interim Report* (unpublished), Middlesbrough: University of Teesside.

Commission of the European Communities (2001) *European Commission White Paper – A New Impetus for European Youth*. Brussels COM (2001) 681.

Children and Young People's Unit (CYPU) (2001a) *Building a Strategy for Children and Young People Consultation Document*. London: Children and Young People's Unit.

Children and Young People's Unit (CYPU) (2001b) *Learning to Listen: Core Principles for the Involvement of Children and Young People*. London: Children and Young People's Unit.

Cooper, C. and Hawtin, M. (eds) (1997) *Housing, Community and Conflict: Understanding Residents 'Involvement'*. Aldershot: Ashgate Publishing Company.

Davies, B. and Markhen, M. (2000) 'Those in favour'. *Young People Now*, April, pp. 30–2.

Elshtain, J. B. (1990) *Power Trips and Other Journeys: Essays in Feminism as Civic Discourse*. London: University of Wisconsin Press.

France, A. (1998) 'Why should we care?': Young People, Citizenship and Questions of Social Responsibility. *Journal of Youth Studies*, Vol. 1, No. 1, pp. 97–111.

Furlong, A. and Cartmel, F. (1997) *Young People and Social Change – Individualization and Risk in Late Modernity*. Buckingham: Open University Press.

Giddens, A. (1991) *Modernity and Self-Identity: Self and Society in the Late Modern Age*. Cambridge: Polity Press.

Hall, T. and Williamson, H. (1999) *Citizenship and Community*. Leicester: Youth Work Press.

Harris, V. (ed.) (1994) *Community Work Skills Manual*. Newcastle: Association of Community Workers.

Lowndes, V., Pratchett, L. and Stoker, G. (2001) 'Trends in public participation: Part 1 – local Government perspectives', *Public Administration*, Vol. 79, No. 1, pp. 205–22.

Malone, K. (1999) 'Growing up in cities: as a model of participative planning and 'place-making', *Youth Studies Australia*, June, pp. 17–23.

May, N. (1997) *Challenging Assumptions: Gender Issues in Urban Regeneration*. York: Joseph Rowntree Foundation.

Measor, L. and Squires, P. (2000) *Young People and Community Safety: Inclusion, Risk, Tolerance and Disorder*. Aldershott: Ashgate.

Prout, A. (2000) 'Children's participation: control and self-realisation in British late modernity', *Children and Society*, Vol. 14, pp. 304–15.

Stilwell, F. (1993) 'Reshaping Australia: urban problems and policies' in Karen Malone, 'Growing up in cities: as a model of participatory planning and "place-making" with young people'. *Youth Studies Australia*, June 1999, pp. 17–23.

Part III

Leisure Pursuits and Gendered Identity

10
Risk, Gender and Youthful Bodies

Robin Bunton, Paul Crawshaw and Eileen Green

Introduction

Psycho-social approaches to risk frequently highlight gender difference in perception of risk and risk-taking depicting boys and young men as relatively greater 'risk takers' than girls and young women (Plant and Plant, 1992; Cutter *et al.*, 1994; France, 2000). Concerns with public health have similarly emphasised gender difference expressed by dispositions to risk and recent UK studies have found that men claimed to ignore health lifestyle advice and actively seek risk-taking to test and demonstrate the inherent resilience of their bodies (Jones, 1993; Watson, 1998, 2002). Such work pre-dates recent concern for risk within sociology and is usually based upon differing assumptions about the reality of risk.

Some more recent work on the gendered body has, however, pointed out the tendency of such studies to reproduce more pervasive gender distinctions by embodying particular orientations to risk. Petersen and Lupton (1996) have suggested that public health discourses have traditionally portrayed women's bodies as risk, 'through their potential for intimate contact with other bodies as seducers and as nurturers' (p. 78). Gilman (1993) has noted that female beauty is often associated with corruption and death, and the female body has been seen as threatening, contagious and unstable in public health and other discourses which portray the female body as inherently subject to loose controls over body boundaries. In recent work on gender and HIV/AIDS, for example, women's bodies remain distinctly 'leaky' as a sign of contagion. Waldby (1997) has illustrated this through highlighting the absence of heterosexual men in the discourse on AIDS. Waldby's cultural analysis shows however that other sexual identities – women, bisexual men and gay men – have all been represented as inherently problematic and 'risky'.

Women's bodies are seen as highly risky and contagious because they emit fluids that are potentially threatening and 'dirty'. Body fluids demonstrate the permeability of the body, its necessary dependence on the outside world and its vulnerability (Grosz, 1994). Leaky bodies seem to worry us and we spend a great deal of time regulating intake and expulsion of food, liquids and substances (Shildrick, 1997; Seymour, 1998). Whilst this concern with the body crosses gender, class and ethnicity, there has been a particular concern for the female body at risk, which is seen as both threatening and vulnerable. If the female body in Western cultures is seen as predominantly moist, flowing, leaky and difficult to contain, men's bodies, by contrast, are represented as dry, hard and well contained and controlled, with the Hellenic muscular idealised body representing control, rigidity and strength. This distinction is based upon a broader Western theme of the division of bodies closer to 'nature' and those further from 'nature' (Cranny-Francis, 1995).

These basic somatic oppositions contribute to a different gendered experience in relation to risk discourse. A recent UK study of young people, heterosexuality and power (Holland *et al.*, 1998) has examined the gendered positioning of bodies in young peoples experience of risk in relationships, particularly sexual relationships. The authors argue that:

> Young people's bodies are given meaning through ideas about the body and sexuality which are social, but these ideas are not entirely separate from bodily constraints and possibilities. (1998, p. 108)

Holland *et al.*'s (1998) study suggests that young women and men experience on the one hand a disembodied femininity and an embodied masculinity on the other. The study confirms Martin's (1989) claim that women tend to see their bodies as separated from themselves, as alienated or fragmented and in need of control. Young women work hard at gaining control over the surfaces and contours of their bodies. Boys in this study, by contrast, would appear to engage more comfortably with their physicality and with the potential the body has for pleasure. The implication is that pleasure is involved in the regulation of power relations and control of the sexual relationship. Girls are under pressure to control their unruly bodies in the sexual encounter and to deny their own pleasure or at least subordinate these to those of the boy. Although this relationship is far from straightforward, there are clear alignments with broader Western typifications of the body. There are indications in this study that the discourses disciplining the body may be of more interest to girls than boys. This finding is similar to Lupton and Tulloch's recent work on young people's orientation towards the risks of HIV/ AIDS (1998). Whilst boys are placed in a difficult situation needing to juggle accepted notions of masculinity, such as avoiding appearing 'emotional' and 'girlie' or a 'poofter', girls are better disposed to health counsellors and to talk about what happens to bodies and how to discipline them. Girls are equally disappointed by boys who are unable to talk openly about them.

The gendered body, then, is expressed through differing dispositions towards risk. The male body has been constructed as hard, invulnerable, dry, controlled and otherwise strongly bounded. By contrast, women's bodies have been characterised as altogether more 'leaky', viscous, flowing, vulnerable open and less strongly bounded (Shildrick, 1997). Such differences related to other more general cultural coding across areas such as crime and relationships. Reporting upon a three-year study of young people's perception and management of risk in a large industrial town in the North East of England which throughout this volume we called Townville, here we explore the ways that 'gendered risk' features in young people's accounts of their lives. We reflect on the nature of risk in classical psycho-social studies of risk and suggest that the gendering of risk is far from straightforward. In particular we question the depiction of young women's behaviour as simply low-risk and suggest that, understood phenomenologically, the gendering of risk is a far more complex phenomenon.

Locating risk

Risk research is not new to sociology. Indeed, Durkheim's focus on suicide may be considered one of the first systematic risk studies. The current perspective and research foci raised in the work of Douglas (1992), Beck (1992) and Giddens (1991) give a different turn to these more familiar concerns, however. Our approach to risk differs here from much of social-psychological approaches which have tended to examine 'objective' risks, and assumed that risk-taking requires some type of correction or intervention strategy (Plant and Plant, 1992). Within such literature risk is viewed as socially problematic. Here we attempt to be more reflexive. Rather than focusing upon risks as phenomena to be reduced in various ways, we attempt to focus on risk, risk perception and risk discourses as a means of examining broader social, cultural, political and economic processes. This concern with how young people 'construct' risk within their own socially embedded and culturally meaningful discourses (or what we here refer to as situated discourses) has become a recurring theme in youth research. Recent studies have considered how young people often reject 'objective' definitions of risky behaviour in favour of constructing their own 'risk hierarchies' (see Abbott-Chapman and Denholm, 2001) and have recognised the situated nature of risk within the life worlds of young people (Lawy, 2002). Here risk becomes something to be negotiated and managed with reference to complex and diverse social and cultural influences such as education, the family and the peer group. This discussion builds on such work to introduce an embodied reflexivity into young people's risk discourses and suggest that different dispositions towards risk have come to play an important part in the construction of the gendered body.

Self-development or actualisation through the management of risk is a life-long accomplishment; though in adolescence and the extended period of 'youth', these processes are likely to be particularly intense (Lupton and Tulloch, 1998; France, 2000; Abbott-Chapman and Denholm, 2001; Lawy, 2002). Adolescent concern with the body and the threats presented by infection and disease such as HIV/AIDS, for example, can illustrate something of young people's, 'heightened sense level of agentive reflexivity in relation to the health of their bodies ...' (Lupton and Tulloch, 1998, pp. 31–2). It might be argued that contemporary youthful identities are, *sin qua non*, 'post-modern' identities (Miles, 2000), representing a period of increased negotiation opportunity. As such this period offers a useful entry point for detailed analysis of the self and body. In our study of Townville's young people, the recurring study in this volume's chapters, we examined 'risk' as a subjective, meaningful or 'members' category and explored aspects of risk calculation and risk management apparent in the everyday lives of young people. Accounts of dangers, concerns, worries and anxieties, as well as notions of fate, chance and luck were examined with reference to broader theoretical concerns with the 'risk society'. Dispositions to risk manifest in everyday settings and in everyday discourse were part of broader strategies for dealing with uncertainty and the unpredictability of contemporary life. Beck (1992) has acknowledged inequity in risk distribution: lower classes bearing a disproportionate burden of risks. We would concur with this and are particularly interested in the distribution of risk and risk perception across class, gender, ethnicity and age groups. Furlong and Cartmel (1997) highlighted such inequalities in describing life for young people in contemporary 'risk society'. They point to class differences in exposure to risks. Similarly, here we explore gendered differences to risk. If, in late modernity, young people must, negotiate a set of risks which were largely unknown to their parents, they do so in ways that are gender specific.

Furlong and Cartmel's (1997) empirical grounding of some more abstract analyses of risk highlighted a problem of the ontological status of risk. The difference between 'objective' risks, manifest at broader societal and institutional discourses, and everyday use of such notions is glossed, for example, in the work of Beck and Giddens. Our own study attempted to locate risk in young people's everyday accounts as 'situated vocabularies' of risk and encompasses more phenomenological elements of risk.

The data presented here can be read at two levels. On the one hand, it could be seen as documenting 'objective' risks experienced by young people in a rapidly changing urban economy, and one in which familiar problems associated with social and economic deprivation and social exclusion are apparent. As such, the data would document the social distribution of risk by gender, age and class (though few of our sample fall into middle-class categories). On the other hand, the data allows examination of the means by which young people draw upon and use risk and associated discourses to construct gendered identities – particularly through the ways they see, care for and develop their own bodies. They can be read as 'accounts of risks' which will reflect broader discourses on the body. We are primarily concerned here with the latter use of the data.

Gendered risk

Our study focused on risk across five different spheres: health and lifestyle, economic and employment, intimate risks, crime and safety and environmental risk. Young people's definitions of 'risk', however, grouped risk with reference to seven different criteria. Risks in their accounts tended to fall into notions of: taking chances, getting or not getting caught, health/lifestyle risks, getting into trouble, pursuing pleasure, being in danger and doing something bad. 'Taking chances' and doing 'the unknown' involved activities such as running in front of cars as a game, being uncertain about what might happen in actions, doing dares, gambling. Getting caught or doing 'what you should not do', included, not doing homework or watching TV late at night. Health and lifestyle risks were more similar to official risk and included smoking, drinking and taking drugs. Getting into trouble for these young people involved stealing, lying, fighting or getting into mischief. Getting pleasure seemed integral to risk and was described as doing 'mad' or 'daft' things for fun or 'the buzz'. Being in danger involved such things as visiting 'dangerous places', being bullied, being near strangers at night. Doing 'Something that is bad' might mean wasting life, wasting health, 'making life a misery'. These categories were not mutually exclusive.

The combination of quantitative and qualitative data allows considerable scope for comparison of girls' and boys' accounts of risk. We highlighted differences from the survey findings running Chi Square significance tests using the independent values of gender, area and age, against a number of questions. No significant differences were found by gender across the seven categories of the meaning of risk or in the risky activities young people claimed to undertake, although young men were more likely to take risks than young women (35.4 men as apposed to 25.6). No significance existed either in the relevance and meaning of chance, which tended to be grounded in play and doing risk. One question we asked was: what three risky things do you do? Again no significant differences by gender were demonstrated, although, 'getting into trouble and illegal things' was more relevant to young men (16.7 per cent – no young women mentioned it) 'being normal' was more risky for young women (28.8 per cent compared to 4.8 per cent of boys).

Differences in the accounts of risk activities were found in relation to area and age group – two other interests of the study. Risk-taking is firmly located in play for a younger group. For the older age group risk was more located in health and lifestyle such as smoking and drinking. 'Being normal' also carried greater risk for the older age group in this sample. The older group reported taking more risks than the younger age group. Significant differences also occurred in our sample by area. Five hundred and eleven young people were included in the survey, although 131 were from Townville (the area of 'objective high risk' that was our focus). We were able to compare responses on the meaning of risk for this group in comparison to other areas that are arguably relatively more advantaged in 'objective risk assessment'. Young people in Townville were more likely to see the meaning of risk grounded in 'danger'. The rest of our sample were more likely to ground risk in 'taking a chance'. This finding is important to the study overall. The qualitative interviews had clustered accounts of risk-taking around issues of places, people and practices. Townville young people interviewed saw threats and danger coming from within their own community, which has particular relevance for women.

Examination of the meaning of risk and accounts of risk-taking activities, then, did not differ significantly by gender. The different constructions of women's and men's bodies referred to earlier as a vulnerable, open or leaky as opposed to hard, closed and contained were not superficially evident in this data. Closer examination of particular features of these accounts, however, illustrates some differences. These are shown here in relation to safety and also in relation to the pleasure, excitement and the fear of risk-taking.

Issues of safety were explored in some detail in the questionnaire with a series of questions about 'what worried' young people in relation to crime. There were high levels of reported contact with crime in Townville. For instance 35.4 per cent witnessed vandalism most weeks or days, 29.1 per cent reported seeing people being threatened by a knife, 31 per cent reported seeing shoplifting, 40 per cent seeing vandalism of a parked car, 52.7 per cent witnessing the stealing or 'Twoccing' (Taking Without Owners Consent) of a car and 33 per cent witnessing the breaking into of a house. Crime risk activities appeared to be a routine everyday aspect of life in Townville. 67.1 per cent expressed worry at drug dealing in the area, 64 per cent were worried about violence against the person. Significant differences existed between genders and age groups. Fifty-three per cent of the sample was concerned about bullying at school, for example, though 66 per cent of the young women as opposed to 45 per cent of young men. Young people in Townville frequently reported feeling unsafe in their own community as a result of threats from others (usually other young people). Significant gender differences did emerge in relation to risk management strategies. Whilst young people in Townville managed risks by travelling in gangs (69 per cent) and going out with friends (79.9 per cent), they appeared to see the streets as potentially dangerous place for individuals. Forty-three per cent of young people said they would not go out after dark as a way of avoiding danger. 55.4 per cent of young women as opposed to 33.2 per cent of young men said that they used this strategy to avoid danger. Young women were also less likely to report carrying a weapon 10.6 per cent as opposed to 36.1 per cent of young men.

Gendered discourses of risk

The qualitative data in the study supported these findings. Young women in particular expressed their fears in relation to presence on the streets, of potentially threatening people as well as to the dangerous practices carried out by themselves and their friends. For example, safety was an issue discussed in a number of focus groups. Young women in particular talked about fear at night as in the following:

> ... especially on the night we can't go out after 7 o'clock, because of the big gangs standing on the corners which sort of stops you, ... intimidates you. You feel scared inside you, they probably not say anything and stuff but you are scared. You feel scared and that is not very nice, that is why you sat locked in the house ... and they just

sat outside all on summers day, but you are locked in. (Group of women aged 20–25)

A younger girl commented

You try not to walk around on you own. I'm not allowed to. I'm not allowed out after 8 o'clock. We're not allowed when it's dark. If she goes out I go with her. We just go to each other's houses and listen to tapes and that. (Aged 12)

Girls in particular also seemed aware that Townville had particularly high risks relative to other districts as one girl in a group of 11–13 year olds commented:

... Compared with places like (another district nearby) people living in Townville have more worries 'coz this is a bad place to live ... well I mean you have got druggies living near you there's so many houses being broken into or burnt, you know that sort of stuff. (Aged 11–13)

The boys we interviewed appeared to be more philosophical about the nature of Townville and the risks it presented. They were less concerned for late night dangers and often normalised the setting. One boy commented:

It depends on what places you mean. If it's posh areas, rich places, there's no crime. But (another district nearby) and that have similar problems. Kids won't go into crime in posh areas, car don't get nicked. There's more youth here. (Member of group aged 11–16)

Arguably, these young people were highly aware of the structural relationship between place and risk.

Further focus group data illustrates how sexual risk, in terms of under-age or perhaps unwanted pregnancy, is a risk apparent for young people in Townville, particularly when combined with alcohol use. Again in response to the question, what are the issues/concerns for young people in Townville? A mixed sex focus group responded:

Young male: Everyone's pregnant! A lot of 16 year olds get pregnant.
Young male: Yeh and a lot of 14 and 15 year olds I know as well.
Interviewer: Do you think they get pregnant because they want to or because they don't know what they're doing?
Young male: They're always drunk at the time.

Young female: No! It could've been an accident you know what I mean!

The respondent's discussion around underage sex and pregnancy illustrates young people's awareness of the potential risks of unprotected sex. They demonstrate that they are also aware of the links between alcohol use and the increased likelihood of engaging in risky sexual practices. The following response illustrates young female's perceptions of the risks apparent for young men in the Townville area.

Young female: I think boys fight more, more boys hang around the streets than girls do.

Interviewer: What kind of things do boys do that you wouldn't dare?

Young female: Well they just think they are tougher.

Young female: They fight because they think they have to well in (Townville) anyway.

This response illustrates young females' perceptions of how within their community a culture of violence exists which exposes young men to the bodily risks of physical attack. Holland *et al.* (1998) and other writers such as Pearson (1983) have commented on the link between working-class communities and cultures of violence and aggressive masculinity. Pearson (1983) argues that historically working-class communities have always been characterised by violence and the above response suggests that young men within Townville, a traditionally working-class area, feel the need to conform to this.

This extract also illustrates female perceptions of the street as predominantly male space. Female respondents are suggesting that boys use the street to their exclusion and make it a site alive with risks for them. Connell (1987) describes the street as a highly gendered institution. He proposes that as so much social activity takes place in the street it can be seen as 'a definite social milieu with particular social relations' (pp. 132–4) and due to the intimidation of women within this milieu it becomes a 'zone of occupation by men' (pp. 132–4). Such concentrations of men are greatest in areas of highest unemployment such as Townville. Men however are also at risk in the street, as discussed above, and need to be aware of the dangers of violence from other men. The above quote demonstrates therefore that young girls are aware that the street is predominantly occupied by men and that it can be a site of intimidation, violence and risk both for themselves and young males.

Risk management strategies

It is clear from these extracts that young people attach meaning to specific types of bodily risks that they feel that themselves and their peers are exposed to. Further focus group data illustrates how young people in the area are aware of the need for strategies to counter these risks, of the necessity for risk management. As stated earlier both young men and young women perceive themselves as at risk from physical violence on the streets of Townville, but both have strategies for managing this risk. For young men in the sample, being involved in the risky practice of fighting was seen as routine, but as a risk that can be managed by sticking together.

> Young male: If you're gonna have a fight with someone and you're on your own you dunno, but if all your friends are with you, you think alright, I'll fight.
> Interviewer: So it makes you feel confident then.
> Young male: Yeah.
> Young male: Yeah if anyone hits him, I batter them.

This suggests that it is important for young men to appear to be tough and capable of fighting. Being in street fights with the prospect of physical injury is clearly a risky practice but one that can be managed by friends 'backing each other up'.

> Young male: You feel safe with your mates cos you know if there's any trouble you've got, they're going to help you out.

Young males in the sample were very specifically aware of the risk of being attacked by other males. For young women it was a more vague but still as pressing a risk of people 'out there' on the street who might harm them in some way.

> Young female: You feel safer when you're with someone, 'cos you might get grabbed.

In differing ways then, both young males and young females use the same strategy of the group to manage the risks apparent to them on the streets of Townville. Further focus group data goes on to illustrate that it is particularly important for young men to be able to manage the threat of physical risk in this context, as the risk of being attacked in the street was described as a daily threat.

> Young male: If you walk down the streets or something you get hit, especially him 'coz he's little for his age they call him ginger cunt and that.
> Young male: It's the big lads, the twoccers that have a go at him 'coz he's little for his age.
> Interviewer: How old are the lads that do this?
> Young male: About 16 or 17.
> Interviewer: So this worries you also?
> Young male: Yeah, there's loads of gangs hang around the fish shop and corner shops and disturb people and that.

Although, as the above illustrates, young men do feel at risk on the street in Townville, place is presented as less of a threat to young men in general. This may relate to the normality of male violence within working-class cultures, and an acceptance its inevitable presence, or perhaps the boys and young men's belief that their group can effectively manage violence. However, these young males did acknowledge the realities of the bodily risks they were exposed to. They discussed ways in which they could negotiate and manage risks and illustrate how such strategies are internalised in male gender identities.

In discussion of sexual risks, young people saw problems in Townville that required a strategy. They frequently talked of girls they knew becoming pregnant under 16 and of the need to use contraception. However, the opportunities for risk management provided by official agencies such as through school were seen as limited.

> Interviewer: So do you get taught sex education at school then?
> Young male: We just get given a box of condoms.
> Interviewer: Is that it?
> Young male: Yeah a box of durex.
> Young male: The girls get tampax and we don't get nowt.

Holland *et al.* (1998) discuss the way that school based provision in sex education is often not suited to the needs of young people and that this is particularly an issue for young men. They suggest that there is often a disparity in the way young men and young women learn about sex. Although young men seem to receive less formal sex education than young women they share a common perception that they do not need to learn about sex; somehow they just know about it (Holland *et al.*, 1998, p. 59). The implication is that poor sex education for young men in schools 'we just get given a box of condoms' is compensated for by the peer group and personal experience.

Risk and excitement

Significant differences were found in relation to risk and excitement, a 'positive' aspect of risk. Risk is always a two-way concept and offers positive as well as negative values to risk takers and managers. Risk profiling and risk management involves the seeking as well as the avoidance of risk, hence some young people were likely to see 'being normal or being good' as a risk. When asked, 'What three risky things do you do?' replies grouped into the following six headings: taking chances, getting caught and not doing as you were told, health and lifestyle, getting into trouble, and doing dangerous things, and being good or 'normal'.

Taking chances, usually in play, involved participation in activities such as, climbing on roofs, dares and riding bikes. Getting caught and not doing as you were told included sneaking out at night and truancy. Health and lifestyle risks were again more familiar and included having sex, smoking, drinking and taking drugs. Getting into trouble and doing illegal things involved, fighting, stealing, selling computer games illegally and stealing car radios. Doing dangerous things included, going out at night, driving fast, walking alone and riding motorbikes. Being good or 'normal' also appeared to involve risk. There were dangers in being a swot, playing football, watching TV, camping, doing adult things or going to the park.

Significant differences were found by gender. When young people were asked whether or not they saw risk-taking as exciting or not. It became clear that young people saw an important aspect of risk-taking as excitement. Only 2.3 per cent of young men never saw risk-taking as exciting and young women indicated that they found risk-taking less exciting (see Table 10.1).

We asked young people if they found risks enjoyable but no gender significance was found here. There were significant differences, however, in relation to reported levels of fear associated with risk-taking. Thirty-four per cent of young men, for example, never find risk-taking frightening whilst 6.9 per cent of young women never find it frightening and 20.7 per cent always find it frightening as opposed to 7.3 per cent of young men (see Table 10.2).

Table 10.1 Do you find risks exciting?* (%)

	Never	Sometimes	Always	It depends	Total
Male	2.3	30.2	32.6	34.9	100
Female	20.7	37.9	13.8	27.6	100

Note: * All results tested as significant at p < 0.05.

Table 10.2 Do you find risk-taking frightening? (%)

	Never	Sometimes	Always	It depends	Total
Male	34.1	30.1	7.3	19.5	100
Female	6.9	51.7	20.7	20.7	100

Whilst enjoyment was not significant in our survey, there was some indication that there may be a more negative association of risk for girls and young women and a more pleasurable association for young men. Older young people across gender tended to report the pleasures of risk as being primarily in the thrill or the buzz. These findings would appear to corroborate those of Holland *et al.* who found young men's accounts of their experience of sexual risk and the body as more pleasurable than young women's (Holland *et al.*, 1998).

Qualitative focus group data supports this contention that there are gender differences apparent in whether or not young people saw risk-taking as exciting or not. Young women appeared to perceive risk as something which was a danger to them and which they must develop strategies to avoid, such as staying in after dark or only going out in groups. The risk of violence for young people on the streets of Townville has been well illustrated, however, further focus group data provides evidence of young men seeing fighting as an enjoyable risk, and also suggests that it is an established part of these young males peer group.

Young male: Wherever you go, whatever you do, you have a good scrap don't you? When you haven't been fixed up by a quarter to two, that's it you know you're in for a scrap.

Young male: That's the crack. You go to the Madison and that to score and if you haven't scored by quarter to two, you look about for the tanks? (girls) no tanks that's it man.

Young male: Scrapping time.

Jones (1993) discussed why young men feel the necessity to engage in such exaggerated masculine behaviour. He attributes this behaviour to the decline in traditional manual labouring opportunities for young males. He concludes that:

> Faced with the disruption of it's traditional identities, the male body has become a site of further exaggeration of gender differences, including the proliferation of hyper-masculine representations and body practices in an effort to transcend and negate gender similarities to construct exclusively masculine discourses within a contemporary culture. (p. 77)

According to Jones (1993) then, young men use their bodies in engaging in risky practices such as fighting as a means of separating themselves from the feminine, as a means of confirming and reaffirming their masculine identities. With traditional routes for doing this, such as through the labour market, blocked, risky practices provide an outlet for exaggerated expression of traditional masculine norms. An exclusively masculine discourse is created which promotes the positive aspects of risk-taking, particularly those which demonstrate the toughness and resilience of the male body.

This is further expressed in other attitudes and dispositions towards risk. For older young people in our sample, risk-taking was deliberately engaged in various ways that involved activities such as dangerous driving, rolling cars or riding motorbikes without a crash helmet.

> Interviewer: Do you or your friends do dangerous things, take risks?
> Young male: Yeah.
> Young male: Roll cars. (16–19 years)

As discussed above, actively engaging in exciting or dangerous practices can be seen as a means of defining and developing masculine identities within the male peer group. This data suggests that young males actively pursue risk-taking as a means of both pleasure and identity formation within the male peer group, and that risk is associated with positive identities. Shilling (1993) discusses a similar theme, but in relation to sporting activities. He suggests that in typical choices of sport for working-class men the body is primarily a means for the experience of excitement even though physical investment in these sports can involve considerable effort, risk of injury or pain (Shilling, 1993, p. 130). The implication is that working-class males actively put their bodies at risk as a means of testing their own masculinity. Shilling suggests that the working class have an instrumental relation to their bodies, that it is a means to an end in the pursuit of labour, pleasure or excitement (Shilling, 1993, p. 130) rather than something in need of care and maintenance. In this Shilling is suggesting that working-class groups such as those in our sample are outside of the discourse which promotes care of the self as an individual responsibility and which signifies a healthy body as a mark of distinction (Petersen, 1996). This would appear to be supported by data which illustrates young people actively seeking risk-taking. However other focus group data illustrates that some young men in the sample would like to engage in more positive body maintenance, but feel that they are excluded from this through financial constraints.

> Young male: It is expensive, it is expensive. The thing is it's alright to start off with when you do start training to keep yourself fit or what ever but after that if you're going to treat it seriously you have to eat all the right foods and everything and it's not er, it's not something you can really afford if you were on the dole, if you know what I mean.

This is perhaps indicative of Beck's (1992) contention that within the risk society it is the working classes that will inevitably experience more risks, and that poverty brings with it an unfortunate abundance of risks. The inability to engage in active care of the self is perhaps one symptom of this inequality. The experience of this inequality has wider ramifications for the life experiences of these young people, as Shilling (1993) notes:

> If people are as reflexively aware of their bodies as Giddens suggests, then we may expect those in positions of subordination, without the time or resources to nurture their bodies, to be particularly prone to feelings of alienation and disaffection. (p. 200)

Discussion

Our study explored the extent to which young people draw on secular discourses of risk and risk management in their everyday lives. Research projects such as our own inform local economic and social policy programmes aimed at instilling new sets of risk management skills, body maintenance regimes and ultimately new forms of self-managed citizenship (Petersen and Lupton, 1996; Dean, 1999). Broader discourses of crime prevention, health promotion, work and enterprise and personal development mediate young bodies but not in a singular fashion. The discourses on risk that contribute to active citizenship are not unitary but are drawn upon differently by young men and women. The young women and men in our study appear to account for risks in different ways and adopt different risk management strategies.

Encountering risk and taking risks was a routine and ordinary event for all the young people in our sample. Young men and women appeared to view risks, dangers, concerns and related concepts in similar ways involving, taking chances, the unknown, getting caught, health and lifestyle risk-taking, getting into trouble, getting pleasure, being in danger and doing something that is bad. Though young men did say that they took more risks than young women in our sample, these differences were not statistically significant. When particular risks were examined in detail, however, such as safety, violence and safety management young women and girls did show significantly different dispositions towards risk. Support for these findings can be found in the analysis of the qualitative data we gathered. These differences were in line with some broader cultural constructions of the 'vulnerable female body'. These dispositions might reflect aspects of the broader discursive construction of the body as well as the everyday position of women in Townville. It is interesting to note here however that, though there were significant differences between girls' and young women's perception of threat and risks (females saw greater risks than males), their reported behaviour differences were not significant. Girls and young women appeared to be taking similar risks despite perceiving or attributing greater threats to them. This contradicts understanding of girls as (relatively) low risk takers. Understood phenomenologically, their risk-taking would appear to be greater than the boys. This finding suggests that simplistic understanding of risk-taking by gender is misleading and that we should be careful before describing girls and young women as non-risk takers.

Significant gender differences apply also to the more positively valued aspects of risk-taking. Young men and women are more likely to take risks for the thrill and 'the buzz' than their younger counterparts. Young men report valuing the excitement of risk more and experiencing the fear of risk less than young women. It appears that they may be taking more pleasure from the risks they take. This difference would seem to reflect some of the more general studies of risk takers (Plant and Plant, 1992) but particular aspects of the pleasures of risk may well warrant further research.

Such constructions of risk and pleasure are suggestive of broader developments in the construction of the modern body. Williams (1998) has argued that the late modern 'healthy' body is always constructed through a process of 'oscillation between bodily control and corporeal transgression: modalities which reflect and reproduce fundamental contradictions within Western culture and late capitalism itself'. Indeed it has been suggested that increasing importance of consumption and leisure in the West has re-valued more sensual forms of embodiment and of knowing oneself (Miles, 1992; Mellor and Shilling, 1997). This would suggest a valorisation of risk-taking in identity construction. Such valorisation of risk-taking has been said to be particularly important for men seeking the ideal male bodily form (see Jones, 1993; Watson, 2000). For young men in our sample this relationship with transgression is illustrated through their engagement with risk as an element of their identity construction (see also Mitchell *et al.*, 2001) yet also through their perceived need to balance this cultivation of risk with attention towards bodily maintenance and control more in line with dominant conceptions of risk avoidance and the construction of the healthy self.

If consumption oriented more sensual forms of embodiment are emerging in recent times, then we might speculate that there will be differing access to them. Young men in our study would appear to be more likely to enjoy what Maffesoli (1996) has termed 'sensual solidarity' and may have more privileged access to the anti-risk discourses that construct it. The work of Holland *et al.* (1998) would appear to support this finding. It is not that young men and women do not have understanding of risk discourses that are constitutive of embodied youthful identity, but rather that they draw upon them differentially. The sample of girls and young women in our study are more likely to draw upon knowledges that discipline and regulate their own bodies, in line with dominant cultural constructions of the female body. Boys and young men appeared more likely to engage with such discourses in a way that reaffirms their identity as men. This differential access suggest that what we are witnessing is the construction of 'gendered discourses of risk' which create ideal male and female bodily forms with reference to risk discourses apparent in late modern societies. This requires a balance between risk and pleasure, safety and danger, the appropriation of which becomes a central part of gendered identity construction as young people struggle with the contradictions apparent in complex risk discourses.

References

Abbott-Chapman, J. and Denholm, C. (2001) 'Adolescents' risk activities, risk hierarchies and the influence of religiosity'. *Journal of Youth Studies*, Vol. 4, No. 3, pp. 279–97.

Beck, U. (1992) *Risk Society: Towards a New Modernity*, London: Sage.

Connell, R. (1987) *Gender and Power*. Oxford: Polity.

Cranny-Francis, A. (1995) *The Body in the Text*. Melbourne: University Press.

Cutter, S., Tiefernbacher, J. and Solecki, W. (1992) 'En-gendered fears: Femininity and technological risk perception'. *Industrial Crisis Quarterly*, Vol. 6, pp. 5–22. Re-printed in Cutter, S. (ed.) (1994) *Environmental Risk and Hazards*. New Jersey: Prentice Hall.

Dean, M. (1999) 'Risk, calculable and incalculable' in Lupton, D. (ed.) *Risk and Sociocultural Theory: New Directions and Perspectives*. Cambridge: Open University Press, pp. 131–59.

Douglas, M. (1992) *Risk and Blame: Essays in Cultural Theory*. London: Routledge.

France, A. (2000) 'Towards a sociological understanding of youth and their risk taking'. *Journal of Youth Studies*, Vol. 3, No. 3, pp. 317–31.

Furlong, A. and Cartmel, F. (1997) *Young People and Social Change: Individualisation and Risk in Late Modernity*. Buckingham: Open University Press.

Giddens, A. (1991) *Modernity and Self-Identity: Self and Society in the Late Modern Age*. Cambridge: Polity Press.

Gilman, S. (1993) 'Touch, sexuality and disease' in Bynum, W. and Porter, R. (eds) *Medicine and the Five Senses*. Cambridge: Cambridge University Press.

Holland, J., Ramazanoglu, C., Sharpe, S. and Thompson, R. (1998) *The Male in the Head: Young People, Heterosexuality and Power*. London: The Tufnell Press.

Jones, A. (1993) ' "Defending the border", men's bodies and vulnerability'. *Cultural Studies from Birmingham*, Vol. 2, pp. 77–123.

Lawy, R. (2002) 'Risky stories: youth identities, learning and everyday risk'. *Journal of Youth Studies*, Vol. 5, No. 4, pp. 407–23.

Lupton, D. and Tulloch, J. (1998) 'The adolescent "unfinished body", reflexivity and HIV/AIDS'. *Body and Society*, Vol. 4, No. 2, pp. 19–34.

Maffesoli, M. (1996) *The Time of the Tribes: The Decline of Individualism in Mass Society*. London: Sage Publications.

Martin, E. (1989) *The Woman in the Body: A Cultural Analysis of Reproduction*. Milton Keynes: Open University Press.

Mellor, P. and Shilling, C. (1997) *Re-forming the Body: Religion, Community and Modernity*. London: Sage Publications.

Miles M. (1992) *Carnel Knowing*. Tunbridge Wells: Kent Burns and Oates.

Miles, S. (2000) *Youth Lifestyles in a Changing World*. Buckingham: Open University Press.

Mitchell, W., Crawshaw, P., Bunton, R. and Green, E. (2001) 'Situating young people's experiences of risk and identity'. *Health, Risk and Society*, Vol. 3, No. 2, pp. 217–33.

Pearson, G. (1983) *Hooligan: A History of Respectable Fears*. Basingstoke: Macmillan.

Petersen, A. (1996) 'Risk and the regulated self: the discourse of health promotion as politics of uncertainty'. *Australian and New Zealand Journal of Sociology*, Vol. 32, No. 1, pp. 44–57.

Petersen, A. and Lupton, D. (1996) *The New Public Health: Health and Self in the Age of Risk*. London: Sage Publications.

Plant, M. and Plant, M. (1992) *The Risk Takers*. London: Routledge.

Seymour, W. (1998) *Remaking the Body: Rehabilitation and Change*. London and New York: Routledge.

Shildrick, M. (1997) *Leaky Bodies: Feminism, Postmodernism and (Bio) Ethics*. London: Routledge.

Shilling, C. (1993) *The Body and Social Theory*. London: Sage Publications.

Townsend, P., Phillimore, P. and Beattie, A. (1998) *Health and Deprivation: Inequality and the North*. London: Routledge.

Treichler, P. (1987) 'AIDS, homophobia and biomedical discourse: an epidemic of signification'. *Cultural Studies*, Vol. 1, No. 3, pp. 263–305.

Waldby, C. (1997) *AIDS and the Body Politic: Biomedicine and Sexual Difference*. London: Routledge.

Walkerdine, V. (1997) *Daddy's Girl: Young Girls and Popular Culture*. Basingstoke: MacMillan Press.

Watson, J. (1998) 'Running around like a lunatic: Colin's body and the case of male embodiment' in Nettleton, S. and Watson, J. (eds) *The Body in Everyday Life*. London: Routledge.

Watson, J. (2002) *Males Bodies: Health, Culture and Identity*. Buckinghamshire: Open University Press.

White, R. (1994) 'Street life: police practice and young people in Australia' in White, R. and Alder, C. (eds) *The Police and Young People in Australia*. Cambridge: Cambridge University Press.

Williams, S. J. (1998) 'Health as moral performance: ritual transgression and taboo'. *Health*, Vol. 2, pp. 435–57.

11
Risk, Motherhood and Children's Play Spaces: The Importance of Young Mothers' Experiences and Risk Management Strategies

Wendy Mitchell

Introduction

Young motherhood and childhood and thus the lives of young mothers and children are much discussed in late modern society. Indeed, both groups are frequently presented as occupying an ambiguous and at times contradictory position: as 'a risk' to society and 'at risk' and thus vulnerable within society. Drawing upon qualitative data, this chapter focuses upon the lives of 14 young mothers in Townville,[1] a town located in the North East of England characterised by high levels of social and economic deprivation. The chapter examines the young mothers ever-present concern about and strategies to manage risk, in relation to safe spaces and leisure experiences for their children. The chapter demonstrates the importance of exploring individual perceptions and understandings of 'risk', whilst simultaneously recognising that these perceptions are socially, economically and culturally grounded in specific local contexts. Exploring the young mothers' understanding of risk and their risk management strategies demonstrates a complex interweaving of three discourses within late modern society. The first centres upon the idea that we are moving towards 'risk society', a society pervaded by ever-present risk anxiety, and a felt need to try and control or at least manage 'risk' (Beck, 1992, 1994, 1998). The second discourse discusses ideologies of motherhood, especially the importance of being or rather perceived as a 'responsible and respectable mother'. The third and final discourse focuses upon the historically fluid and often contradictory concept of childhood, particularly with regard to children's leisure. The chapter examines how these discourses are interwoven within the mothers' lives, especially how and why they are utilised and the impact they have upon both the mothers' and their children's lives, including the mothers' own sense of 'self'. Structurally, the chapter is divided into three sections. The first section, reviews the literature surrounding the three discourses noted above, thus highlighting a number of key issues young mothers may face in late modern society. Before exploring how the Townville mothers make sense of these discourses, the study's sample is introduced with the aid of some basic demographic factors. The study's research methods are also summarised. The third section presents the empirical data, exploring and discussing how the Townville young mothers actively seek to manage risk in their own and their children's lives, especially their children's play spaces. The chapter concludes with a consideration of these risk management strategies in the wider socio-economic context. As we enter the twenty-first century, society is frequently presented as increasingly heterogeneous, however, this chapter demonstrates the continuing importance of traditional class and gender inequalities. Indeed, a central theme pervading the mothers' management strategies is their awareness of the gendered nature of risk in Townville.

Risk society and ideologies of motherhood

As previously discussed by Bunton, Green and Mitchell in their introductory chapter, society today is increasingly associated with the movement towards 'risk society'. Indeed, the literature surrounding late modern society highlights and debates a number of interrelated changes and developments, such as a greater sense of 'ontological insecurity' (Giddens, 1991) and increasing individualism, succinctly depicted by Lash (1994) as 'reflexive modernisation'. In addition, theorists such as Beck (1992) and Giddens (1991) suggest that traditional structures and boundaries, especially those of class, gender and ethnicity are no longer clear cut or static but are gradually becoming more contested, blurred and less localised. How far this has or is gradually occurring remains, however, much debated. Indeed, other theorists (Roberts, 1996; Furlong and Cartmel, 1997; Scott *et al.*, 1998) argue that Beck and Giddens over-estimate this blurring, class, gender and ethnicity continues to permeate young people's lives, as does the importance of local places and spaces. This has been succinctly summarised by Furlong and Cartmel (1997, p. 114) as an 'epistemological fallacy'.

However, in contrast to this, a number of visible changes have been noted by Beck in the sphere of intimate relationships. In late modern society, Beck (1992), Beck and Beck-Gernsheim (1995) suggest that intimate and personal relationships are regarded as increasingly fragile and transitory. For example, whereas in the past, marriage was seen as 'for-ever', today it is argued that individuals are more willing to end a relationship if it is not felt to be personally fulfilling. Hence, living with a partner can be both a transitory and emotionally painful experience (see Mitchell and Green, 2002, pp. 2–3, for a more in-depth discussion). In contrast, parent–child, especially mother–child relationships are regarded as potentially more durable and secure (Beck, 1992; Beck and Beck-Gernsheim, 1995; see also Becker and Charles, 2003 work exploring 'the family'). As a result of this, it is suggested that adults increasingly place a desire to find themselves through another onto their child rather than another adult (Beck and Beck-Gernsheim, 1995, pp. 72–3). Jensen (1994, p. 74) similarly associates late modernity relationship changes with a growing 'feminization of childhood', as women increasingly have primary responsibility for children emotionally, practically and economically.

Feminists however, such as Smart and Neale (1999) criticise Beck (1992) and Beck and Beck-Gernsheim's (1995) ideas as idealising the concept of motherhood and mother–child bonds. Indeed, these concepts raise a number of powerful and persistent ideologies that continue to permeate Western society. For example, as I have argued previously (Mitchell and Green, 2002, p. 5), motherhood is frequently 'romanticized and idealized as the supreme physical and emotional achievement in women's lives' (Phoenix and Woollett, 1991, p. 13). Hence, 'mother' and 'womanhood' are viewed as two sides of the same coin (Oakley, 1979) and it is often presumed that all women are 'waiting' or 'wanting' to be mothers (Letherby, 1994). Endemic within these ideals are essentialist assumptions about women fulfilling their 'natural' biological and maternal instincts (Woodward, 1997). Motherhood is also pervaded by the 'ethic of care', summarised by Henderson *et al.* (1989, p. 122) as the 'belief that self and other are interdependent'. Relationships are thus viewed as an integral part of being a woman, for mothers this is frequently translated into ideals of selflessness, especially the idea that a 'good', 'responsible' mother puts her child before herself. Feminists have and continue to contest these ideas, however, analyses of motherhood have been diverse, some have prioritised and others have marginalised the importance of motherhood in women's lives. Although in many ways a shared experience, motherhood can, as Ribbens (1994, p. 28) has noted, similarly raise contradictory and ambiguous feelings in women. This diversity mirrors the wider post-modernist feminist belief that women cannot be viewed as a homogenous category; diversity and differentiation must be acknowledged and explored (Silva, 1996; Skeggs, 1997; Jackson and Scott, 2002).

Furthermore, it is also important to recognise that many of these ideals are premised upon a very specific, socio-historical type of motherhood, Smart (1996) describes this as 'normative motherhood', that is, white, married and middle class. Consequently, not all mothers and/or types of mothering are viewed positively. Those who do not meet these normative standards are frequently problematised within society and portrayed as 'bad' or inadequate mothers, one of the clearest and most current examples, which will form the focus of this chapter are lone mothers, especially teenage mothers. Indeed, the fecund body is often experienced diversely by middle-class and working-class females and discussed very differently by social commentators (Walkerdine *et al.*, 2001). In many ways, teenage motherhood is an easy target to problematise because, as Phoenix and Woollett (1991) highlight, teenage mothers are felt to have entered motherhood at the 'wrong' age, that is, too young. Indeed, their very identity highlights society's ambiguous and often contradictory notions of adulthood. Biologically, the young mothers may have achieved womanhood but socially, they are often not equated with adult status. Politically, lone mothers, especially young mothers have also become increasingly marginalised and viewed as 'dangerous', linked with moral panics around and growing fears for 'the underclass' (Murray, 1994; McIntosh, 1996; Rosenneil and Mann, 1996). However, there is also a vast literature associating teenage motherhood (both mother and child) with health problems and socio-economic disadvantages (Simms and Smith, 1986; Hudson and Ineichen, 1991; Magee, 1994; Martin and Colbert, 1997; Kissman, 1998). Lone mothers, particularly teenage mothers thus face a number of contradictory and paradoxical discourses: on one hand they are perceived as 'a risk' to society, on the other, they are felt to be 'at risk'. Hence, recent Government (DoH, 1999) and European Union (Berthoud and Robson, 2001) reports portray teenage motherhood as a problem that needs to be addressed and a group requiring greater support.

Children, risk and play

In late modernity it also comes as no surprise that society's perception of children is frequently contested. Historically, it is acknowledged that the concept of childhood has changed over time. Associations of childhood with 'innocence', 'weakness' and a need for 'discipline' have been linked back to the renaissance (Ariès, 1961). More recently, sociological and cultural analyses have moved away from developmental and social-isation models to an understanding of childhood as a socially con-structed and culturally specific but heterogeneous experience (James and Prout, 1990; Mayall, 1994; Qvortrup *et al.*, 1994; Hill and Tisdall, 1997; James *et al.*, 1998). Similarly, children's rights discourses have proliferated (Children Act, 1989; United Nations, 1989; Alderson, 1995; Franklin, 1995).

However, it is increasingly feared that clearly defined moral and social boundaries between children and adults are becoming confused and ambiguous (Wyness, 2000). Hence, there is anxiety that some children are 'out of place' (Wyness, 2000). At the heart of this anxiety there appear two contradictory and paradoxical discourses surrounding children and the concept of 'childhood' (Scott *et al.*, 1998; Holloway and Valentine, 2000). On one hand, there is recognition of children's autonomy but on the other, an increasing focus upon the need for protection. Valentine (1996) has summarised this as a perception of children as 'angels' and 'devils', underpinned by a series of moral panics around childhood and symbol-ised by images of child murderers, teenage gangs roaming the streets and a rise in youth crime. Hence, some children ('angels'), especially pre-teenage children are viewed as vulnerable and in need of protection, whereas others ('devils'), are viewed as dangerous and 'out of control' and thus a risk to society (see also Valentine and McKendrick, 1997).

Interwoven within these contradictions and concerns there are specific socio-economic changes. Here, we will highlight the decline of family authority and the 'domestication' and 'commodification' of children's play, as they are interwoven with the lives of Townville's young mothers. The erosion of family authority is frequently associated with the decline of the idealised nuclear family and fears of 'the underclass'; particularly absent fathers and as discussed above, teenage mothers (Murray, 1994). Leading to a perception of children being inadequately disciplined, a dearth of 'appropriate' adult role models and moral guidance and thus in danger of becoming 'out of control'. Concerns about the changing nature of children's play evolve from a perception of play as a fundamental right for all children, as demonstrated by article 38 of the UN Convention on the Rights of the Child (1989). Indeed, spontaneous and independent play is frequently viewed as important for children's social, emotional and cog-nitive development and enhancing their geographical awareness of local spaces (Matthews, 1992; Aitken, 1994; Valentine and McKendrick, 1997).

However, there is increasingly felt to be a 'relative absence of time, space and opportunity for children to play' in Western society (Wyness, 2000, p. 16), especially in terms of spontaneous, independent play. In contrast, children's play is frequently characterised as home based and/or more formally organised by adults. Within the literature (Corsaro, 1997; Valentine and McKendrick, 1997; Holloway and Valentine, 2000; Wyness, 2000), this movement is often associated with parents' and in general, society's heightened fears of danger, especially 'stranger danger' on the streets and the growth of dual earner families. The latter leading to an extension of more formally organised childcare, such as crèches and after-school clubs. Consequently, commentators, such as Hendricks (1994), Näsman (1994) and Zeiher (2001) argue that children's leisure has gradually moved from being located within local neighbourhoods towards more isolated and geographically dispersed spaces of child oriented leisure. However, with the advent of mass communication, especially mobile phones and e-mail, this raises the potential for temporal and spatial boundaries amongst children being eroded (Zeiher, 2001). Public policies may seek to accommodate children's independent play outside the home, via parks and adventure playgrounds but this provision is often felt to be inadequate and low priority, especially in times of economic decline (Valentine and McKendrick, 1997; Kelley *et al.*, 1998; Zeiher, 2001). These trends may provide an overview of the changing nature of children's play but it is important to recognise that socioeconomic inequalities can impact upon children's play (Valentine and McKendrick, 1997; O'Brien *et al.*, 2000). Similarly, despite the current negativity, organised and structured play is frequently a stimulating experience for many children (O'Brien *et al.*, 2000).

The ensuing empirical analysis of young mothers' experiences of life in Townville draws together the above three spheres of literature surrounding risk society, responsible motherhood and children's play. The data demonstrates that these discourses are frequently interrelated within the mothers' lives and simultaneously recognises that their individual subjective perceptions and experiences of risk anxiety and active management strategies, especially in relation to ensuring their children's safe play are grounded in the wider socio-economic context within which they live. However, before presenting this data, the sample of young mothers are introduced.

Action Risk project

This chapter explores the lives and experiences of 14 young mothers interviewed as part of the wider project, *Action Risk*[2] located in Townville, an area characterised by high levels of social and economic deprivation (see Bunton, Green and Mitchell's introductory chapter for an overview of the whole project). The young mothers participating in *Action Risk* ranged in age from 15 to 24 years. Each mother had between one and three children; the youngest was six weeks and the oldest, six years. The ideas discussed here are those of predominately white mothers. Four Asian mothers were also interviewed; however, due to subtle ethnic differences their ideas will not be explored, as they require a separate discussion in their own right. Thirteen of the mothers were single never married, one was divorced and five lived with partners (see Table 11.1). It is important to recognise that the sample may not be statistically representative of all young mothers in Townville, as a potential population was identified with the aid of relevant professionals (health visitors, teachers) and then chosen on a self-selecting rather than random basis.

Table 11.1   Sample of Townville mothers

Name*	Age (yrs)	Number of children	Marital status
Paula	22	One child – 2 years, pregnant with second	Lives with partner
Susan	20	Two children – 3 years and 5 months	Lives with partner
Heidi	21	Three children – 6 years, 3 years and 7 months	Lives with partner
Sally	22	One child – 10 months	Lives with partner
Kim	22	Three children – 4 years, 2 years and 7 months	Lives with partner
Debbie	16	One child – 5 months	Moves between mother and partner and his family
Jenny	24	One child – 3 years	Divorced lone parent
Jane	17	Two children – 3 years and 6 months	Single lone parent
Sharon	22	Two children – 5 years and 3 years	Single lone parent
Liz	20	One child – 3 years	Single lone parent
Amanda	19	One child – 11 months	Single lone parent
Karen	20	Three children – 4 year old twins and 2 years	Single lone parent
Kelly	16	One child – 6 weeks	Single lone parent living with parents
Tanya	15	One child – 3 months	Single lone parent living with mother

Note: * Names have been changed to protect the mothers' anonymity.

As noted above, the concept of 'the underclass' is frequently associated with lone mothers, however; this chapter will seek to avoid this term, due to its social presumptions and negativity (Baldwin *et al.*, 1997). The author also recognises the importance of listening to children and their subjective ideas; however, the ideas of the mothers' children were not explored due to their young age and the specific age limitations of *Action Risk*. The mothers were individually interviewed using a flexible topic guide in either local community buildings (the local women's centre and primary school) or at the women's own homes. The interviews lasted between an hour and an hour and a half and were all tape-recorded. After transcription, the researchers read and re-read the interviews in order to identify and explore key concepts and themes, drawing upon grounded theory principles (Glaser and Strauss, 1967).

Risk, motherhood and children's play spaces

Townville's dangerous streets

Over two-thirds of the mothers viewed life in Townville as potentially risky and dangerous. Only two mothers questioned whether Townville itself was particularly risky, as other local areas were felt to be just as dangerous. However, there was a general feeling that one needed to be competent and street wise to cope with everyday life. Hence, it comes as no surprise that they focused their risk anxiety upon their young children and the belief that they were not street wise. Indeed, the mothers presented their young children as key members of Townville society that needed to be protected; they were the vulnerable 'angels' (Valentine, 1996). Assessments of everyday risks and dangers focused upon four areas: 'stranger danger', joyriders, syringes and playground domination.

Over half (10) of the mothers feared there were dangerous 'outsiders' in the neighbourhood, that is, people who had come into the area rather than Townville residents. For many, this 'stranger danger' had crystallised into a belief that child abductors and paedophiles 'lurked out there' on the streets of Townville, especially from the local bail hostel.

Susan: I wouldn't let Sophie play out on the front, on the road, there's a hostel.
Interviewer: The bail hostel?
Susan: Yes, I won't let her out of my sight. I won't even let her in the back garden on her own and it's all closed in.

Interviewer: Sometimes when I've talked to people they're worried about the bail hostel because it's quite near, does it ever worry you?

Paula: Yeah, it does but I think it will be worse once the new one is finished being built ... from what I've been told it's supposed to be a high security one for paedophiles and people like that. I don't want no one grabbing my kids. I would worry me more if I had a girl, you know if I had a daughter.

This fear of child abductors and paedophiles in Townville was of great concern to the young mothers. Risk assessments are not always based on objective or expert facts but rather, as Douglas (1992) suggests, value judgements and shared cultural beliefs. Hence, establishing the validity of these beliefs is not a central issue here, a fear of child abductors and paedophiles in Townville, whether fact or fiction, was very real to the mothers and thus had a profound effect upon their risk assessments and the care of their children. Indeed, within *Action Risk*, concerns about male 'stranger danger' generally pervaded girls' and young women's consciousness and thus in many ways policed their behaviour (Foreman *et al.*, 2000; Green *et al.*, 2000). Previous studies have indicated that parents' fears are frequently gendered, girls are viewed as more 'at risk' than boys (Stanko, 1990; O'Brien *et al.*, 2000). In Townville, as noted above, the young mothers' fears were similarly gendered. However, mothers of boys also noted concern, thus highlighting, as Valentine (1997) and Valentine and McKendrick (1997) suggest, that 'stranger danger' fears are frequently linked to all young children, irrespective of gender.

Risks associated with the growing volume of traffic are well established in the literature (Kelley *et al.*, 1998; O'Brien *et al.*, 2000). In Townville, the young mothers' (eight) fears focused upon a very specific type of traffic, namely, young male joyriders.

Jane: It's just all the daft people, the older people about 18/19 who have learnt to drive skidding about and the people that haven't even got a licence skidding about.

Kim: Joyriders, we usually get them around here and lads on motorbikes being stupid. I saw a car chase the other night where I live.

Joyriding and taking cars without consent have been much discussed by the media, frequently in terms of moral panics surrounding ideas of youth 'out of control' and juvenile crime. This in turn heightened the mothers' anxiety and fear for their children.

Within *Action Risk*, the issue of drugs raised a number of complex discourses. As Crawshaw's chapter similarly notes, amongst many teenagers (13 years plus) there was a subjective divide between different types of drugs. Hard drugs (such as heroin) and drug users or 'smack heads', as they were frequently discussed were viewed as dangerous and a risky pursuit. However, 'softer' drugs (such as cannabis) were not equated with the same degree of 'risk', indeed, some young people linked these with relaxation and recreation (Foreman *et al.*, 2000). Discussions with the young mothers similarly associated 'hard' drugs with risk. Three quarters (11) focused their risk anxiety upon used syringes lying around Townville, which were not always restricted to public streets and alleyways but could spread into private spaces, such as gardens and yards.

Tanya: There's loads of smack heads and stuff like needles on the floor and that.

Kim: I found one [needle] in my garden but I don't know if it was a drug needle or what ... it might have been nothing, it might have been something, I just put it in the bin.

Interviewer: Did it worry you?

Kim: Yeah, with all the drugs and that, that are about.

This in turn raised a wider and more diffuse fear of AIDS.

Liz: There was a kid where my mother lives [still in Townville], over the road from her, he found a needle and picked it up ... he had to go for an AIDS test.

It is interesting to note that dangerous 'outsiders', joyriders and needles were perceived as threatening, irrespective of the age of one's child. They were feared by mothers with school age children, toddlers and babies. However, for those with babies, risks such as joyriding and needles on the streets were somewhat theoretical, as their children were not yet walking. Despite this, they were still felt to be pertinent and thus feared for the future.

As noted in the literature and also discussed in Foreman's chapter (Chapter 9), parents frequently highlight a lack of public playgrounds for children. Seven Townville mothers similarly stressed a dearth of play-grounds; especially safe play areas. As one would expect, the majority had school age/toddling children, however, it was still an area of concern for one mother (Sally) with a baby. In Townville, playgrounds were associated with risk not only in terms of 'stranger danger' but also dangerous 'insiders', that is, local residents, such as teenage gangs. Indeed, these highly visible 'youth' were frequently viewed as problematic and in need of control, in many ways they began to symbolise Valentine's (1996) 'devils':

Interviewer: Are there any parks in Townville to take the kids?

Sally: Not really, there's one, the other one's rubbish 'cause there's loads of big kids on it ... they put mud all over the seats of the swings and slides and everything ... There needs to be more play areas and stuff, we want more of 'em and to keep the big kids off.

Young mothers' risk management

Faced with an ever-present fear of danger from a range of subjectively perceived and objectively experienced risks, coupled with recognition of the importance of play for their young children, the mothers actively developed risk management strategies. These strategies sought to both protect their children and provide stress reduction coping mechanisms for themselves. Indeed, they frequently drew upon 'problem-focused' coping mechanisms (Lazarus and Folkman, 1984). For example, as discussed above, they identified problems and dangers on Townville's streets and as a result sought alternative solutions, such as closely supervising their children's leisure experiences and movements. Hence, it comes as no surprise that nine mothers with school age/toddling children stressed that their children do not play out on the streets or go out alone. In contrast, they play inside the home, or, if outside are supervised. These mothers thus follow the familiar pattern of children's play and leisure time being increasingly adult supervised and controlled (Valentine and McKendrick, 1997; Kelley *et al.*, 1998; O'Brien *et al.*, 2000).

Heidi: Well most of the time we'll be either at home or at the park, you know they don't really go far ... [later] I don't let them play out the front. Like in the summer, now and again if I'm sat on the step but most of the time they are out the back.

In addition, it was also clear that they sought to rationalise and make sense of the situation for themselves in order to mentally adjust to it, even if they could not change it (Lazarus and Folkman, 1984). Hence, as noted above, many of the mothers (including some with only babies) frequently focused upon tangible symbols such as paedophiles and 'smack heads', which were viewed as external, that is, they were 'out there' on the streets and not directly in the home. Kelley *et al.* (1998) in their study of parents, risk and children have similarly noted this externalisation of risk. In many ways the mothers recognised that these are public risks that they frequently cannot control, that is, who is on the streets of Townville and what is dropped. However, this does not mean that they do not want to regain a sense of internal, personal control over their own and their young children's lives. Subjective perceptions of control, however small can help foster feelings of security and even power (Van Veldhuizen and Last, 1991; DeWinter *et al.*, 1999). Thus, mothers with school age/toddling children felt more secure knowing exactly where their children were and regulating their movements. Hence, the Townville mothers, in a similar manner to Roberts' (1995) discussion of parental prevention of childhood accidents, gained a sense of security by controlling their child's exposure to risks rather than actually changing the external risk situation. It is important to recognise that the mothers in this sample were able to physically control their child's movements, due to their young age. Although beyond the scope of this study, it would be interesting to explore the mothers' feelings of security as their children mature and become physically more independent and mobile. However, it is clear that the mothers' present strategy reflects, as Petersen and Lupton (1996) suggest, the onus within 'new public health' policies to focus upon and promote active and individual self-governing behaviour rather than focusing upon wider macro issues. Here, for example, in Townville, the ever-present reality of social and economic deprivation.

Social and economic inequalities

In late modernity, some theorists have noted a growing trend towards parents adopting individualised 'compensatory measures' in order to balance the felt need to protect one's children with a recognition of the importance of providing play opportunities beyond the family home (Kelley *et al.*, 1998, p. 19). With the growing dispersion of children's leisure activities to isolated and increasingly privatised centres, it is argued that parents spend large amounts of time transporting their children (especially young children) to and from specific child orientated activities and clubs (Kelley *et al.*, 1998; Zeiher, 2001). Thus, in many ways it is felt that young children's leisure worlds have geographically broadened and their range of activities expanded. However, some theorists (Adler and Adler, 1994; Ward, 1994; Kelley *et al.*, 1998; O'Brien *et al.*, 2000; Zeiher, 2001) have also noted the importance of social and material resources and thus the persistence of inequalities. Despite this, the everyday reality for those who do not have these resources to draw upon is less frequently explored.

Discussions with the young mothers in Townville clearly highlighted that they were isolated and excluded from this trend to individualised 'compensatory measures' (Kelley *et al.*, 1998): materially, socially and/or personally. Exclusion generally arose from a lack of disposable income and reliance upon public transport. Hence, six felt they could not afford to pay for clubs or activities:

> Susan: There's not much for them to do really ... everywhere you go
> you have to pay to get in, the swimming baths or places like
> that, so she's in all the time.

Even free activities or public places were often inaccessible if they were beyond Townville, as public transport was not only expensive but also problematic with young children and pushchairs.

> Interviewer: Some people have told me that there is a good play-
> ground for the kids over in North Park, is that right?
> Karen: Yes, ... I haven't been over there for ages, but it's good
> down there.
> Interviewer: Is there any reason why you haven't been?
> Karen: It's too far. Yes, especially to trail all three kids.
> Interviewer: Could you go on the bus?
> Karen: That means getting two tickets, one from here to the
> town and then to North Park. I just can't afford to get
> that many buses.

A significant number (eight) recognised that their child's leisure world was geographically limited to a narrow sphere and that a car would not only make their life a great deal easier but would also extend their leisure lives.

> Karen: Go more places, do more things, take the kids out at the week-
> ends, I'd love a car.

For the small minority of mothers (three) who sometimes had access to a car, trips out were looked forward to but simultaneously reinforced their dependent status, as many could not drive and thus they had to rely upon others.

> Jenny: I like it when I can take him [son] to the beach but the beach and picnics and all the rest are with my Mum and Dad, they've got a car.

Indeed, isolation from organised child-orientated play activities may disadvantage the young mother's children in the future. If, for example, as Adler and Adler (1994) suggest, these play centres and activities enable children to experience certain valued skills, knowledge and resources, that is, Bourdieu's 'cultural capital' that are increasingly socially valued.

However, the young mothers were by no means passive victims. Social and economic circumstances clearly dominated their experiences but they actively drew upon other coping resources to broaden their lives (see Lazarus and Folkman, 1984 for a general discussion of coping resources), such as their relationships with extended kin in or near Townville. For example, safe leisure time could be spent away from one's own house within the homes of kin.

> Sharon: Like Saturdays and Sundays ... we go to Mam's for their dinner, Sunday dinner around our Mam's and then it's back home.

Similarly, kin could also be relied upon to supervise children's play if a mother had to 'nip out'. Those without the support of a partner particularly valued this.

The impact on mothers' self-identity

One may presume that the young mothers' isolation from individualised 'compensatory measures' could impact upon their self-perception as a parent, that is, feeling they are inadequately providing for their child(ren). However, this was clearly not the case for many of the mothers (eight). In contrast, discussions revealed that they viewed their active risk management as a signifier of being a 'good' mother. As noted previously, the 'ethic of care' and ideals of 'selflessness' are endemic within ideologies of motherhood. Indeed, half of the Townville mothers highlighted that they continually put their child(ren) first:

> Amanda: She is number one, you are not number one, she is number one. So it is basically, you have got to look after her first, I mean you can look after yourself but you're that busy, you just take care of what she needs first and you come second.

Despite this, some (five) were very aware that as young mothers' they were frequently negatively stereotyped as irresponsible and potentially 'bad' mothers.

> Heidi: When you walk in the streets and like when older people look down at you, when you are walking in the streets and people see that I've got three kids now and I'm young, you know I'm only 21, you can tell, you know what they're thinking.

Hence, it comes as no surprise that many stressed and actively sought to demonstrate that they were responsible and respectable mothers. Thus, in a similar manner to Phoenix's study of young mothers (1991a,b) and as I have previously highlighted (Mitchell and Green, 2002, pp. 15–16), they emphasised their own success as a 'good' mother by mentally distancing and physically contrasting their behaviour as responsible and caring with 'other' mothers in Townville. These 'others' were viewed as 'uncaring', 'irresponsible' and thus potentially 'bad' mothers.

> Heidi: I see a lot of kids playing outside, like running across the road and stuff like that, I'm thinking, 'where are the mam's?' and they are nowhere to be seen.
> Interviewer: How does that make you feel?
> Heidi: You feel sorry for them, you think they are not getting looked after properly, like I wouldn't let my kids play out like that ...
> Jenny: No, I mean there are mothers down my street that just let their kids do what they want. But there is no way I would let him do what he wants ... when you see some kids around here they are left to do what they want. I don't know how they haven't been snatched, they [mothers] are not bothered about the cars that go up and down the street, whereas I am, I would not let Bob play out the front. If he wants to play out, he can play out the back.

Using their subjective perceptions and symbolic understandings of Townville space, these mothers set personal boundaries of respectability and responsibility. Hence, although these 'other' mothers may live on the same streets, how and what parts of Townville space they use (i.e. allowing their children on the streets unsupervised) clearly differentiates them (see also Lupton, 1999). They are viewed as risk-taking mothers who do not responsibly manage their children's use of public space.

Hence, the ethic of care has become intricately interwoven with space management and the mothers' associations of 'respectability'. This distinction between acceptable and unacceptable behaviour, highlights, as Valentine (1997) and Holloway (1998) have previously demonstrated, the power and importance of locally based discourses of 'normative mothering'. Indeed, Holloway (1998, p. 31 and p. 46) depicts these as 'moral geographies of mothering' acting as both a resource to guide behaviour and a means to define oneself.

The use of this subjective distancing is thus an important emotional coping mechanism and in many ways raises the mothers' self-esteem and enables them to mentally escape negative social stigmatisation. However, as I have previously argued (Mitchell and Green, 2002, pp. 16–17) this is a somewhat temporary measure, as it does not actually challenge the gendered and class based stereotypes surrounding young single mothers (Skeggs, 1997). In many ways, the mothers' association paradoxically reinforces and perpetuates these stereotypes. Furthermore, as they discuss 'responsible and respectable mothering' and the 'ethic of care', the mothers simultaneously engage in a Foucauldian form of self-surveillance. Indeed, Foucault's (1988) discursive 'technologies of the self' are frequently dual edged. On one hand, they may appear to offer reflexivity and possibilities for self-liberation but on the other, each individual is constantly involved in monitoring the self. Hence, the mothers are constantly aware of their own behaviour and seek to modify any actions perceived as transgressing 'responsible mothering'. Although individually based, this self-surveillance impacts upon wider society and, as Skeggs notes, continues to foster an environment of gendered social control. This association between risk, protecting children and parenting in general has also been noted by Scott *et al.* (1998), O'Brien *et al.* (2000) and Wyness (2000).

Risk management and mothers' leisure

Adopting risk management strategies of close child supervision and home-based activities had a corresponding impact upon many of the mothers' personal leisure time. In fact, over half (eight) emphasised that they had very little time for their own leisure, as house work and childcare responsibilities kept them busy.

Sharon: I like to read, I read books and magazines and watch the television. I haven't got much time to do anything
Amanda: It's quiet when Zoë has gone to bed, that's the only time I relax. I'm sort of uptight all day.

This reiterates many previous studies of women's, especially mothers' leisure, which emphasise that mothers generally have less leisure time, space and opportunities than their male counterparts (Deem, 1986; Wimbush, 1988; Henderson *et al.*, 1989; Green *et al.*, 1990). Inequalities are frequently associated with a range of ideological, material and practical constraints, which are simultaneously interwoven with relations of class, gender and ethnicity. In Townville, we have already seen that many of these constraints, such as the gendered ethic of care and lack of money and resources, continue to impact upon the young mothers' lives and thus permeate their personal leisure experiences. However, one cannot presume that home based activities and time spent amusing or just being with one's children is always viewed as restrictive or 'work'. As noted by Kay (1987, 1996), mothers can experience these activities as leisure for themselves and thus enjoyable. Indeed, in a similar manner to Kay's study (1987), a small but significant number of the Townville mothers felt their children gave leisure experiences more meaning.

> Heidi: Like with the kids it's a lot more fun, like when we go out to a restaurant or something like that, it's a lot more fun with the kids. There is a lot more laughs and you see the kids run around and stuff.

Thus, although the home may be a place of work, it was also viewed as a potential leisure space for themselves. Hence, they adopted a variety of activities to distance themselves from the risk anxiety associated with childcare in order to relax, even though they remained in the home.

> Paula: On a night when Jack is in bed I just love the peace and quiet, I can do stuff for myself. I like knitting and sewing, so I sit down and do that or have a nice long soak in the bath.
> Jenny: I'm not a heavy smoker because I can't afford to be ... but when he goes to bed, I think, 'oh get on the setee and have a cigarette and relax' ... I know it's not very healthy smoking but it's my treat, it's mine, you know it's something for me.

This highlights, as many theorists have noted (Wearing, 1990; Mowl and Towner, 1995; Wearing and Fullagar, 1996) the importance of viewing leisure as a relative and relational experience. Furthermore, the latter comment is important as it demonstrates a complex balancing of conflicting discourses of risk and motherhood (see also Graham, 1984;

Hudson and Ineichen, 1991; Lupton, 1999; Mitchell *et al.*, 2001). On one hand, smoking is viewed as unhealthy and risky but on the other, it relieved stress and created personal time and space, thus enabling this mother to invert the 'ethic of care' to, as noted by Bialeschki and Michener (1994, pp. 68–9), 'care of the self'. However, within these strategies to relax, subjective perceptions of being a responsible mother remained. In fact, gendered ideas of responsibility frequently pervaded the mothers' independent leisure. For example, going out for a drink or to a nightclub with friends was regarded as flexible, dependent on the availability of material and social resources, such as saving enough money for a 'night out' and a responsible babysitter to supervise the children.

Karen: Sometimes I even have to save up from the beginning of the month and when the end of the month comes, I just have enough to go out.
Sharon: I go out once a fortnight on a Friday just down the bottom [i.e. Townville] … my mam has them both, that's once a fortnight.

Concluding comments

This chapter may initially present a rather bleak picture of every-day life in Townville for the mothers and limited play opportunities for their children, in terms of both public play areas and detachment from organised activities beyond the local community. Social and economic factors, such as unrelenting poverty and deprivation, the persistence of negative social stereotypes associated with young motherhood and a perceived threat of danger on Townville's streets clearly impact upon their own and their children's lives. Indeed for both, their experiences of Townville are limited to a narrow geographical sphere, focusing upon the home or houses of kin. However, one cannot presume that the mothers are passive victims of their circumstances. Indeed, their risk anxiety surrounding safe spaces and activities for their children has demonstrated that they work hard to manage perceived areas of risk, establish a sense of personal control and feelings of greater security for themselves and their children. Indeed, the mothers' subjective interpretations of risk and the various coping strategies adopted have illustrated how three diverse and at times contradictory sets of discourses, surrounding risk society, responsible and respectable motherhood and the concept of childhood are interwoven. These discourses are not only utilised to make sense of life in Townville, they simultaneously impact upon the mothers' identity.

Although these coping mechanisms may be individually employed and rationalised by the mothers, their perceptions of risk and management strategies still remain firmly grounded in wider socio-economic issues. Hence, although the mothers may reflexively assess their actions, sense of 'self' and the 'choices' that they feel they have, these interpretations are, as Lash (1994) has similarly noted, made within the everyday and somewhat traditional class and gender relationships that continue to pervade Townville. Indeed, gendered perceptions of motherhood and being a 'good, responsible' mother continue to underpin their lives. The specific coping mechanisms many employ, for example, the use of 'othering', externalisation of risk and the symbolic management of space demonstrates this. In many ways, this reiterates and further develops the aforementioned gendered nature of risk discussed in Bunton, Green and Mitchell's introductory chapter. Thus, many of the mothers are not only acutely aware of patriarchal feminine stereotypes, especially around mothering and 'appropriate' behaviour but also actively seek to incorporate these into their everyday lives. However, it is important to recognise the dual edged nature of gendered risk. On one hand, these strategies enable the mothers to raise their self-esteem and regain a personal sense of control and security in an increasingly insecure world. On the other hand, they not only perpetuate social stereotypes but also crucially introduce an element of self-surveillance and thus self-limitation. This paradox exemplifies the complexity of the mothers' lives. In a similar manner to Holland *et al.*'s (1998) analysis of risky female sex amongst teenagers, what initially may appear to be irrational and/or self-limiting actions are in fact rational strategies to manage risk, especially when one occupies a position (i.e. young mother) that is frequently socially stigmatised and economically disadvantaged.

Notes

1. This chapter develops ideas of risk and mothering previously introduced in Mitchell, W., Crawshaw, P., Bunton, R. and Green, E. (2001) and Mitchell, W. and Green, E. (2002).
2. *Action Risk* – three-year project (April 1997–March 2000) funded by the Department of Environment's Single Regeneration Budget.

References

Adler, P. and Adler, P. (1994) 'Social reproduction and the corporate other: the institutionalisation of afterschool activities'. *Sociological Quarterly*, Vol. 35, pp. 309–28.

Aitken, S. (1994) *Putting Children in their Place*. Washington DC: Association of American Geographers.

Alderson, P. (1995) *Listening to Children*. London: Barnardos.

Ariès, P. (1961) *Centuries of Childhood*. Harmondsworth: Penguin.

Baldwin, D., Coles, B. and Mitchell, W. (1997) 'The formation of an underclass or disparate processes of social exclusion? Evidence from two groupings of "vulnerable youth" ', in Macdonald, R. (ed.) *Youth, The 'Underclass' and Social Exclusion*. London: Routledge, pp. 83–95.

Beck, U. (1992) *Risk Society: Towards a New Modernity*. London: Sage.

Beck, U. (1994) 'The reinvention of politics: towards a theory of reflexive modernization' in Beck, U., Giddens, A. and Lash, S. (eds) *Politics, Tradition and Aesthetics in the Modern Social Order*. Cambridge: Polity Press, pp. 1–55.

Beck, U. (1998) 'Politics of risk society' in Franklin, J. (ed.) *The Politics of Identity*. London: Routledge.

Beck, U. and Beck-Gernsheim, E. (1995) *The Normal Chaos of Love*. Cambridge: Polity Press.

Becker, B. and Charles, N. (2003) 'Layered meanings: the construction of "the family" in the interview', paper presented at the *British Sociological Association Annual Conference*. University of York, 11–13 April 2003.

Berthoud, R. and Robson, K. (2001) 'The outcomes of teenage motherhood in Europe', *EPAG Working Paper 22*. Colchester: University of Essex.

Bialeschki, M. D. and Michener, S. (1994) 'Re-entering leisure: transition within the role of motherhood'. *Journal of Leisure Research*, Vol. 26, No. 1, pp. 57–74.

Corsaro, W. (1997) *The Sociology of Childhood*. California: Pine Forge.

Deem, R. (1986) *All Work and No Play: The Sociology of Women and Leisure*. Milton Keynes: Open University Press.

Department of Health (1989) *Children Act*. London: HMSO.

Department of Health/Social Exclusion Unit (1999) *Teenage Pregnancy*, cm 4342. London: Stationery Office.

De Winter, M., Baerveldt, C. and Kooistra, J. (1999) 'Enabling children: participation as a new perspective on child-health promotion'. *Child: Care, Health and Development*, Vol. 25. No. 1, pp. 15–25.

Douglas, M. (1992) *Risk and Blame – Essays in Cultural Theory*. London: Routledge.

Foucault, M. (1988) 'The dangerous individual' in Kritzman, L. D. (ed.) *Michel Foucault: Politics, Philosophy, Culture*. New York: Routledge.

Foreman, A., Bunton, R., Crawshaw, P., Green, E., Mitchell, W. and Seabrook, T. (2000) *Risk Community: A Study of Risk and Young People*, Final Report (unpublished). Centre for Social and Policy Research: University of Teesside.

Franklin, B. (ed.) (1995) *The Handbook of Children's Rights*. London: Routledge.

Furlong, A. and Cartmel, F. (1997) *Young People and Social Change: Individualization and Risk in Late Modernity*. Buckingham: Open University Press.

Giddens, A. (1991) *Modernity and Self-Identity: Self and Society in the Late Modern Age*. Cambridge: Polity Press.

Glaser, B. and Strauss, A. (1967) *The Discovery of Grounded Theory*. Chicago: Aldine.

Graham, H. (1984) *Women, Health and the Family*. Brighton: Wheatsheaf Books.

Green, E., Mitchell, W. and Bunton, R. (2000) 'Contextualising risk and danger: an analysis of young people's perceptions of risk'. *Journal of Youth Studies*, Vol. 3, No. 2, pp. 109–26.

Green, E., Hebron, S. and Woodward, D. (1990) *Women's Leisure, What Leisure?* London: Macmillan.

Henderson, K., Bialeschki, M., Shaw, S. and Freysinger, V. (1989) *A Leisure of One's Own: A Feminist Perspective on Women's Leisure.* State College, PA: Venture Publishing Inc.

Hendricks, B. (1994) 'No room for children – the changing dimensions of provision of children's play in urban areas' in Henry, I. (ed.) *Leisure: Modernity, Postmodernity and Life-styles, Leisure in Different Worlds 1.* Eastbourne: The Leisure Studies Association, pp. 217–26.

Hill, M. and Tisdall, K. (1997) *Children and Society.* London and New York: Longman.

Holland, J., Ramazanoglu, C., Sharpe, S. and Thomson, R. (1998) *The Male in the Head: Young People Heterosexuality and Power.* London: The Tufnell Press.

Holloway, S. (1998) 'Local childcare cultures: moral geographies of mothering and the social organisation of pre-school education'. *Gender, Place and Culture,* Vol. 5, No. 1, pp. 29–53.

Holloway, S. and Valentine, G. (2000) 'Spatiality and the new social studies of childhood'. *Sociology,* Vol. 34, No. 4, pp. 763–83.

Hudson, F. and Ineichen, B. (1991) *Taking it Lying Down – Sexuality and Teenage Motherhood.* Basingstoke: Macmillan.

Jackson, S. and Scott, S. (eds) (2002) *Gender: A Sociological Reader.* London: Routledge.

James, A. and Prout, A. (eds) (1990) *Constructing and Reconstructing Childhood.* London: Falmer Press.

James, A., Jenks, C. and Prout, A. (1998) *Theorising Childhood.* Cambridge: Polity Press.

Jensen, A. M. (1994) 'The feminization of childhood' in Qvortrup, J., Bardy, M., Sgritta, G. and Wintersberger, H. (eds) *Childhood Matters: Social Theory, Practice and Politics.* Aldershot: Avebury.

Kay, T. (1987) *Leisure in the Lifestyles of Unemployed People* (unpublished PhD thesis). Loughborough: Loughborough University.

Kay, T. (1996) 'Women's leisure and the family in contemporary Britain' in Samuel, N. (ed.) *Women, Leisure and the Family in Contemporary Society: A Multi-National Perspective.* Oxford: CAB International, pp. 143–59.

Kelley, P., Hood, S. and Mayall, B. (1998) 'Children, parents and risk'. *Health and Social Care in the Community,* Vol. 6, No. 1, pp. 16–24.

Kissman, K. (1998) 'High risk behavior among adolescent mothers: the problem in context'. *Early Child Development and Care,* Vol. 143, pp. 103–12.

Lash, S. (1994) 'Reflexivity and its doubles: structure, aesthetics, community' in Beck, U., Giddens, A. and Lash, S. (eds) *Reflexive Modernization.* Cambridge: Polity Press, pp. 110–73.

Lazarus, R. and Folkman, S. (1984) *Stress, Appraisal and Coping.* New York: Springer.

Letherby, G. (1994) 'Mother or not, mother or what? Problems of definition and identity'. *Women's Studies International Forum,* Vol. 17, No. 5, pp. 525–32.

Lupton, D. (1999) *Risk.* London: Routledge.

Magee, C. (1994) *Teenage Parents – Issues of Policy and Practice,* National Youth Federation, Dublin: Irish Youth Work Press.

Martin, R. (1988) 'Truth, power, self: an interview with Michel Foucault', October 25, 1982, in Martin, L., Gutman, H. and Hutton, P. H. (eds) *Technologies of the Self: A Seminar with Michel Foucault*. London: Tavistock.

Martin, C. and Colbert, K. (1997) *Parenting – A Life Span Perspective*. New York: The McGraw-Hill Companies Inc.

Matthews, M. H. (1992) *Making Sense of Place*. Hemel Hempstead: Harvester Wheatsheaf.

Mayall, B. (ed.) (1994) *Children's Childhood's – Observed and Experienced*. Bristol: The Falmer Press.

McIntosh, M. (1996) 'Social anxieties about lone motherhood and ideologies of the family – two sides of the same coin' in Silva, E. (ed.) *Good Enough Mothering? Feminist Perspectives on Lone Motherhood*. London: Routledge, pp. 148–56.

Mitchell, W., Crawshaw, P., Bunton, R. and Green, E. (2001) 'Situating young people's experiences of risk and identity'. *Health, Risk and Society*, Vol. 3, No. 2, pp. 217–33.

Mitchell, W. and Green, E. (2002) ' "I don't know what I'd do without our Mam" Motherhood, identity and support networks'. *The Sociological Review*, Vol. 50, No. 1, pp. 1–22.

Mowl, G. and Towner, J. (1995) 'Women, gender, leisure and place: towards a more "humanistic" geography of women's leisure'. *Leisure Studies*, Vol. 14, pp. 102–16.

Murray, C. (1994) *Underclass: The Crisis Deepens*. London: IEA Health and Welfare Unit.

Näsman, E. (1994) 'Individualization and institutionalisation of childhood in today's Europe' in Qvortrup, J., Bardy, M., Sgritta, G. and Wintersberger, H. (eds) *Childhood Matters: Social Theory, Practice and Politics*. Aldershot: Avebury, pp. 165–88.

Oakley, A. (1979) *Becoming a Mother*. Oxford: Martin Robertson.

O'Brien, M., Jones, D., Sloan, D. and Rustin, M. (2000) 'Children's independent spatial mobility in the urban public realm'. *Childhood*, Vol. 7, No. 3, pp. 257–77.

Petersen, A. and Lupton, D. (1996) *The New Public Health – Health and Self in the Age of Risk*. London: Sage.

Phoenix, A. (1991a) *Young Mothers?* Cambridge: Polity Press.

Phoenix, A. (1991b) 'Mothers under twenty: outsider and insider views' in Phoenix, A., Woollett, A. and Lloyd, E. (eds) *Motherhood, Meanings, Practices and Ideologies*. London: Sage, pp. 86–102.

Phoenix, A. and Woollett, A. (1991) 'Motherhood: social construction, politics and psychology' in Phoenix, A., Woollett, A. and Lloyd, E. (eds) *Motherhood, Meanings, Practices and Ideologies*. London: Sage, pp. 13–27.

Qvortrup, J., Bardy, M., Sgritta, G. and Wintersberger, H. (eds) *Childhood Matters: Social Theory, Practice and Politics*. Aldershot: Avebury.

Ribbens, J. (1994) *Mothers and their Children – A Feminist Sociology of Childrearing*. London: Sage.

Roberts, H. (1995) 'Empowering communities: the case of childhood accidents' in Roberts, H., Smith, S. and Bryce, C. (eds) *Children at Risk: Safety as a Social Value*. Milton Keynes: Open University Press.

Roberts, K. (1996) 'Individualisation and risk in East and West Europe' in Helve, H. and Bynner, J. (eds) *Youth and Life Management – Research Perspectives*. Yliopistopaina: Helsinki University Press, pp. 226–40.

Rosenneil, S. and Mann, K. (1996) 'Unpalatable choices and inadequate families – lone mothers and the underclass debate' in Silva, E. (ed.) *Good Enough Mothering? Feminist Perspectives on Lone Motherhood*. London: Routledge, pp. 191–210.

Scott, S., Jackson, S. and Backett-Milburn, K. (1998) 'Swings and roundabouts: risk anxiety and the everyday worlds of children'. *Sociology*, Vol. 32, No. 4, pp. 689–705.

Simms, M. and Smith, C. (1986) *Teenage Mothers and their Partners – A Survey in England and Wales*. London: HMSO.

Skeggs, B. (1997) *Formations of Class and Gender*. London: Sage.

Silva, E. (ed.) (1996) *Good Enough Mothering? Feminist Perspectives on Lone Motherhood*. London: Routledge.

Smart, C. (1996) 'Deconstructing motherhood' in Silva, E. (ed.) *Good Enough Mothering? Feminist Perspectives on Lone Motherhood*. London: Routledge, pp. 37–57.

Smart, C. and Neale, E. (1999) *Family Fragments?* Cambridge: Polity Press.

Stanko, E. (1990) *Everyday Violence*. London: Routledge.

United Nations (1989) *The Convention of the Rights of the Child*. Geneva: UN.

Valentine, G. (1996) 'Angels and devils: moral landscapes of childhood'. *Environment and Planning D: Society and Space*, Vol. 14, pp. 581–99.

Valentine, G. (1997) ' "My sons' a bit dizzy" "My wife's a bit soft": gender, children and cultures of parenting'. *Gender, Place and Culture*, Vol. 4, No. 1, pp. 37–62.

Valentine, G. and McKendrick, J. (1997) 'Children's outdoor play: exploring parental concerns about children's safety and the changing nature of childhood'. *Geoforum*, Vol. 28, No. 2, pp. 219–35.

Van Veldhuizen, A. and Last, B. (1991) *Children with Cancer – Communication and Emotions*. Amsterdam: Swets and Zeitlinger.

Walkerdine, V., Lucey, H. and Melody, J. (2001) *Growing up Girl: Psychosocial Explorations of Gender and Class*. Basingstoke: Palgrave.

Ward, C. (1994) 'Opportunities for childhoods in late twentieth century Britain' in Mayall, B. (ed.) *Children's Childhood's – Observed and Experienced*. Bristol: The Falmer Press, pp. 144–53.

Wearing, B. (1990) 'Beyond the ideology of motherhood: leisure as resistance'. *Australian and New Zealand Journal of Sociology*, Vol. 26, No. 1, pp. 36–58.

Wearing, B. and Fullager, S. (1996) 'The ambiguity of Australian women's family leisure: some figures and refiguring' in Samuel, N. (ed.) *Women, Leisure and the Family in Contemporary Society: A Multi-National Perspective*. Oxford: CAB International, pp. 15–33.

Wimbush, E. (1988) 'Mothers meeting' in Wimbush, E. and Talbot, M. (eds) *Relative Freedoms – Women and Leisure*. Milton Keynes: Open University Press, pp. 60–74.

Woodward, K. (1997) 'Motherhood: identities, meanings and myths' in Woodward, K. (ed.) *Identity and Difference, Culture, Media and Identities*. London: Sage, pp. 240–82.

Wyness, M. (2000) *Contesting Childhood*. London: Falmer Press.

Zeiher, H. (2001) 'Children's access to space and use of time', paper presented at the *Cost A19 Children's Welfare Meeting*, 26–29 October, Trondheim: Norway.

12

Risking It? Young Mothers' Experiences of Motherhood and Leisure

Rebecca Watson

Introduction

Feminist analysis of dominant discourses on lone motherhood (Silva, 1996) and young mothers (Phoenix, 1991a,b) offers useful insight as to why it is meaningful to consider young mothers' experiences in the context of 'risk'. Feminist leisure studies correspondingly provides an interesting platform from which to examine leisure as a site of multiple actions and interactions for young mothers (Wearing, 1998). This extends beyond a focus on risk and leisure (Rojek, 1995, 2000) in public spheres experiencing major economic and social transitions on a macro, global scale (Beck, 1992), albeit with implications for localised, micro, social and cultural relations. As yet, there appears to be little research that examines everyday contexts of 'risk' whereby individuals and groups negotiate, react and respond to demands of responsibility for the self and for others, in this instance, caring for and bringing up children. This chapter examines the experiences of a small number of young mothers (who had their first child under the age of 25) in a large city in the north of England. In-depth qualitative research enables an assessment of shifting identities for young women as they become mothers and face a number of uncertainties in relation to caring for and bringing up children. At the same time, the women create and achieve time and space for themselves. Their experiences highlight the multiple axes of gender, race and class shaping their everyday lives and indicate that uncertainty is often commonplace. The chapter therefore considers the extent to which risk is experienced as different aspects of uncertainty. Concurrently, the women are active in negotiating and to an extent overcoming these uncertainties as they employ a number of strategies in responding to a variety of constraints.

In the discussion that follows, I will demonstrate how these strategies represent resistance to dominant forms of 'respectability' that remain evident in everyday discourse on mothering. How and where women are accepted as 'respectable' (Skeggs, 1998) has a marked impact on mothers who often perceive and experience themselves as 'other', often having a determining effect on the young mothers positioning of themselves. Thus, it is easy to see why and how young mothers are constructed in relation to risk, both as '*a* risk' to moral values surrounding marriage and the family and '*at* risk', as vulnerable and welfare dependent (see Mitchell's chapter). Arguably, all women, in numerous and different contexts face risk in terms of the physical and emotional demands that becoming a mother places upon them. This can be via embodiment and a changing sense of self (Bailey, 2001), or in relation to external factors including the 'risk' of bringing up children in 'a world such as this' alongside the positioning of mothers in dominant discourse (Smart, 1996).

Empirical data highlights a number of key themes in relation to risk and uncertainty faced by young mothers and the chapter is organised around four key sections. Following a brief outline of the research methodology and an introduction to the mothers discussed here, the first section examines the extent to which the women may be seen as having taken a risk in becoming 'young mothers'. Second, the ways in which they face uncertainty in relation to close relationships, housing and financial instability are then considered. Third, attention is paid to how the mothers take a number of 'calculated risks' in order to protect and achieve their own time and space for leisure, thus creating and re-creating identities that enable them to see themselves as more than (just) 'being a mum'. The fourth section 'resisting respectabilty' builds on this to look at ways in which the women are active in generating new locations/positions. Finally, a brief conclusion summarises risk and leisure for the mothers in the study and outlines themes for further, future analysis. The implication is that we re-position young mothers as subjects rather than simply deviant and/or 'risky' others. Theoretical analysis is grounded in data and the women's experiences are contextualised alongside relevant literature throughout. The underlying theoretical premise is critical engagement with processes of gender, race and class and it is argued that these can only be fully understood via the detailed analysis that this data produces. Tracing the contours of risk and leisure running throughout these processes is thus an illuminating venture.

The study

Data is taken from a study of women living in Leeds and was collected between 1997 and 1999. Interviews (14) and participant observation (approximately 25 over the research period) were used to explore and examine sites and meanings of leisure for young mothers. The methodology adopted a critical reflexive approach that highlighted a number of salient issues in 'researching difference' (Watson and Scraton, 2001). Table 12.1 gives an overview of interviewees whose experiences are discussed here. Participants were asked to describe their ethnicity during the interviews and this is presented along with age, number of children and marital status. Pseudonyms are used (self-selected by participants) to protect anonymity.

Taking a risk? Becoming and being a young mother

Common stereotypes of 'good' and 'bad' mothering are often constructed on the basis of good, married, over 25, middle class and white in contrast to bad, 'single', teenage, working class and black (Phoenix, 1988, 1991, 1996; Reynolds, 1997). The 'good' mother is also constructed as one who stays largely within the private sphere of the home (Hill-Collins, 1994) while lone mothers and working-class mothers, across racial categories, are often associated with menial paid labour

Table 12.1 The young mothers

Name (pseudonym)	Age (1st child born at)	No. of children	Ethnicity (own description)
Kelly	18	1	White
Samaira	20	3	British Pakistani
Shakila	22	2	Asian
Neeta	22	2	British Sikh
Nasra	23	3	Asian
Trisha	19	2	British West Indian
Manda	19	1	British-African-Asian
Lisa	24	1	White
Summaya	22	1	Asian British
Claire	25	2	White British
Emma	22	1	White British
Keira	21	1	Asian British
Alisha	21	2	British Asian
Jenny	25	2	White British

(Glenn *et al.*, 1994; Standing, 1997; Watson, 2000). For 'young' South Asian mothers, 'culture' is used as a blanket term to perpetuate general-isations surrounding arranged marriage and restrictive family life (Parmar, 1982; Puar, 1996; Bhopal, 1998). Evidently, a number of perva-sive ideologies of motherhood continue to be reproduced and refigured within society (Silva, 1996, Mitchell's chapter). It is necessary therefore, to explore individual women's experiences of becoming a mother under 25, to explore experiences of, and reactions to, dominant discourses on mothering and motherhood.

> ... many mothers are socially constructed as pathological and differ-ences between mothers are not adequately studied or written about. (Phoenix, 1991, p. 13)

Exploring difference allows for micro levels of analysis to be mapped onto broader structural issues (Brah, 1996) through a deconstruction of different mothering experiences as a means of addressing power rela-tions (Glenn *et al.*, 1994) and in assessments of risk. Through becoming and being young mothers, women are recipients of dominant discourse and in many respects take a risk in challenging prescriptive moral values associated with becoming and being a 'good' mother. Experience is a product of complex interrelationships of gender *and* race *and* class, both as a result of, and as constitutive of, practices that recreate social rela-tions, albeit in a multiplicity of ways.

Jenny, for example, talked about how she felt read and positioned in terms of dominant discourses of mothering. She said:

> I mean M's black and looks black and L is mixed race, well they're both mixed race and L looks white and I do find that there's a difference somehow because I think with M there was more of that 'you're a white single parent with a black child.' ... I don't know even if people think so much about whether I'm a single parent when they see a child as white but I think there's this sort of stereotype of a white woman with a black child, you know, 'been up to no good' and all that sort of stuff.

Although her comments draw attention to the pervasiveness of gen-dered ideologies surrounding lone motherhood, it is also clear that Jenny's son being black significantly affected this. The risk of being judged clearly shapes perceptions and experiences of mothering, reflect-ing a public gaze that is both resultant and constitutive of gendered, racialised and classed relations.

Age similarly continues to be central in marking women as 'young mothers' that is often heightened by class (Phoenix, 1988, 1991) and notions of respectability (Skeggs, 1998). As Kelly said:

I didn't feel young at 17, I felt grown up. I felt more grown up then than I do now in some ways.

Kelly also recognised however, that she was regarded by other people as a 'young mum' and she was aware of being constructed as 'deviant' (Silva, 1996). She said:

I tell you when I did feel young, I felt that when I was pregnant, you know when I was showing, I felt that everyone was looking at me thinking I was young. You know, what-is-it? Parent class, antenatal and stuff, I didn't do any of that because they made me feel ashamed, even though it wasn't a problem for me. But it seemed to be for them (laughs).

There is nothing here to indicate Kelly's racial identity (white British), suggesting an absence/silence of whiteness and its relationship to the construction and re-construction of gender (Frankenberg, 1997). This continues to be commonplace in leisure and sport research (Birrell, 1990; Scraton, 2001; Watson and Scraton, 2001; Carrington and McDonald in Scraton, 2001; King, 2002).

In contrast to the positioning of Kelly as a young mother, stereotypes of South Asian women as passive recipients of 'traditional' forms of marriage (Bhopal, 1998; Puar, 1996) continue to be utilised by the dominant white majority to label South Asian 'young mothers' as 'normal' within different ethnic populations. This is commonly a product of the 'problematicization of culture' approach (Puar, 1996) that marks South Asian women as homogeneous and subordinate to culturally prescribed values. It is interesting to consider the experiences of the South Asian mothers in my study, to examine individual circumstances that challenge this view. Some were married, some had never been married and some were lone mothers. They negotiated their location as young mothers in many different ways, as did the white mothers and the African-Caribbean mothers. For some there was more uncertainty and a sense of risk-taking than for others. As Shakila said;

If I think about it, you know, 19 was so young, to get married, to start a family, I mean you don't know what it's going to be like. I don't think you realise how much your life is going to change. You don't know what's going to happen in the future.

Neeta was married at the same age as Shakila and appears to be a lot more certain about her actions at the time:

> It was an arranged marriage and I was okay with that, it's what I wanted. I'd trained as a nurse, I was 19 and I wanted to get married and start a family.

Samaira had experience of being rejected by her family on becoming pregnant in what her family considered to be 'unsuitable' circumstances. Samaira said this was exacerbated by her parents' view that she should have a 'traditional Asian' arranged marriage. She said:

> I did feel upset. You know, I had a son and for the first four years, his grandparents hadn't even see him. You know, they didn't agree with what I'd done. They thought I'd brought shame on the family. They didn't think about what I went through, you know, the risks of running away to get married to someone else, and we didn't have a decent place to live to start with and I was expecting.

Evidently, there is a sense in which the women took a risk in becoming mothers in relation to how they had changed and were regarded and positioned by other people. Risk has different meanings when we look at individual experiences and accounts. However, there is a theme that emerges around acceptance and rejection in relation to *social* risks, in addition to young mothers being seen as 'at risk' pathologically (Phoenix, 1991). Social risk requires attention to the interplay of gendered relations. For example, we still know little about race, ethnicity and risk from different subject positions. Considering diverse experiences demonstrates that ongoing processes of negotiation are central features of everyday life for the mothers in this study. Living within complex interrelationships of gender, race and class mean that periods of uncertainty are commonplace. Whether risk equals uncertainty, is an ambivalent claim and ensuing questions of subjectivity and identity are too detailed to address here (Brah, 1996; Rose, 1996). Nonetheless, uncertainty remains a feature of the mothers' experiences.

Facing uncertainty

In this section, I look more closely, at how shifting relationships impact on the mothers' sense of stability and security and consider how these changes are negotiated. Financial constraints as a feature of uncertainty are also discussed, highlighting class and economic status and their interrelationships with gender and race.

Data clearly demonstrate that the mothers live within a variety of different relationship forms and show that there has been a real shift from notions of married, nuclear, family forms. As Trisha said:

> My kids have different fathers, and C's dad stays here so he can help with childcare. But I wouldn't call it 'living with'. He can only stay two nights otherwise it's classed as cohabiting, and we get our own benefits, I couldn't afford it otherwise. Besides, I've had quite enough of him by then and I want my own space.

Kelly decided that it was not going to work out with her boyfriend at the time:

> As soon as I got pregnant I thought 'I've had enough. It'll only get worse, and I'll be better off on me own'.

Similarly, Manda said she soon realised that she was going to be on her own with a baby:

> I hadn't ever really thought about having a baby. But when I got used to the idea, I realised it were going to be me, you know, on my own. I mean he does see his Dad, sometimes, but he lives in London and it's me that's brought him up.

Whereas Trisha had been able to negotiate a working relationship whereby she got some support for her son's childcare and was not taking sole responsibility, clearly some of the other mothers felt they would be better off as lone parents. There is evidence of the women having taken active decisions here and it is useful to remember that they are not simply passive recipients of dominant discourse on the 'right way' to bring up children. Although relationships may be relatively short term and lead to further uncertainty, the risk of going it alone was often an active decision where individuals weighed up whether they saw themselves better off as lone mothers.

A number of women received support from other family members, often mothers and sisters, who lived nearby. Not all of the mothers however, had support from immediate or close family. For example, Lisa said:

> Well me mum's in Leeds, but I mean they don't come, I don't really have 'owt to do with them. There's me brother, he comes and stays

but apart from him, I don't bother with any of them, they don't come here and see me. I'm not bothered really. I mean they never bothered anyway, I mean when R came along.

The mothers in the study faced economic insecurity and this affected them in a number of ways. Not least, it meant little or no disposable income for spending on leisure. The nature and availability of paid work was a key feature of the mothers' day-to-day experiences. Low or no income, and not always being in relationships where financial support from fathers could be depended upon all added to constraints on every-day life for young mothers and their children. Mothers who took part-time evening work put themselves in risk situations in a number of ways. First, they risked loss of benefits and/or court proceedings if they were found to be earning undeclared 'cash-in-hand'. Second, they faced a num-ber of risks associated with both servicing men's leisure in public leisure sites and moving about the city at night (Green *et al.*, 1990; Scraton and Watson, 1998). Third, they faced risk in terms of being positioned as 'bad mothers' by working out of the home in the evenings. This reflects a his-torical continuity of working-class women positioned within city centre spaces as liminal and dangerous (Wilson, 1991; Skeggs, 1999).

In terms of leisure, not going out in the evenings was often a restric-tion that a number of mothers placed upon themselves. A 'night out' was often regarded as an extravagance because it involved wanting new clothes, finding and possibly paying for a baby-sitter, and having enough money for taxis and a 'decent' time once out. Lisa talked about how she had to plan for this.

> I've got to find the money if I want to go out, and I have to plan it. I'll work it out to a week where I haven't got a lot to pay out, I've got me gas, TV and video, and me TV licence direct debit, so they come out in three consecutive weeks. So it's like in that last fourth week, that's my money, so my wage is actually mine that week, and if I want to go out then I can, not that it's a lot to go out on mind.

Financial constraint is clearly a common barrier, not only in access to leisure, but for everyday items too. This is echoed in other research on young mothers' coping strategies (see Mitchell's chapter). As Trisha said:

> And when it comes to like fashion, and shoes, and even coats, I mean there's times when ... there's necessity items but sometimes they're luxury items and you have to make do, you have to make do with

whatever. You know, I'm the one making ends meet and sometimes I realise I can't make ends meet.

Most mothers in the study did not have formal qualifications and had fragmented work experience due to demands of mothering and the nature of paid work available to them. It is useful to consider class as a social and cultural category (Skeggs, 1998), rather than simply an economic label (Brah, 1996). It is arguably patriarchal relations and continuities surrounding a sexual division of labour (Walby, 1997) that result in women's secondary positions in the labour market, but interrelationships with race are also clearly significant (Phoenix, 1988, 1991; Brah, 1996). Despite some evidence of a 'feminisation' of the workplace in terms of increases in the numbers of women entering paid employment (Leeds Development Agency, 1999), there is little evidence that women are securing well paid, stable incomes with employee benefits. Financial insecurity is a risk to health and well-being but this is not something particularly new that young and/or lone mothers have to face. It has long been a feature of their experiences (Hill-Collins, 1994). The view that individuals take out precautions to protect themselves within a risk society, such as healthcare plans, insurance against loss of income and so on (Beck, 1992; Adams, 1995), are not options open to these women. They are more likely to be drawn to unofficial moneylenders and are not always able to gain credit cards/agreements. As a consequence, coping strategies include what may be considered as calculated risks.

Calculated risks

Wimbush's (1986) focus on social processes, constraints upon and meanings attached to mothers' leisure in historical context is insightful. Mothers' leisure is defined by Wimbush as sociability, enjoyment, privacy, self-gratification and relaxation. This leisure is achieved via negotiation of structural inequalities, primarily gender and class. Conflict and tension result through women's internalisation of the pressures of being a mother (Richardson, 1993), and therefore it is common for mothers to feel they have little control over their leisure (Wimbush, 1986). The mothers in my study did create and protect their own time and space for leisure (Wearing, 1990; Watson, 2000) within the context of external constraining features including social, economic and cultural factors (Deem, 1986; Green *et al.*, 1990). In some senses, we can see young mothers 'taking risks' to achieve leisure, calculated risks that may at times jeopardise their chances of being constructed and read as 'good' mothers. In some instances, they felt they were recipients of a discourse that regards young women becoming mothers a product of their own risk behaviour (Phoenix, 1991; Silva, 1996). The women in my study took risks in a range of different contexts in order to maintain and explore their sense of self 'outside' mothering responsibilities. This section draws on data to highlight the negotiation of gendered and racialised public space for leisure and considers individual meanings attached to 'leisure' that may be regarded as escape from the responsibilities of bringing up children.

In spatial terms, perceptions of safety continue to have a significant impact on women's use of out of home leisure. This is compounded by perceptions of local places and spaces that have to be navigated and negotiated in everyday contexts. As Summaya said:

> I heard so many horror stories about coming to live here (inner city area of Leeds). You know, people said don't go out with your handbag. But it gets ridiculous. I mean, you can't just stay in all the time if you've got a baby. You need to go to the park, you need to go to the shops.

Summaya's statement was not about fear in relation to race, rather it was a comment about public spaces as gendered where women often feel vulnerable and at risk. Not necessarily in terms of sexual attack but the potential and/or actual violence associated with muggings. Different women talked about their negotiation of space after dark, and there was variance in perceptions of risk. At times this included fear of sexual attack (Valentine, 1989; Deem, 1996; Skeggs, 1999). However, *all* the women suggested that they made arrangements with others for out of home leisure, visits, education, courses and classes and paid work that might be during the evenings, to minimise perceived risks of women out on their own at night (Green *et al.*, 1990; Scraton and Watson, 1998). Kelly and Lisa both lived in the same block of flats and had similar opinions towards going out at night. Kelly said:

> Once it gets to say, like I'm scared of the dark. I would not go out on me own to walk at all. I wouldn't walk to the shop round the corner or anything like that.

Lisa who said her attitude had changed since there had been a sexual assault not very far from where she lived, echoed this:

> I mean at one point it wouldn't bother me but it like, because of all these rapes and things that have gone on, I mean that's put me off

just going to the shops. If it wasn't for the fact of hearing about them, I don't think I'd be that bothered but it worries me.

This worry and fear is clearly evidence of a gendering of space where women continue to see themselves as vulnerable (Hanmer, 1992). Claire had been mugged before she had become a mother and this has always made her wary of being on her own.

Ever since then, I've never gone, I mean my friend still walks across the park at night; she really worries me. If I'm with a few of us, if we're all together, then I'll walk. Otherwise, I'd always have to get a taxi.

Manda on the other hand, made a distinction between where it was 'safe' to walk on her own, and where she felt it was not, reflecting a different strategy towards risk in public spaces. Whereas Lisa and Kelly did not feel happy about going to the local shop, Manda said:

I think it's all right round here, I mean you see gangs of kids but they're only young and it doesn't bother me because it's familiar, I mean I've always lived round here. I used to hate walking through town on me own on a night but I don't mind it so much now.

Emma felt that she should be more careful about moving round the city at night once she became a parent. This had consequences for her leisure in that she felt she should not put herself 'at risk' and must always have extra money for taxis. She explained:

I think it is different now, just in case anything happened to me, for her (daughter's) sake. I mean I don't think anything would but you have to be careful. For years I'd walk home through the university and I was never really bothered, but I don't know, maybe round here it's different.

Keira also talked about a sense of responsibility as a mother that made her less likely to take risks. She said being on her own with her daughter meant that she was less likely to go out in the evenings on her own. When she did have to be out in the dark, for example, due to work, she was conscious of not walking where it was 'too quiet'.

Well I wouldn't walk where it's gonna be pitch black, and I always walk on the main road. It depends how I feel. You know, sometimes

I'll just get a taxi, and other times I'll catch the bus. So I suppose it kind of bothers me but then sort of doesn't bother me either.

Both Samaira and Alisha said that they did not feel comfortable walking around after dark. Summaya commented on her perception about going out in the evenings after a recent visit to Pakistan.

I was actually thinking about the after dark thing quite recently. I mean, when I was in Pakistan, I went out to the shops at night, and walked round to visit people, and yet I wouldn't do that here, which is silly really because statistically it's far more dangerous in Pakistan than in England.

Evidently, she felt more relaxed in Pakistan although she was not clear as to why this was so, beyond a general feeling. Looking more closely at Summaya's comments suggests she had a greater sense of anonymity in Pakistan, whereas, she may well have felt conspicuous as being constructed as the 'other' in the UK, despite living in a multi-racial area.

At the same time, however, it is interesting to look at ways in which the mothers took risks in order to achieve their leisure and a sense of self (Wearing, 1998). This included, for example, movement across public space at night, despite perceptions demonstrated above that this was not a sensible or responsible action. As Manda said:

I've been silly at times, well at times I still am. I mean, I've come through the park on me own late at night. If I get scared I just run, and I have thought I should really get a taxi, you know that I shouldn't be risking it, but if you're waiting for a taxi and you know you've got to get back, for a baby-sitter or for work the next day or whatever. And it is mad but it can be exhilarating, you know, it's just you, you're taking a bit of a risk and it's fine.

Data demonstrate that various everyday situations for the women involved different degrees of risk in different contexts. In some ways young, often lone mothers, living, working and moving across public city space, face situations that reflect a historical legacy for working-class and black women (Hill-Collins, 1994), as opposed to reflecting responses to a more recent risk society.

Drinking (alcohol) was a common feature for some, but not all the mothers. There was variance across the mothers' perceptions of 'having a drink' as part of leisure that cut across ethnic identity. The young mothers talked about the importance of maintaining an identity based around socialising, including music and friendship groups (Wimbush, 1986; Green *et al.*, 1990; Green, 1998). Emma, for example, had negotiated time and childcare to attend a music festival for a weekend away.

It was excellent; I got a free pass because I knew someone who was playing. And we got plenty of free beer, free food, the works. It was brilliant; you know, to be away from it all, the responsibilities, being able to get out of it for a while.

Emma's sense of 'free time' clearly included time and space to 'let go' and included recreational drug use. This was also the case for Manda, and had been part of Kelly's leisure experiences prior to becoming a mother. Interesting questions surround the use of recreational drugs for mothers and there appears a lack of research that considers this use as a coping strategy and/or release from the pressures of caring for young children. There is a 'moral panic' discourse surrounding young mothers who may have substance abuse problems, but this detracts attention from women who may be drinking and/or using drugs as a feature of their leisure in ways that they see as 'safe' or at least as taking 'calculated risks'. Degrees of control and autonomy depend on the disposition of individuals as well as social, cultural and economic positioning that affect mothers' sense of self and self-worth. Mothers involved in this form of risk-taking were conscious of being read by others as irresponsible and/or 'bad mothers'. These feelings were also affected by ethnicity to differing degrees. Keira drank wine as part of socialising in 'mixed' company (i.e., not just South Asian) but she did not want to 'risk an argument' when attending what she referred to as 'events in the community'.

More 'acceptable' forms of risk-taking might include trying new physical activities that involve 'controlled' risk in managed environments. For example, two of the South Asian mothers, Nasra and Shakila had been abseiling as a result of using a local community group for educational and leisure purposes (Watson, 1998). Their self-confidence was clearly increased by the new experience. As Nasra said:

I was scared, I mean I'd never done anything like that before. But then the buzz, once you've proved to yourself you can do it, amazing!

Shakila echoed this sentiment by saying 'brilliant, absolutely brilliant'! From the various leisure experiences of young mothers in the study, sites of acceptability and respectability are made visible and thus we need to consider women's active engagement in risking new positions that refigure dominant views of how young mothers 'should' behave. However, it is important that we do not construct a dichotomy of good/bad risk as this may serve to recreate moral prescription surrounding 'acceptable' behaviour for mothers and young mothers.

Resisting respectability

Evidently, an ideology of respectability (Green *et al.*, 1990, p. 116) impacts on women's sense of themselves whereby they internalise messages relating to (in-)appropriate behaviours, thus placing limits on, for example, their leisure in public spaces and as shown above, the kinds of leisure that mothers are engaged in. The discursive practice of young working-class (white) women attempting to achieve respectability in public spheres has been usefully discussed by Skeggs (1998) and demonstrates how these practices inform and shape attitudes towards mothering and marriage. There are different consequences for different women as data presented here are testimony to. For example, there are complexities surrounding the 'shame' of being a young mother, an unmarried mother, being in the 'wrong' kind of marriage, being separated and so on. These positions are marked as a result of interrelationships of gender, race and class whilst at the same time, the variety of actors engaged in mothering needs to be recognised. They point to the continuity, albeit through periods of transformation, surrounding these interrelationships and demonstrate that young mothers are prepared to take certain risks and face uncertainty as they navigate and negotiate respectability. This section focuses on the impacts of gender and then ethnicity. Experiences of, and consciousness around ethnicity continue to be more 'visible' in the accounts of the South Asian mothers and point to difference as an area for further analysis.

Resistance to dominant discourse was evident in reflections the women made about themselves as young mothers. In particular, there was recognition that 'blanket terms' and commonly used descriptions of young mothers were inappropriate and inaccurate. As Lisa said:

> Everybody used to think it were a single mothers' hostel here (the flats) because yeah, for a while, everybody seemed to be a single mum. But they're not, and even if they are, it doesn't mean you're automatically going to get on. And it certainly doesn't mean you all have the same ideas about bringing up your kids.

Being a 'single mum' had been experienced by many of the mothers at some point. It was by no means a label that could be applied unproblematically and was both rejected and reclaimed by individual women. Lisa went on to say:

> Well I think to myself sometimes 'God, I'm sick of being on my own', and I'd like a bit of adult company but it's like, to be taken over, I'd feel like I were being taken over and I wouldn't feel like I've got me own space. Like now, I can do what I want, it's my house, I pay the bills, I sort the rent. But to go out with someone that's okay, because it's 'okay, I'll meet you in town' and then I'll come home ... on me own if that's what I want!

Kelly also demonstrated resistance to being positioned as a certain 'type' of lone mother:

> Being a mother changed me. I was, my life was in a rut, I was with the father but I knew it wasn't going to last. I knew I wasn't going to stay at home stuck with a baby. I was going to work, I am going to work, I'm going to college and having him was the start of it all.

Manda felt becoming a young mother was a positive thing and suggested that studying to become qualified for future paid work was bound up in her identity as a parent. Far from being or becoming welfare dependant (Standing, 1997), she resisted a dominant discourse that positioned her as 'problematic and irresponsible' (Phoenix, 1996, p. 176). Manda said:

> I think probably in all me life I've probably only signed on for a year in total and that's when R were younger and I were like doing me A-levels, and I'm like, I was gonna go and get a job. Maybe if I hadn't had R, I might have been; I mean I might not have got it together.

Young, lone mothers take risks in rejecting 'traditional' views of the family. However, they are agents who are prepared to take these risks and are thus active in refiguring discourse on mothering and the family. They risk periods of hardship but evidently, are prepared to face these in order to achieve independence and a sense of being in control.

Resistance to dominant discourse was also evidenced in experiences of the South Asian mothers (four of the six women discussed here were married in different circumstances, as discussed in the first section). These experiences were qualitatively different between individuals and there is evidence that some women are becoming more 'independent' from family, tradition and culture (Puar, 1996; Bhopal, 1998) in making life choices, whilst some women are actively seeking to maintain principles of 'traditional' religious faith (Afshar, 1994). What is clear is that there are few grounds on which to generalise experiences of South Asian mothers (Puar, 1996), as there are few grounds to homogenise, for example, white working-class mothers (Phoenix, 1988). Rather, we need to consider both individual experience and shared accounts of social and economic relations by accounting for micro, localised features and not simply falsely generalising experience on the basis of ethnic identity (Brah, 1996; Mirza, 1997; Modood *et al.*, 1997). Samaira said:

> I mean we got together because that's what we wanted and we said we'd get married and settle down because you know, like for Asians, it's very difficult, things can be very strict and you can't always make people understand.

Samaira risked and then experienced rejection by her family. She put herself at risk for a period when she was isolated from close friends and family, but felt that these risks were worthwhile.

Summaya had had an arranged marriage but felt that she would make active changes in the upbringing of her daughter. She says:

> I feel I'm going to be able to relate to my daughter differently. I will want to try and explain things to her. When I was about 13 and friends started going out with boys and we weren't allowed, well not that we didn't, we just knew we wouldn't talk about it at home. It was disapproved of and we knew that. Whereas now, I would want to talk to her about Islam, explain; see how she feels, rather than simply saying, 'No, we don't do that sort of thing'.

Keira often felt that she was at risk of being received negatively not only by her immediate family but also by her Hindu community more broadly.

> Say like one of our big priests is coming down from India, then I'd go down to Leicester. You know, as part of the wider Hindu community we're expected to get involved. You're talking thousands of people and we all have a part to play. It's really good fun. Lots of preparation and lots of dressing up. Last time, I looked after overseas guests who were visiting. And yet, at the same time I'm looking over my shoulder to see who's looking at me and my daughter. You know because

my mum says it's shameful for me to have her and not be married. But I have got a life and I still want to take part in things that are important to me.

Evidently, she was quite prepared to take those risks in order to achieve leisure that was meaningful to her.

Alisha had experiences of being uncomfortable and positioned as the 'other' at a local leisure centre. She clearly felt the impact of stereotypes around South Asian women's lack of involvement in active leisure.

I mean you don't know what to wear and when you've got tracksuits on and everyone else is wearing leotards, you feel the odd one out and you see them thinking, 'oh, they're the Asians, she can't wear that' (leotard).

She faced uncertainty about her identity in relation to how she felt about herself and how she perceived other people would construct her. South Asian women use leisure spaces differently and therefore, levels of involvement in domestic and out of home activities should not be generalised. Samaira and Nasra went swimming at the public baths and were willing to risk the reactions of family and community members. Nasra discussed her negotiation of dress/undress:

I go swimming with my children and that's a conscious decision that I have made. Some women make a conscious decision to always be covered up in public, so they're not about to start going swimming at the local baths. But there doesn't seem to be recognition from swimming pools that Muslim families aren't about to just start swimming in mixed sessions.

Experiences across a range of leisure sites are too numerous to catalogue here but those presented point again to the different contexts and different constructions of risk that young mothers negotiate in daily life.

Discussion and conclusions

Mothers in the study do take risks but at this stage, it is not clear that this is a reflection that 'postmodern life (...) seems to be besieged by risk' (Rojek, 1995, p. 152). Historically, there are numerous continuities surrounding young mothers experiences of risk that point towards gradual, rather than dramatic, change. Changing relationships need to be regarded as the outcome of individual negotiation and agency. Feminist perspectives argue it is women who are creating new family positions and locations and challenging dominant discourse, as opposed to simply suggesting that it is new forms of risk and uncertainty that create them. Evidently, there is a need to address shifting sites of structure and agency. Macro issues of economic insecurity and social position (e.g. housing, types of paid work, experiences of racism, fear of public space after dark and so on) have a persistence that has arguably always shaped the experiences of young mothers in urban environments. In a way, they have always been read and represented as a 'risk(-y)'population. We therefore need micro analysis of localised, embedded and embodied experiences to explore changes in family and household circumstances and thus examine resistance and (re-)negotiation to mothering ideology. Processes of gender, race and class continue to shape women's perceptions and experiences of mothering and consequently create, as well as constrain, multiple situations in which leisure is achieved and enjoyed.

We can consider risk-taking and leisure for the mothers in this study both in terms of leisure to escape risk and leisure as risk. In the former, mothers evidently require time and space to themselves outside of mothering roles and responsibilities, leisure in which they can recuperate, relax and temporarily be 'away from' everyday pressures. Leisure as risk is where they engage in situations that offer excitement, exhilaration, something different. The meanings and contexts for this are multiple and leisure as escape, in addition to leisure as risk, is clearly intertwined. Interestingly, young mothers seem less visible within current leisure studies work where there is a juxtaposition of leisure as risk, read 'new', exciting, dangerous and involving conspicuous forms of consumption (Rojek, 1993), with 'serious leisure', read 'authentic', morally/spiritually valuable, voluntary, middle class (Stebbins, 1992, 1997). Such approaches are in danger of missing the fundamental premise of where risk emerges, that is, in the everyday contexts of uncertainty, negotiation and resistance. We therefore need more discussion of public–private boundaries and relationships to illuminate further the interplay between leisure and risk for young women with children.

There remains a paucity of research that considers difference *and* similarity of young mothers' experiences across different ethnicities that has long since been recognised (Parmar, 1982; Phoenix, 1988). This remains highly problematic in trying to understand the identities, experiences and needs of different ethnic populations and individuals living in the UK across health, employment and leisure issues (Brah and Shaw, 1992;

Brah, 1996). Assessments of risk are often in danger of re-enforcing constructions of the 'other', rather than challenging them and breaking them down. Young mothers' experiences of leisure, risk and ethnicity have really only been introduced here. For example, risking new forms of respectability for a number of South Asian mothers was clearly an issue. Leisure is evidently an important context in which this resistance occurs, be that through the use of public spaces for leisure and/or through social and family networks. Further research in this area will provide exciting opportunities in which to explore the creation, maintenance and reproduction of identities within the dynamic sphere of leisure.

References

Adams, J. (1995) *Risk*. London: UCL Press.
Afshar, H. (1994) 'Muslim women in West Yorkshire: growing up with real and imaginary values amidst conflicting views of self and society' in Afshar, H. and Maynard, M. (eds) *The Dynamics of Race and Gender*. London: Taylor and Francis, pp. 127–50.
Bailey, L. (2001) 'Gender shows: first-time mothers and embodied selves'. *Gender and Society*, Vol. 15, No. 1, pp. 110–29.
Beck, U. (1992) *Risk Society*. London: Sage.
Bhopal, K. (1998) 'South Asian women in East London: religious experience and diversity'. *Journal of Gender Studies*, Vol. 7, No. 2, pp. 143–56.
Birrell, S. (1990) 'Women of color, critical autobiography, and sport' in Messner, M. and Sabo, D. (eds) *Sport, Men, and the Gender Order*. Champaigne, IL: Human Kinetics Books, pp. 185–99.
Brah, A. (1996) *Cartographies of Diaspora: Contesting Identities*. London: Routledge.
Brah, A. and Shaw, S. (1992) *Working Choices: South Asian Young Muslim Women and the Labour Market*. London: Department of Employment (Research Paper No. 91).
Deem, R. (1986) *All Work and No Play: The Sociology of Women and Leisure*. Milton Keynes: Open University Press.
Deem, R. (1996) 'Women, the city and holidays'. *Leisure Studies*, Vol. 15, pp. 105–19.
Frankenberg, R. (1993) *White Women, Race Matters: The Social Construction of Whiteness*. London: Routledge.
Glenn, E. N., Chang, G. and Forcey, L. R. (1994) (eds) *Mothering: Ideology, Experience and Agency*. London: Routledge.
Green, E. (1998) 'Women doing friendship: an analysis of women's leisure as a site of identity construction, empowerment and resistance'. *Leisure Studies*, Vol. 17, No. 3, July.
Green, E., Hebron, S. and Woodward, D. (1987) *Women's Leisure in Sheffield: A Research Report*. Department of Applied Social Sciences: Sheffield City Polytechnic.
Green, E., Hebron, S. and Woodward, D. (1990) *Women's Leisure, What Leisure?* London: Macmillan.

Hanmer, J. (1992) *Women, Violence and Crime Prevention: A Study of Changes in Police Policy and Practices in West Yorkshire.* University of Bradford Research Paper No.1.

Hill-Collins, P. (1994) 'Shifting the center: race, class and feminist theorizing about motherhood' in Glenn, E., Chang, G. and Forcey, L. (eds) *Mothering: Ideology, Experience and Agency.* New York: Routledge, pp. 45–65.

King, C. (2002) 'Play the white man: racialised narratives in soccer governance', paper presented at the *Race, Nation, Sport. One Day Conference* organised by the British Sociological Association Race and Ethnicity Study Group, University of London, 13 September 2002.

Leeds Development Agency, 1999, www.leedsgovt.org.uk

Mirza, H. S. (1997) (ed.) *Black British Feminism: A Reader.* London: Routledge.

Modood, T. (1997) ' "Difference", cultural racism and anti-racism' in Werner, P. and Modood, T. (eds) *Debating Cultural Hybridity: Multi-cultural Identities and the Politics of Anti-racism.* London: Zed Books, pp. 154–72.

Parmar, P. (1982) 'Gender, race and class: Asian women's resistance' in The Centre for Contemporary Cultural Studies (eds) *The Empire Strikes Back: Race and Racism in 70s Britain.* London: Hutchinson.

Phoenix, A. (1988) 'Narrow definitions of culture: the case of early motherhood' in Westwood, S. and Bhachu, P. (eds) *Enterprising Women: Home, Work, and Culture Among Minorities in Britain.* London: Routledge.

Phoenix, A. (1991a) *Young Mothers?* Cambridge: Polity Press.

Phoenix, A. (1991b) 'Mothers under twenty: outsider and insider views' in Phoenix, A., Woollett, A. and Lloyd, E. (eds) *Motherhood, Meanings, Practices and Ideologies.* London: Sage.

Phoenix, A. (1996) 'Social constructions of lone motherhood: a case of competing discourses' in Silva, E. B. (ed.) *Good Enough Mothering? Feminist Perspectives on Lone Mothering.* London: Routledge, pp. 175–90.

Puar, J. K. (1996) 'Resituating discourses of "whiteness" and "Asianness" in Northern England: 2nd-generation Sikh women and constructions of identity' in Maynard, M. and Purvis. J. (eds) *New Frontiers in Women's Studies: Knowledge, Identity and Nationalism.* London: Taylor and Francis.

Reynolds, T. (1997) '(Mis)representing the black (super)woman' in Safia Mirza, H. (ed.) *Black British Feminism: A Reader.* London: Routledge, pp. 97–112.

Richardson, D. (1993) *Women, Motherhood, and Childrearing.* London, Macmillan.

Rojek, C. (1993) *Ways of Escape: Modern Transformations in Leisure and Travel.* London: Macmillan.

Rojek, C. (1995) *Decentring Leisure: Rethinking Leisure Theory.* London: Sage.

Rojek, C. (2000) *Leisure and Culture.* London: Palgrave.

Rose, N. (1996) 'Identity, Genealogy, History' in Hall, S. and DuGay, P. (eds) *Questions of Cultural Identity.* London: Sage, pp. 128–50.

Scraton, S. (2001) 'Reconceptualising race, gender and sport: The contribution of black feminism' in Carrington, B. and Mcdonald, I. (eds) *Racism and British Sport.* London: Routledge.

Scraton, S. and Watson, B. (1998) 'Gendered cities: women and public leisure space in the "postmodern" city'. *Leisure Studies,* Vol. 17, pp. 123–37.

Silva, E. B. (1996) (ed.) *Good Enough Mothering? Feminist Perspectives on Lone Motherhood.* London: Routledge.

Skeggs, B. (1998) *Formations of Class and Gender.* London: Sage.

Skeggs, B. (1999) 'Matter out of place: visibility and sexualities in leisure spaces'. *Leisure Studies*, Vol. 18, No. 3, July, pp. 213–32.

Smart, C. (1996) 'Deconstructing motherhood' in Silva, E. B. (ed.) *Good Enough Mothering? Feminist Perspectives on Lone Mothering*. London: Routledge, pp. 37–57.

Standing, K. (1997) 'Who is a single mother? The shifting subjectivities of single mothers', paper presented at *Transformations: Thinking through Feminism*. Lancaster University, July 1997.

Stebbins, R. (1992) *Amateurs, Professionals and Serious Leisure*. Montreal: McGill University Press.

Stebbins, R. (1997) 'Casual leisure: a conceptual statement'. *Leisure Studies*, Vol. 16, No. 1, pp. 17–26.

Valentine, G. (1989) 'The geography of women's fear'. *Arena*, Vol. 21, pp. 385–90.

Walby, S. (1997) *Gender Transformations*. London: Routledge.

Watson, B. (1998) *'Mothers' Time Well Spent'*, A Report for GROW (Giving Real Opportunities to Women Community Group), Leeds Metropolitan University.

Watson, B. (2000) *Motherwork–motherleisure: Analysing Young Mothers' Leisure Lifestyles in the Context of Difference*, Leeds Metropolitan University PhD thesis.

Watson, B. and Scraton, S. (2001) 'Confronting whiteness? Researching the leisure lives of South Asian mothers'. *Journal of Gender Studies*, Vol. 10, No. 3, pp. 265–77.

Wearing, B. (1998) 'Beyond the ideology of motherhood: leisure as resistance'. *Australian and New Zealand Journal of Sociology*, Vol. 26, No. 1, pp. 36–58.

Wilson, E. (1991) *The Sphinx in the City: Urban Life, The Control of Disorder and Women*. London: Virago Press.

Wimbush, E. (1986) *Women, Leisure and Well-being*. Edinburgh: Centre for Leisure Research.

13

The 'Logic of Practice' in the Risky Community: The Potential of the Work of Pierre Bourdieu for Theorising Young Men's Risk-Taking

Paul Crawshaw

Introduction

This chapter attempts to explore the salience of the work of Pierre Bourdieu for theorising young men's experiences and understandings of risk within a working-class community in the North East of England; here called Townville. Two key areas of his work will be discussed. First, more recent writings on inequality and social suffering in contemporary societies (1998, 1999) and their relevance to the experiences of young men in Townville will be considered. Second, the potential of his 'theory of practice', with particular emphasis on the concept of 'habitus' (1977, 1984, 1990), to contribute to an understanding of young men's risk-taking will be explored.

Pierre Bourdieu is internationally recognised to be a seminal social theorist, philosopher and researcher whose work has had significant impact upon the disciplines of anthropology, sociology, cultural studies and education, amongst others. His work has spanned four decades and encompasses a wide variety of areas from anthropological studies of communities (1962), critiques of cultural forms such as photography and art (1990) to overtly political challenges to neo-liberalism (1998, 1999) as well as extended theoretical discussions (1977, 1990). This broad sweep of work encompassing a number of intellectual fields is in many respects characteristic of grand theorists such as he is increasingly recognised to be. One of the key aspects of the work of Bourdieu is his ability to combine theory with a rigorous empiricism (Bourdieu and Wacquant, 1992), a goal, which the study of risk and young people documented here, strives to achieve. In many ways, this feature of his work prompted the discussion of its potential for theorising some of the findings of the study discussed below. Before exploring some of Bourdieu's key ideas in more detail, it is worthwhile spending some time reflecting on recent theory concerned with risk and late modernity, which in many ways informed the development of this research.

Risk and late modernity

Late modernity has been characterised by growing risk and uncertainty (see Giddens, 1991; Beck, 1992). This is a result of changes in both technology and knowledge which have led to greater control over all areas of the social, but which, as a result of globalisation and the increasingly transnational dangers presented by developments such as nuclear power, are capable of creating global risks. The result is ever-growing uncertainty and a movement towards what Beck (1992) describes as the 'risk society', within which risk becomes the key organiser of social relations, over more traditional divides such as class or gender. Alongside these developments, a process of detraditionalisation is also said to have taken place as a result of changes in production and increasing globalisation which have weakened traditional ties linked to work, families and communities and led to increased uncertainty or 'ontological insecurity' (Giddens, 1991, p. 84). Beck and Giddens (and more recently Beck and Beck-Gernsheim, 2002) argue that this results in a process of individualisation, whereby people feel more and more responsible for their own lives. Such changes are linked to the rise of what has been described as 'reflexive modernisation' (Beck et al., 1994). According to theorists, within reflexive modernisation, we see an increasing disembedding of traditional structures and identities and consequently a growing need for social actors to form their own biographies 'reflexively' without traditional drivers such as work and community. As Beck (1994) notes, under the conditions of reflexive modernisation ' … individuals must produce, stage and cobble together their biographies for themselves' (p. 13).

Theorists argue that such a process of disembedding creates increasing insecurity and the need for individuals to manage the ever-increasing risks of late modernity on an individual basis. Furlong and Cartmel (1997) refer to this as an 'epistemological fallacy'; that late modernity creates ever greater risk, but processes of detraditionalisation and globalisation which fragment traditional markers of identity such as work and community, lead to individuals increasingly perceiving the need to manage such structurally determined risk on an individualised basis.

These changes have particularly affected the lives of young people, who, as a result of the construction of youth as a dependent, transitional and marginal phase of the life-course, face an increasing number of risks which they must manage on an individual basis (Furlong and Cartmel, 1997, p. 1).

The research presented here suggests that for young men, risk was indeed a key feature of their daily experiences and something which they perceived the need to manage. The very ubiquity of risk in their lives led to a consideration of the potential of the work of Bourdieu for theorising 'risk as practice' and this will form the basis of the discussion which follows.

Epistemologies of risk

One of the key findings of the research discussed here has been to uncover the complexity of risk discourses in the lives of young men and the challenges this presents for researchers and policy makers alike. Consequently a concern with understanding young people's own subjective understandings of risk emerged early in the research process. Such an approach coincides with Bourdieu's (1977, 1990) broader project of transcending the dualism between objectivity and subjectivity, and consequently his work has much to offer epistemological approaches to understanding risk.

In-depth interviewing and focus groups were the key research methods used. Focus groups were held in two different settings, the local youth and community centre and two local schools. These involved groups of various sizes with up to six participants conducted by both a researcher and a youth and community worker. Such discussions were loosely structured, with the facilitators introducing themes designed to explore what life was like for young men in their area, but also providing scope for the participants to discuss issues of concern to themselves. In-depth interviews were also conducted in two contexts, again the two local schools, and to access an older sample of young men via local post-16 training providers. Such qualitative methods of data collection were employed because of their potential to elicit young men's own understandings of risk and danger in their own terms and based upon their own experiences (Walker, 1985).

One of Bourdieu's key concerns has been to uncover the relationship between objectivity and subjectivity in practice (Bourdieu, 1977, 1990). For Bourdieu this represents a key challenge of sociological research. He refers to objectivism as a tool used to in order to 'constitute the social world as a spectacle' (1990, p. 52). Such an objectivist viewpoint is rejected as being incapable of explaining how the social world is actually constructed through processes of practice which serve to produce and reproduce the seemingly 'real' structures which objectivism makes the object of it's study. Bourdieu argues, that we must 'step down from the sovereign viewpoint from which objectivist idealism orders the world' (1990, p. 52), and rather, situate ourselves within 'real activity' (p. 52). Such an approach has the potential to challenge the apparent realism of structure and recognise that such structures themselves, although ostensibly observable and measurable, are only constituted through practice. Wary of such an epistemological shift descending into relativism, Bourdieu suggests that it is the 'habitus', the durably installed generative principles which produce and reproduce the practices of a class or class fraction (1977, p. 72) which allows us to understand how such seemingly objective structures are both produced through practice and set limits to it within their own specific, typically class based fields. In this way, Bourdieu's ideas offer an epistemological and methodological third way (Grenfell and James, 1998, pp. 1–2) between objectivist structuralism and subjective constructionism.

Such concerns were apparent in the research discussed here, which attempted to explore young people's 'subjective' understandings and experiences of risk, outside of 'objective', 'official' and 'adult' discourses. This has been described elsewhere as an attempt to understand young people's own 'situated discourses of risk' (Bunton et al., 1998), that is their own subjective understandings of risk which, as our research has illustrated, are not necessarily congruent with objective definitions. Within the official discourses of health promotion, crime control and the personal and social education which characterises youth and community work, risk is typically presented as negative, as something to be managed and avoided, and increasing effort is put into surveying and profiling risk within communities as diverse as drug users and school children as well as whole populations. Such discourses attempt to render risk calculable, knowable and hence avoidable through the use of technologies of expertise such as crime statistics and epidemiology. These technologies present us with official accounts of risk and suggest measures for avoidance, which appear rational.

Such rational and objectivist accounts of risk do not necessarily have meaning for all social groups. However, as the work of Mary Douglas (1984, 1992) has illustrated, risk is often constructed within communities with reference to norms and values, boundaries and pollution, cleanliness and dirt. In this context, risk is essentially subjective; what is understood as risk may only have meaning within particular situated discourses specific to particular cultures. In the early phases of this research, it soon became apparent that young people's subjective understandings of risk were not necessarily the same as adult or official definitions. This became a dominant theme throughout the project and such findings were presented to policy makers in an attempt to influence decision-making (see Foreman *et al.*, 2000). Through focusing, as Bourdieu advocates, on 'real activity' (1990, p. 54) this chapter attempts to theorise young men's often risky practices as the product of the habitus within which they find themselves and which their practices inevitably reproduce. The hope of such an exercise is to challenge the notion (as Bourdieu does throughout his work on practice) that practice can be understood in an objective way. The discussion will suggest that official discourses which condemn young people's behaviour as irrational and risky and attempt to intervene on such a basis are misguided as they are incapable of understanding the 'logic' of such practices which are determined by the historically constructed and reconstructed habitus of such a group.

Field, practice and 'habitus'

For Bourdieu, society is not homogenous, but must be understood as consisting of a number of fields which operate according to their own internal logics or dynamicism which is both the product and the producer of the specific habitus appropriate to it (Williams, 1995). Bourdieu's theory of practice, where practice refers to 'what people do', is thus premised upon understanding the relationship between individual practice, the fields in which such practices take place and what he describes as the habitus. It is the habitus which allows us to begin to identify the 'logic of practice' (1990) within specific fields. The goal is thus to be able to say why certain groups engage in certain practices and others do not that is, why are specific cultural practices such as listening to classical music predominantly associated with higher social class groups. It is habitus, which in many respects provides the cornerstone of Bourdieu's theory, as a means of describing the durably installed generative principles which produce and reproduce the practices of a class or class fraction (Bourdieu, 1977). In *Outline of a Theory of Practice* (1977) habitus and its relationship to practice is defined in a characteristically oblique way:

> The structures constitutive of a particular environment (e.g. the material conditions of existence characteristic of a class condition) produce

habitus, systems of durable, transposable dispositions, structured structures predisposed to function as structuring structures, that is as principles of the generation and structuring of practices and representations which can be objectively 'regulated' and 'regular' without in any way being the product of obedience to rules, objectively adapted to their goals without presupposing a conscious aiming at ends or an express mastery of the operations necessary to attain them and, being all this, collectively orchestrated without being the product of an orchestrating action of a conductor. (1977, p. 72)

Bourdieu thus argues that the structures, which make up a particular environment produce habitus and that this in turn structures, practice. Thus, it is always overarching structures in the form of, for example, class conditions, which determine the habitus of both individuals and social groups and therefore their practices. The habitus can consequently be defined as:

A socially constituted system of cognitive and motivating structures which provide individuals with class dependent predisposed ways of relating to and categorising both novel and familiar situations. (Shilling, 1997, p. 129)

It is formed in the context of people's social locations and inculcates in them a worldview based upon and reconciled by these positions. As such, it tends towards reproducing specific social structures. The habitus thus becomes a way in which we can describe localised strategic actions (Robbins, 2000, p. 27) which moves us beyond the determinisms of structure and the subjectivisms of agency. It is important to note that Bourdieu does not suggest that the action of the habitus is to determine 'mechanistic' and fixed responses in practice, but rather that it limits the options that individuals have through providing both cultural norms and historical precedents which in turn determine strategies of action or practice. Habitus can therefore be understood as:

... the values and dispositions gained from our cultural history that generally stay with us across contexts (they are durable and transposable). These values and dispositions allow us to respond to cultural rules and contexts in a variety of ways (because they allow for improvisation), but the responses are always largely determined – regulated – by where (and who) we have been in a culture. (Webb *et al.*, 2002, pp. 36–7)

In *Distinction* (1984), Bourdieu uses his concept of habitus to explain class specific consumption practices and offer a sociological critique of taste. Consumption practices and patterns are described as linked to the habitus of certain groups through a historical construction of taste that becomes unconscious and continually reproduced through practice. Such consumption practices can be risky that is, alcohol consumption or cigarette smoking, but may have a 'cultural logic' within their specific habitus. The potential of such an understanding of consumption for the study of health behaviours and the development of health promotion interventions has been noted (Bunton and Burrows, 1995). This is valuable for the present discussion, as the findings presented here challenge dominant discourses which position young men as a group who 'choose' to participate in risky activities, as has been suggested in other research (Plant and Plant, 1992). Rather, our research suggests that because of their class and geographical position (which of course are not discrete – see Sibley, 1995) young men find themselves exposed to risks that they need to manage. Thus, we must seek to understand the structures that construct the habitus of these young men as risky; an area based on traditional tough working-class masculinity and now facing high levels of crime as a result of increasing exclusion. Such symptoms of structural changes have exacerbated the incidence of risk within the working class 'field' of this area and lead to increased need for risk management. An understanding of such changes are significant as the habitus is identified as having a distinct teleological character (Bourdieu, 1990) and thus becomes 'an amalgam of social, cultural and economic positions' (Robbins, 2000, p. 35) subject to change, but always acting upon practice with reference to history.

> The habitus, a product of history, produces individual and collective practices, more history, in accordance with the schemes generated by history. It ensures the active presence of past experiences which deposited in each organism in the form of schemes of perception thought and action tend to guarantee the correctness of practices and their constancy over time more reliably than all formal rules and explicit norms. (Bourdieu, 1990, p. 54)

Bourdieu thus describes the habitus as history turned into nature (1977, p. 78). If risk and it's management are understood as part of everyday practice, it can be argued that young men find themselves acting out their routine and daily practices with reference to a habitus, a core structure of which is the understanding of, and responses to risk. The practices carried out within a particular habitus are often identified as uncon-scious. That is, they are so much in line with both the past and present experiences that actions are carried out, or practices engaged in, without individuals consciously evaluating their meaning. Experience of the social field determines the availability of responses and courses of action without the need to consciously reflect upon them. In this way, for Bourdieu, practice is, at least partially, unreflexive. This is significant here, as has been noted, recent theory relating to the study of risk in late modernity has increasingly suggested that individuals are required to be more reflexive as a result of detraditionalisation and growing uncertainty (see Giddens, 1991; Beck, 1992). Bourdieu suggests that because of the influences of history and culture in determining behaviour, practice is often unreflexive, without necessarily being mechanistic. Webb *et al.* (2002) suggest that this is because 'habitus is, in a sense, entirely arbi-trary; there is nothing natural or essential about the values we hold, the desires we pursue, or the practices in which we engage' (p. 38). Rather, they are culturally and historically specific.

What are the implications of this for the experiences of the young men who form the focus of this discussion? As working-class young men who find themselves in an increasingly disadvantaged and excluded commu-nity, their habitus is characterised by the features historically associated with such areas. Traditionally, these could be more easily identified as dominant tough working-class masculinity and this is borne out by research findings. Latterly, in line with both global and local change dis-cussed earlier this traditional construct of masculinity has become more complex. With the increasing decline of the area of Townville as a result of such changes, this has in many ways exacerbated the traditional tough nature of masculinity with growing crime and drug use and a concomi-tant increase in violence and disorder which in many ways provided the impetus for this study. The habitus of these young men is therefore deter-mined by the historical imperatives of working-class masculinity, their structurally determined position as young people, which is marginal (a marginalisation further exacerbated by exclusion which I have argued elsewhere, see Crawshaw, 2002) and a high degree of exposure to risk. Risk therefore becomes one of the key determinants of young men's habitus; a structuring structure which determines practices in the con-texts of their daily lives. As a result, risk is normalised and comes to determine their daily practice and experience which manifest them-selves in the form of engaging in risky practices but also, significantly, risk management strategies which become an ordinary part of the expe-riences of both themselves and others. Risk thus becomes routine and unremarkable, although it may not appear so to the objective observer. As Bourdieu notes:

> One of the fundamental effects of the orchestration of habitus is the production of a commonsense world endowed with the objectivity secured by consensus on the meaning of practices and the world, in other words the harmonisation of agents' experiences and the continuous reinforcement each of them receives from the expression, individual or collective, improvised or programmed, of similar or identical experiences. (1977, p. 80)

It is thus the homogeneity of the habitus which 'causes practices and works to be immediately intelligible and foreseeable and hence taken for granted' (p. 80). If risk is so implicit in the practices of these young people, the attempts of a research project such as ours to explore risk as an objective phenomenon is potentially exposed as flawed. As noted, risky youth were identified as a key concern of diverse professionals in Townville and this project was an attempt to contribute to the management of risk. It soon became apparent, however, that young people's understandings of risk were not necessarily congruent with adult definitions. Our research suggested that young people constructed their own 'situated discourses of risk' (Bunton *et al.*, 1998) in response to their environment, which was perceived as imbibed with risk and danger. For example, where adults and control cultures might identify groups of young people on the street as risky, for young people themselves such behaviour was described as a risk management strategy, as they perceived themselves as at risk from both adults within their own community and strangers as well as other young people. Such a theorisation of risk as a relative concept is not a new approach to understanding risk within communities.

The anthropological work of Mary Douglas has offered valuable insights into how risk is constructed with reference to dominant cultural norms and values within communities (Douglas, 1984, 1992). Building on earlier concerns with cultural understandings of dirt and pollution (see Douglas, 1984), Douglas has argued that risk is not absolute and therefore cannot be measured objectively. Rather, risks are constructed with reference to the cultural norms of a particular community. She argues that although some risks are 'real', what is understood as a risk is specific to a particular community and is mediated by social and political processes (p. 29). We must therefore understand risk as relative concept. Risk and danger cannot necessarily be measured objectively from some ostensibly objective and superior vantage point because they are always contingent upon micro cultural understandings, which are negotiated within communities themselves. Such a conception of risk allows it to be explored as a result of the social, economic and cultural contexts of young people's lives. If habitus acts, as Bourdieu suggests, as a structuring structure that determines individuals practice, it might therefore be argued that this would determine both young people's exposure and response to risk. Young people may experience increased exposure to risk as a result of class condition, which in turn determines locality and in the instance of Townville exclusion, but how they understand and manage this is determined by their own specific class habitus which normalises risk and strategies for its management as part of everyday experiences. Thus, as Douglas (1992) argues, risk might indeed be real, but they are understood differently, responded to and managed in ways that are determined by class habitus. The nature of class specific habitus and the implications of this for the reproduction of inequality have been ongoing concerns of the work of Bourdieu and are particularly relevant for this study of disadvantaged young people.

Life in Townville: inequality and social suffering

An ongoing theme of Bourdieu's work has been inequality and how this is sustained within societies, with particular emphasis upon the link between economic position and access to particular forms of capital. Although implicit in early work (see Bourdieu, 1977, 1990) these concerns have been more explicit in recent writings on inequality, both globally and within his home country of France, and the 'social suffering' (Bourdieu, 1999) that results. For Bourdieu, inequality is identified as a symptom of the dominance of neo-liberal economic forces operating at an international level (Bourdieu, 1998). It is manifested in the form of poverty, exclusion and suffering, the results of the downsizing of traditional industries, the dominance of global markets and rising unemployment and the growth of low-paid work.

These features are all too apparent in the area that provided the focus for this study. In many respects, Townville reflects the conditions of post-industrial late modernity. It has undergone serious economic decline in the past two decades as a result of the downsizing of traditional industries such as steel manufacture, resulting in high levels of unemployment (see Bunton, Green and Mitchell's introductory chapter for a more detailed demographic account). Housing policy has promoted depopulation of the area and this has led to an increasing number of empty properties and the creation of large areas of open space. The town has suffered from a lack of investment from local commerce and this has resulted in the closure of the majority of shops in the main commercial area with few facilities being left for local residents apart from a bank, public houses, social clubs and newsagent/convenience stores. The resulting exclusion is exacerbated by the town's geographical positioning as a peripheral estate, lying outside the main urban centre of its locality and being effectively isolated by the proximity of a main road. This is particularly relevant for young people.

Bourdieu likens the social suffering which results from inequality as an experience akin to feeling left behind by wider society, of lacking dignity as a result of an inability to consume and access basic material resources, and ultimately of social exclusion (1999). The effects of such changes in communities like Townville are severe. Young men involved in this research suggested that their daily lives and experiences were delimited, lacked opportunity and diversity and were often felt to be without purpose:

> Interviewer: *What do you do in your spare time?*
> Young man: Like we just sometimes, like just hang about, that's all we do, that's all we can do.
> Young man: Not much of a life.
> Young man: Not much, there's like nothing to do at all. (all 15 years)

This was described as leading to contact with the police from whom they felt they received excessive surveillance:

> You're either playing football or you're locked up. (17 years)

Young men recognised that they were part of an excluded and often stigmatised group because of the deprivation and concomitant problems of crime which characterised their community. This was particularly significant in terms of their exposure to, and experience of, drug and alcohol related problems.

> It's so bad these smackheads (drug users) walk about with the carrier bags and been shoplifting all day and they come back to Townville trying to sell some stuff off and they sell them to all sorts, you name they sell them from this to that. (Group aged 15–17 years)

> Hard drugs and that because young kids are seeing them everyday and that and their Mam's and Dad's are on them. It's not a very good atmosphere to grow up in. (17 years)

Living in Townville bestowed a negative identity as a result of the town's reputation as a deviant and undesirable community:

> They think we are all, like thieves and all that. As soon as they see one person from Townville and say they are a nice person and they don't even know 'em, they'll think, 'oh he's a thief, you've gotta watch this you've gotta watch that'. (15 years)

In this way, young men recognised that their area was disadvantaged, and that the resulting exclusion affected both their lives within the community and interaction outside of it. Young men also expressed powerful feelings of uncertainty, insecurity and mistrust, indicative of the 'ontological insecurity' which is increasingly understood to characterise late modernity (Giddens, 1991).

> It's like risky, very risky right. In Townville you can't trust anybody. When you get older you feel like you don't really want to live in Townville anymore but you get on with it because you live here. (17 years)

Such feeling led to people wanting to leave the area. As one young man noted:

> It's not the type of town to raise kids in. Like my sisters had a kid down here, she lived here for about a year and in March she moved out, just didn't want to bring her kid up down here. (Group aged 15–17)

Recent risk theory has suggested that it is the most disadvantaged groups within communities which experience the greatest degree of exposure to risk. As Beck notes:

> Risk are distributed inversely in proportion to the distribution of wealth. (1992, p. 19)

This proposition appears to be borne out by the experiences of young men in Townville who describe their lives as imbibed with risk as a result of factors associated with exclusion and disadvantage such as high crime rates, prevalence of drug use and lack of safe spaces.

Risk as practice

For young men involved in this research, exposure to risk was presented as a routine part of their daily experiences. Particular 'risks' highlighted were drugs, crime, street violence and police harassment. As a result, many daily practices involved awareness and management of risk in a variety of contexts. For example, drugs were presented as risky, in terms of the dangers of use, but also because of the risks that drug users presented within their community. In both contexts, drugs were presented as a normal part of life in Townville.

> You just go to the corner shop right and you see 'smackheads' (drug users) walking down from the hostel to go and get some stuff. (Group aged 15–17)

> Because there's loads of 'smackheads', I feel uncomfortable walking around by myself. (Group aged 16–19)

The result of the ubiquity of risk presented by drug users was that young men had to incorporate strategies for risk management into their daily practices, which typically involved staying in groups when on the streets, particularly after dark.

> I don't think much of the area. You have to walk around in crowds because there is that many druggies walking around. (Group aged 16–19)

Paradoxically, young men did acknowledge that they would participate in drug use, but in ways that they perceived as less risky than the behaviour of the 'smackheads'. As one young man noted:

> I smoke the tack (cannabis), that's it, that's all I do. There's nowt really wrong with that, you know, that's sorted that, all that does is like chills you out and you can have a laugh and that. Smack is a hell of a lot, it's not the same at all I believe. (Group aged 16–19)

Bourdieu (1984) notes the importance of distinction in consumption practices both between and within social groups. For Bourdieu, particular consumption practices are bound up with cultural logics which have meaning within specific groups. This has been discussed with reference to health promotion (Bunton and Burrows, 1995) and also class based health inequalities (Williamson, 1995). In this context, it allows us to understand how risky practices are understood differentially in certain cultural contexts. Although, from an 'objective' perspective, drug use may be understood as a risky practice *per se*, for these young men it was much more complex. Hierarchies of drug risk were identified with young men suggesting that some practices were risky and others not. This was partially determined by the perceived health risks of different kinds of drug use, but also by the different cultural identities attributed to the users of respective drugs. Thus 'smack' (heroin) was understood in a specific way, and 'smackhead' to indicate a certain type of person:

I've lived in Townville that long, that it, smack, is a dirty drug. What puts me off, I probably would have tried it by now, what puts me off that, is just seeing, if you look round, people doing a turkey (experiencing withdrawal). (Group aged 15–17)

Young men in the sample saw themselves as distinct from this group, despite discussing their own engagement in drug use, which might be judged as risky by adults or within health promotion discourses. It was also apparent in other contexts that young men found themselves participating in risky practices as a result of their social and class position, but also because of their gender. Masculinity has frequently been identified as a risky identity, that is, that men actively pursue risk in order to attain masculine status and reaffirm their identities as men within the male peer group (Jones, 1993). This has been increasingly documented in studies concerned with men's health and risk (see Watson, 2000). The relationship between masculinity and risk is rarely so simple, however. Men may be more likely to engage in risky practices than women, or at least be less likely to take action to avoid risk (Watson, 2000), however, constructions of masculinity within cultures often limit the number of practices available to men and work to place them in risky contexts simply by virtue of their being male (see Jones, 1993). Following Bourdieu, we could begin to theorise the existence of a masculine habitus, determined by historical and cultural constructs of masculinity, which both exposes and predispose men to risk-taking; behaviours which may often have their own cultural logic within patriarchal societies. As some young men noted:

In Townville the lads always think you have to be hard like you have to fight all the time. (15 years)

If you can't at least throw a few fists here, then there's no point in you staying. (15 years)

Such accounts suggest that to be male is risky identity in Townville. Bourdieu suggests that the habitus sets limits to action, not through determining a Pavlovian conditioned response, but rather influencing practice, because:

> ... being the product of a particular class of objective regularities the habitus tends to generate all the reasonable common sense behaviours which are possible within the limits of these regularities and which are likely to be positively sanctioned because they are objectively adjusted to the logic characteristic of a particular field whose objective future they anticipate. At the same time it tends to exclude all extravagances – behaviours that would be negatively sanctioned because they are incompatible with the objective conditions. (Bourdieu, 1990, p. 54)

Thus, young men's behaviours are determined by the habitus in which they find themselves. To engage in a risky practice such as fighting is consistent with the nature of that habitus, as such behaviour is sanctioned within its own historical logic of working class 'tough' masculinity. Such practices inevitably have an impact upon the body, and Bourdieu employs the concept of 'bodily hexis' to describe the physical attitudes and attributes which emerge in an individual as a result of the relationship between particular fields and habitus (Webb *et al.*, 2002). For these young men, it would seem that a key feature of their 'bodily hexis' is the ability to engage in physical confrontation, with holding one's own (or 'being able to through a few fists') being an essential part of their identity as young men.

It was further suggested that young women did not experience such risks, but that it was being a young man which attracted greater risk. This reflects gender oppositioning long identified in research into femininity and masculinity (see Connell, 1995).

> I reckon girls have an easy life in Townville. When you're a girl nobody says nowt to you. When you're a boy it's all like who are you? Do you wanna have a fight?

Socially constructed gender differences are an important manifestation of bodily hexis, which Bourdieu notes leads to specific embodied activities becoming the domain of men and women, with men, from their position of domination being called upon to perform the 'external' acts associated with physical prowess, domination and violence (see Bourdieu, 2001, p. 38). These are not, of course, distinct from broader discourses of masculinity apparent in wider society and found in various forms throughout different cultural milieu. However, they are all broadly based upon aggression and dominance, albeit in different ways (this refers to the now well established notion of 'hegemonic masculinity'; see Carrigan *et al.*, 1985). Such a habitus structures young men's relationships within their community and has a key role in determining their daily practices.

For these young men it is difficult (if not impossible) to act outside of this limited field of practice determined by the habitus in which they find themselves, that of working-class young men. Bourdieu suggests that in this way habitus does present limits to action and determines the availability of responses and practices for any given group in the contexts in which they find themselves. Therefore, what might be understood from an objective viewpoint as risky (in this instance fighting), has its own internal logic. This logic is determined by the precedent of historical experiences, that is, in this particular class habitus, a tough working-class culture demands a specific response to challenge or threat. Furthermore, for the sample of young men discussed here, the historical construction of masculinity as aggressive and tough demands assertion of this in the form of demonstrating physical prowess. In such a context, the risks presented by fighting are less significant than being seen as deviating from accepted norms and practices. This illustrates the teleological nature of Bourdieu's theorisation of practice, which is always based upon precedents about what constitutes appropriate behaviour within what he describes as 'a determinate class of conditions of existence' (1990, p. 54). Such responses are not necessarily mechanistic in the sense of being pre-programmed and therefore essentially predictable, but are gleaned from the available store of responses which are themselves determined by collective history or experience within a particular group. As Bourdieu notes:

> It is of course never ruled out that the responses of the habitus may be accompanied by a strategic calculation tending to perform in a conscious mode the operation that the habitus performs quite differently, namely an estimation of chances presupposing transformation of the past effect into the expected objective. But these responses are first defined, without any calculation, in relation to objective potentialities immediately inscribed in the present, things to do or not to do, things to say or not to say in response to a probable upcoming future. (1990, p. 53)

Thus, action is not wholly the product of forces outside of the individual in a truly 'structural' sense, but such practices are ultimately predefined by the structures of the habitus. Within this masculine and working-class habitus, practice is always informed by the expectations and precedents set by that habitus which themselves correspond to the historical structures which constitute the habitus itself.

Discussion

This chapter has attempted to present some tentative discussion of the salience of the work of Pierre Bourdieu for theorising young men's risk-taking. As has been noted, Bourdieu's work attempts to present a 'theory of practice' (1977) which emphasises the importance of structures in both its production and reproduction. He argues that practice always takes place within specific habitus, structuring structures, which as a result of both history and culture create possibilities for action within specific contexts (Bourdieu, 1977, 1990). This appears to be particularly relevant to the experiences of young men in Townville. For these young men, risk is depicted as an everyday experience and their responses to this are characterised by the history and culture of their community, often subverting more official risk discourses. Thus practices that may objectively appear risky, such as drug use and fighting, are not necessarily understood as such. This potentially offers a valuable perspective on young people and risk more generally. In contrast to existing work (see Plant and Plant, 1992), the discussion presented here does not aim to argue that young men are active risk seekers, but that rather the conditions of their habitus constructs risk as an ordinary event. If habitus is inseparable from the structures that produce and reproduce them (Bourdieu, 2001, p. 40), and consequently practice is inextricably linked with broader structures, it would seem that structure is still of profound importance as class based habitus determine practice through inculcating appropriate responses which are determined by history and culture. As has been noted, this is not to suggest that practice is mechanistic (Robbins, 2000), rather, the number of potential responses in any given situation or event are limited.

The present discussion has attempted to consider how risk can be theorised as practice with its own particular cultural logic. Such a proposition contradicts perspectives that see risk-taking as an inevitable condition of youth (see Plant and Plant, 1992), and is also in contrast with some of the recent work relating to the rise of the risk society (Beck, 1992) and reflexive modernisation (Beck *et al.*, 1994). Within such discussions, late modernity is characterised as increasingly reflexive with the diminishing importance of traditional markers of identity such as class. Bourdieu's work challenges this through suggesting that at a micro level, structure remains of profound importance in constructing class based identities through the production and reproduction of habitus and practice. Critics of Bourdieu's work have argued against this and suggested that his theory over privileges structure and negates individual agency in practice (Kauppi, 2000). However, it is not Bourdieu's aim to suggest that practice is purely determined by structure and thus mechanistic. It is rather the class of conditions that are produced by habitus, which are in turn produced by overarching structures which govern the characteristics of fields, inevitably impinge on practice in a profound way. In this way, the goal is, as noted earlier, to transcend the dualism between objectivism and subjectivism in order to understand the logic of practice within certain social groups.

It would appear that such a perspective offers a valuable insight into young people's risk-taking. If the researcher assumes the position of detached observer, they are wholly incapable, Bourdieu would argue, of understanding the cultural logics that determine practice at a micro or subjective level. Rather, they must acknowledge the significance of the structures which determine the 'class of conditions' that constitute field and habitus, and seek to understand these through focusing upon 'real activity'; that is, the daily lives of young people in which practices and the habitus that determine them are continually produced and reproduced. Bourdieu describes the habitus as history turned into nature (1977), to explain how as practices become routinised they become normalised and naturalised. If practices such as risk-taking take on such characteristics in a community like Townville, researchers must therefore step down from their 'sovereign' viewpoint, to understand the lives of young people and recognise their complexity in the context of history and culture rather than individual choice and determination. This is not to suggest that risk-taking is an inevitable condition of such a social group, but that the habitus of that group sets limits to action and those who find themselves within it respond accordingly.

References

Beck, U. (1992) *Risk Society: Towards a New Modernity*. London: Sage.
Beck, U., Giddens, A. and Lasch, S. (1994) *Reflexive Modernisation: Politics, Aesthetics and Tradition in the Modern Social Order*. Cambridge: Polity Press.
Beck, U. and Beck-Gernshiem, E. (2002) *Individualisation*. London: Sage.
Bourdieu, P. (1962) Trans. Ross, A.C.M. *The Algerians*. Boston: Beacon Press.
Bourdieu, P. (1977) *Outline of a Theory of Practice*. London: Cambridge University Press.
Bourdieu, P. (1984) *Distinction: A Social Critique of the Judgement of Taste*. Massachusetts: Harvard.

Bourdieu, P. (1990) *The Logic of Practice*. Cambridge: Polity.

Bourdieu, P. (1998) *Acts of Resistance: Against the New Myths of our Time*. Cambridge: Polity.

Bourdieu, P. (1999) *The Weight of the World: Social Suffering in Contemporary Societies*. Cambridge: Polity.

Bourdieu, P. (2001) *Masculine Domination*. Cambridge: Polity.

Bourdieu, P. and Wacquant, L. (1992) *An Invitation to Reflexive Sociology*. Cambridge: Polity Press.

Bunton, R. and Burrows, R. (1995) 'Consumption and health in the "epidemiological" clinic of late modern medicine' in Bunton, R., Nettleton, S. and Burrows, R. (eds) *The Sociology of Health Promotion: Critical Analysis of Consumption, Lifestyle and Risk*. London: Routledge, pp. 206–22.

Bunton, R., Crawshaw, P. and Green, E. (1998) 'Risk, gender and youthful bodies', unpublished conference paper, *International Sociological Association XIV World Congress Conference*, Montreal, Canada, August 1998.

Carrigan, T. Connell, B. and Lee, J. (1985) 'Towards a new sociology of masculinity'. *Theory and Society*, Vol. 14, No. 5, pp. 551–600.

Connell, R. (1995) *Masculinities*. Cambridge: Polity.

Crawshaw, P. (2002) 'Negotiating space in the risky community'. *Youth and Policy*, Vol. 74, pp. 59–72.

Douglas, M. (1984) *Purity and Danger*. London: Routledge.

Douglas, M. (1992) *Risk and Blame: Essays in Cultural Theory*. London: Routledge.

Foreman, A., Bunton, R., Crawshaw, P., Green, E., Mitchell, M. and Seabrook, T. (2000) *Risk Community: A Study of Risk and Young People*. Final Report, Centre for Social Policy Research, University of Teesside.

Furlong, A. and Cartmel, F. (1997) *Young People and Social Change: Individualisation and Risk in Late Modernity*. Buckingham: Open University Press.

Giddens, A. (1991) *Modernity and Self Identity*. Cambridge: Polity.

Grenfell, M. and James, D. (eds) (1998) *Bourdieu and Education: Acts of Practical Theory*. London: Falmer Press.

Jones, A. (1993) 'Defending the border: men's bodies and vulnerability'. *Cultural Studies from Birmingham*, No. 2, pp. 77–123.

Kauppi, N. (2000) *The Politics of Embodiment: Habits, Power and Pierre Bourdieu's Theory*. Peter Lang: Berlin.

Plant, M. and Plant, M. (1992) *The Risk Takers: Alcohol, Drugs, Sex and Youth*. London: Routledge.

Robbins, D. (2000) *Bourdieu and Culture*. London: Sage.

Shilling, C. (1997) *The Body and Social Theory*. London: Sage.

Sibley, D. (1995) *Geographies of Exclusion*. London: Routledge.

Walker, R. (1985) *Applied Qualitative Research*. Aldershot: Gower.

Watson, J. (2000) *Male Bodies: Health, Culture and Identity*. Buckingham: Open University Press.

Webb, J., Schirato, T. and Danaher, G. (2002) *Understanding Bourdieu*. London: Sage.

Williams, S. (1995) 'Theorising class, health and lifestyles: can Bourdieu help us?' *Sociology of Health and Illness*, Vol. 17, No. 5, pp. 577–604.

14
Every Good Boy Deserves Football

Simon Pratt and Elizabeth Burn

This chapter critically analyses contemporary constructions of football in England and how it is being employed through current educational initiatives to address the issue of 'disaffected' young males. We intend to problematise how football has been supplied in schools, under the label of educational enrichment activities, supposedly inclusive of class and racial differences. We suggest that this particular discourse of football is actively re-establishing traditional forms of hegemonic masculinities. We draw on media coverage as well as research into school practices in order to highlight this trend. The chapter explores how class, race and gender are embedded in a football culture that is itself constructed against a background of rapid educational, economic and social change. We question how young male identities are affected by these developments in a society where risk-taking is increasingly part of young men's experiences.

The provision of football to 'disaffected' white and black working-class boys as a way of raising academic achievement through football focused curriculum initiatives and homework clubs linked to local football teams (Francis, 1998) is not an innocent act. The Learning FC Guide which uses football to teach English and Maths (Henry, 2000; Pettecrew, 2000) and the Community Sports Programme: Learning through football (Playing for Success, DFES, 1997) are two examples of recent projects that are increasingly to be found in inner city schools, in areas of high social deprivation: '... Tackling social problems among children and adults in some of the most deprived areas of the country' (Brown, 1999, p. 23). Raphael Reed discusses how notions of masculinity are embedded in this discourse of positive role models for boys: 'Engaging the support of Premier club footballers in after-school study centres is supposed to help' (1998, p. 63). It is set in a political context of the present backlash against girls, that places them as responsible for failing boys, as identified by Weiner *et al.* (1997, p. 1) in Cohen (1998, pp. 19–20) '... girls' achievement since the 1980s has something to do with boys' failure', as if 'backlash period' has sprung forth 'as a result of a decade of equal opportunities policy making deliberately aimed at girls and young women'.

The Teacher Training Agency slogan 'Every Good Boy Deserves Football' (TTA, 1999), that titles this chapter is part of a publicity campaign aimed at recruiting more male teachers to provide positive role models for boys, in order to challenge the feminised (Miller, 1996) classroom with its assumed bias against boys. This reassertion of the patriarchal agenda is evidenced in the way football can operate in primary schools to exclude other groups; as Lenskyi observes, 'the primary product of sport is hegemonic masculinity' (1986, p. 15). Skelton (1996, p. 185) found in her study that schools themselves can operate to 'uphold normative conceptions of masculinity through structure, pedagogy and curriculum'. She further implicates football as one of the ways of reinforcing this regime, as well as promoting an essentialised and homogenised view of boys.

We intend to examine how existing cultural definitions of hegemonic masculinities are both maintained and reconstituted (Thornton in Haddad, 1993) through the ritualised performance of football and its place in the formal and informal school curriculum. Gendered, classed and racialised landscapes frame the relationship between football and education. This is visible in present government initiatives to control the disaffected working-class male (Mac An Ghaill, 1994; Sewell, 1997). These gender discriminatory practices, used to address 'boys, fears, anxieties and displacements which may be expressed in violent or prejudicial ways' (Raphael Reed, 1998, p. 73) means that female pupils and staff, together with more marginalised masculinities (Jackson, 1990) are denied equal access to status, curriculum and teacher attention.

Increasingly, research into masculinity is concerned with 'risk-taking' amongst young men and the term itself can be employed to refer to risky or unsocial behaviours that challenge the existing order as well as being applied to young men who risk non-conformity to dominant masculine norms. Furlong and Cartmel (1997a, p. 6) declare that: 'the risk society is not a classless society, but a society in which the old social cleavages associated with class and gender remain intact; on an objective level, changes in the distribution of risk have been minimal. However, subjective feelings of risk have become a much more significant feature of young people's lives and this has implications for their experiences and lifestyles.' Whilst recognising the potential for derision and abuse that young men face when not conforming to their peer group culture, we also support Salisbury and Jackson's argument that: 'boys need to learn how to open up more about themselves and take the occasional risk of being vulnerable in groups rather than keeping their guards up' (Salisbury and Jackson, 1996b, p. 222). We also acknowledge that the notion of risk-taking itself needs to be explored further. Furlong *et al.* (1997b, p. 98) suggest that we need to review our understanding of risk and vulnerability, recognising increasingly a changing society where: 'the complexity of modern youth transitions' makes risk-taking 'a normal part' of young men's experiences. Present practices that 'insert' football into the curriculum in order to address what the media sees as working-class boys' disaffection have not considered the element of risk-taking and how this impacts on the diversity and complexity of boys' lives.

Research by Connolly (1998) in three inner city primary schools demonstrates how the setting up of a football team as part of their equal opportunity policy to be more inclusive of Black boys, in fact led to elitism and further exclusion for both girls and certain boys depending on their ethnicity or ability: 'Not surprisingly football was a very male affair. Girls were systematically excluded from participating in games during playtime' (Connolly, 1998, p. 85). Women staff were also marginalised by the development of football in the school: 'this emphasis on developing a masculine rapport had the consequence ... of allegiances between the boys and male teachers, sometimes at the expense of female teachers' (Connolly, 1998, p. 87). In the light of these research findings that demonstrate the negative effects of using football to address inequalities, we need to question the governments' assumption that football is the panacea to academic under-achievement and social disaffection. The recognition that lack of academic achievement in these particular schools may be 'seen as a reflection of the middle class bias of schooling in capitalist societies' (Thrupp, 2000, p. 4) is sadly missing from this highly simplistic cataplasm. However, we do not wish to dismiss the positive opportunities for working-class children to utilise an important cultural activity within the school context, but we do need to acknowledge and challenge the present exclusionary practices that are to be found in the professional game today. Hutchinson (1996, p. 178) traces the egalitarian roots of football which 'travelled in the kit-bags rather than with the diplomatic copy'. At the same time as we see increasingly middle class appropriation and consumption of this sport, with the Prime Minister himself supporting a northern working-class club (Newcastle United) and the future king supporting an inner city West Midlands team (Aston Villa). Matthew Brown describes this in the football magazine *When Saturday Comes* as '... the game's metamorphosis from working-class obsession to symbol of the classless, commercially vibrant new Britain we are all supposed to believe in'. We see how few working-class families can actually afford a season ticket – as campaigner, teacher Jane Duffy argues: 'We don't want to see the heart of our stadiums ripped out for the guests of corporate clients' (Williams, 2000, p. 11). We recognise that school itself is a site for contradictory and vying power relations (Mac An Ghaill, 1994); however, these relations are also informed by changing economic conditions. We now see the McDonaldisation (Ritzer, 1993) of football into education with its accompanying financial spin-offs. The costs of the merchandise as well as the entry to the match are economically prohibitive for many working-class families. Furlong and Cartmel (1997a, p. 59) contend that: 'as well as having an impact on the use of leisure time, changing transitional experiences, together with more aggressive and sophisticated marketing techniques, have also affected young people's lifestyles and the patterns of consumption which tend to symbolize cultural identification.'

We question the quality of some of the materials produced in the name of the game and targeted at raising standards in core curriculum subjects. One example of this is a series of Football Maths 'fill-in workbooks' (Shaw and Shiels, 1999) targeted at parents that draw on strategies that include low-level computation sums that have been extensively criticised by the National Numeracy Strategy (NNS) (1999). Teaching initiatives focused on football do not have to be of a simplistic, low-level kind. The training pack *My England* (Bennathan, 1999) forms part of a very well thought-out and educationally sound schools theatre project (ARC Theatre Ensemble). The drama offers a range of high quality resource materials that enable teachers to work with pupils in exploring and challenging racism, homophobia and sexism. We applaud the use of drama to invite young pupils themselves to resist the way football is 'sold' as a right-wing fascist pursuit.

Outdated 'essentialist sociological models of the school' (Skelton, 1996, p. 185) fail to recognise that the complex relationship between boys and football that occurs outside of school can also be viewed in a positive and affirmative way. A different reading of football culture (Pratt, 2000) suggests that a structured activity such as a team sport offers a safe place for young males to construct their masculine identity providing 'a human need for closeness and loyalty' – interaction with others sharing the same interest, without leaving them open to accusations of homosexuality. Thornton describes the joy and friendship often generated by sport. '... I can never deny that I was part of that community of laughter, energy and joy. Sport is a part of a deep need for community, trust and plain old fun' (1993, p. 126). We recognise the need to consider the importance of providing a space where male friendship can be learnt and lived out: 'the most important thing was just being out there with the rest of the guys – being friends' (Messner, 1990, p. 429).

The costs for this team sport can also be seen in a more negative light, such as: an exposure to and possible acceptance of, and participation in, competitive, hegemonic 'laddish' practices; hierarchical pecking orders; the denial of other masculinities; and the legitimisation of failure among those males who lack sporting ability (Sabo, 1985; Parker, 1996; Skelton, 1997; Pratt, 2000). Competitive sport is rule-bound and limited by hegemonic masculine competition, where the 'constant tackling, kicking throwing, yelling, jumping, lunging, running hard' (Salisbury and Jackson, 1996b, p. 208) does not allow for, nor encourage: 'the development of intimate, empathic, cooperative peer relationships, even though they expect it to' (Pratt, 2000, p. 3). The features of hyper-masculinity include: competition; violence; dissent; ritualised identities; rule keeping; hierarchical structures; unconditional loyalty to the club, idolisation of 'stars' and subscription to enforced rituals. These features are paraded and confirmed in daily media coverage of the sport and its professional players. There is also evidence of 'public revulsion over the squalid behaviour of professional footballers' (The Express, 16.02.00, p. 81). Salisbury and Jackson (1996b) view such 'squalid' male behaviour as an effect of the public performance of establishing hegemonic hyper-masculinity through heroic risk-taking. They argue that: 'this proving of masculinity through living on the edge, through playing chicken with your life is a central part of learning to become a "real lad"'. These professional footballers are risking losing their livelihood whilst gaining kudos from young male fandom.

One months' random trawl of a range of national daily newspapers produced clear evidence of the representation of hyper-masculine discourse in football coverage (Bairner, 1999; Head, 1999). We list a range of headlines to illustrate this point:

GOLDEN BOY (The Observer, 19.12.99)
STUFFED (The Mirror, 23.12.99)
BATES IS HAPPY TO WIN WEMBLEY WAR (Evening Standard, 23.12.99)
DAMIEN'S GIVEN 'EM A DUFFING (The Sun, 23.12.99)
GUNNER GET YOU (The Daily Star, 28.12.99)

NUTCASE (The Mirror, 7.01.00)
HUMILIATED (The Mirror, 7.01.00)
RED RAGE (Daily Express, 7.01.00)

These emotionally charged headlines illustrate Robson's view that football provides a means by which 'individuals engage in a public, collective and ritualised pageant of identity' (2000, p. 220). The reader is invited to celebrate the aggressive, militaristic ceremony that is often placed within a confrontational arena that can draw on negative cultural discourses. George Orwell (1950) might have thought that 'sport is war minus the shooting' as discussed in *Heart of the Matter*, BBC1, 26.03.00 – For a kick-off, however, the phallic image of the gun is still prevalent in football coverage. For example the symbolic shoot-out that is representative of 'The Wild West' is replicated in the following excerpt from the sports page of one daily newspaper:

Striker quick on the draw again as Sunderland hit back.
Phillips is the irresistible force whose current form demands that he be Alan Shearer's striking partner in England's friendly against Argentina on February 23rd. In the Wild West he would have been the fastest draw in town. Anyone foolish enough to question that would have ended up on Boot Hill.

Somehow you have the feeling that England manager Kevin Keegan will simply load Phillip's revolver and hand him licence to create mayhem on the international stage.

It was a repetitive theme that came from the lips of managers and players alike without hesitation. 'He's just a natural finisher', they observed in unison. (Daily Mail, 7.2.2000, p. 72)

Lorber and Farrell (1991) quoted in Hasbrook and Harris (1999, p. 314) *Wrestling with Gender*: 'A noticeable process in the production of hegemonic masculinity is the establishment of heterosexual rather than homosexual preferences and relationships.'

We also found many press cuttings that featured clear racial, classed and sexualised stereotypes within the texts, such as

Northern nous v Southern savvy (Guardian, 18.12.99)

The miracle of it all is that they have lasted so long together this irascible product of the Govan shipyards and the plummy, middle class boy from Cheshire who inherited the keys to the kingdom of Old Trafford (Daily Mail, 17.12.99)

Fulham still firing blanks (The Mirror, 29.12.99)

Hormones that lights the soccer fan's fuse (Metro, 13.1.00)

Phil yer boots (The Sun, 21.1.00)

Kev has it away (The Sun, 21.1.00)

The fiery Italian again lost his cool

What next? A Frenchman who doesn't spit, likes the English, never sulks and wants to stay here (The Mirror, 29.12.99)

... wise is allowed to strut his stuff among the pampered Continental poodles and prove once again that the Brits have something to offer (The Sun, 15.01.00)

The preponderance of football coverage in all national newspapers and particularly tabloid press sensationalism, demonstrates how as suggested on the *Heart of the Matter* television programme (BBC1, 26.3.00 – For a kick-off) 'football's real power is found among the masses'. Media representations do not only reflect the present 'state of play' but are agentic in developing contemporary social, political and economic ideologies. The media can perform the role of moral guardians, such as 'The Mirror' tracking down 'Britain's most wanted soccer thug ... who battered mum at Cup final' (31.3.00, p. 7), whilst the 'Daily Mails'' WANTED poster, offering £2000 reward (30.3.00, p. 25) again draws on the Wild West discourse we have earlier discussed. This sense of mission and salvation can also be seen to be applied in educational initiatives in schools that use football to address working-class boys' truancy and disaffection. A recent fictionalised account by a secondary school teacher in a northern inner city location highlights this form of 'bribery'. A social worker persuades a disaffected white working-class teenage boy to return to his secondary school:

... There's nowt in the world that could get us back into school', explained Gerry calmly ...
The social worker raised a hand. 'What about if I give you two tickets for the football?' she asked. (Tulloch, 2000, p. 109)

Other media representations are also influential in further positioning football and its fans. The iconisation of 'Gazza' makes visible his Northern working-class roots, as is evidenced by the blurb on his video 'Gazza: The Real Me'.

All the media want to discover the 'new' me, but really I'm still the 'old' me. That's why me and my mate, Danny Baker of television fame (I know he's a Millwall fan, but I don't hold it against him) thought we would get together and make a video of 'THE REAL ME'. Join me on a tour back to my roots, which include the World Famous Dunston Excelsior Club ...

Notice how infamous Millwall fans are identified as 'Other'. Robson (2000, p. 229) explores how this particular football club is defined as a centre of 'aggressive white nativism' – linked to neo-fascist, right-wing political movements.

The complex ways in which media discourses employ contradictory and exclusionary racial, classed and gendered representations of football personalities and their fans further evidences the need to explore carefully how these serious issues are reinterpreted in school settings. The cultural capital embodied by the sport gives it the power to shape and define male hegemonic attitudes and behaviours, which Jackson argues are being re-asserted. 'The erosion of English, imperial power and authority has led to a deep crisis of English, white masculine identities in boys and men' (1998, p. 81).

All of the media coverage that we have explored in preparation for this chapter supports the notion of working-class boys being compensated for 'humiliating economic and social circumstances' (Kehily and Nayak, 1997, p. 85; Jackson, 1998). The status of football is thus being used by the current education agenda to engage certain boys. It draws upon an idealised hegemonic masculine ideal (Messner, 1990, p. 417), that also re-affirms raced, classed and sexual discriminatory practices:

> Sport is a domain of contested national, class and racial relations, but the hegemonic conception of masculinity in sport also bonds men, at least symbolically as a separate and superior group to women. (Messner, 1992, p. 19)

Furlong *et al.* (1997b, p. 82) in their study of youth work with young people at risk in six socially deprived areas of Scotland found that: 'in several instances providers identified youth male behaviour as presenting particular problems'. Furthermore, this finding supports Laberge and Albert's assertion that: 'it is possible that sport plays an especially potent role in the construction of masculinity among working class boys' (1999, p. 256).

In order to address the current discourse of moral panic about male disaffection, the New Labour government is addressing these imperatives by actively supporting this re-assertion, commodification and modernisation of the 'People's Game' – that is football (Blake, 1999). Appropriating it by setting up after-school clubs at football stadia, in order to communicate with disaffected working-class boys, this missionary-like approach has undertones of football being used once again as a civilising process reminiscent of the nineteenth-century ideology (Robson, p. 221). The meanings which inhere in participation in the game may therefore be seen as transposable to the other spheres of activity in which practical mastery defines the bases of social participation (Robson, p. 222).

This moral panic is embedded within the new 'managerialist strategies' (Arnot *et al.*, 1999) where Equal Opportunities initiatives have been transformed into the discourses of '... value addedness, raising standards, individual rights and responsibilities, and entitlement' (Arnot *et al.*, 1999, p. 100). In her study of a working-class, inner city primary school, Skelton (1996) argues that since the 1988 Education Reform act which established the market philosophy in education, 'teachers working in areas with disenfranchised pupils' (1996, p. 192) are more likely to be placed in a position of having to earn respect and authority by employing masculine forms of authority 'into its control strategies' (ibid., p. 192). This supports our earlier discussion of Connolly's (1998) research into similar inner city primary schools where one of the control strategies employed by the male teachers was the setting up of a football team.

The introduction of the NNS in Primary Schools in September 1999 has resulted in the higher achievement of boys (Rafferty, 1997). It should be noted that this project was first piloted in schools located in areas of high social and economic deprivation in order to raise standards. The NNS employs football itself as a pedagogical tool and this may be implicated in raising boys' mathematical achievement. In our position as teacher educators we have anecdotal evidence from a range of male and female teachers who are employing football as an incentive to learn. One example is worth noting:

> I went to teach a Year six class whose supply teacher had not turned up, and I admit I used the football results to interest the boys for my Numeracy Hour – and it worked! (Inner city white female acting headteacher)

Out of school activities are similarly employing football as an enticement for encouraging boys to engage in learning as well as sport. This is evidenced by professional football clubs' active involvement in inner city educational initiatives, for example, out of school clubs at football grounds, such as Bobby Charlton Soccer Schools (Shaw and Shiels, 1999). The Schools Fantasy League is another example of how the government is linking football and the curriculum as part of its Maths 2000 strategy (McGavin, 2000), which encourages children to develop numeracy skills in the context of collating football results.

All these programmes assume that all inner city boys are interested in football with its accompanying reassertion of hegemonic masculinity. We have argued extensively in this chapter of the dangers of buying into the present conceptualisation of football as inclusive of all males. Our evidence shows that there are a range of both boys and girls who, by non participation in 'the love of the game' are further disadvantaged and excluded from these educational developments. Mills (2001, pp. 61–2) suggests that boys who take risks by resisting: 'dominant masculinizing practices' are more vulnerable than girls to derision by their peer group and this view of risk-taking means that boys who do not support the current football mania are in danger of losing their 'mantle of masculinity'. Additionally, those who are entering into this trend could be replicating negative, stereotypical masculinist imagery, as represented in our analysis of media citations.

In reflection, the current middle-class respectability and populism of football, in terms of fan attendance at matches, corporate hospitality, privatisation and so on does not sit easily with media representations of the sport, with aggressive and violent hyper-masculine identities (Parker, 1996) typified by over-paid professional footballer excesses. These issues are further complicated by: the place of sport in male working-class cultural traditions; and as a real, practised feature of men's every day lives. We must recognise the exclusionary practices in favour of the white male that remain around both the sport itself and society at large.

However, we assert that the exploration of football and its media constructions can be employed as a useful context for examining the ways boys (and by omission girls) are controlled and positioned within these contested relations, as well as the active positioning and investment of certain boys in constructing their masculinity through the playing of football. The deconstruction of media hype surrounding the sport itself can provide opportunities to both resist and reconfigure hegemonic masculinity. We agree with Salisbury and Jackson (1996a, p. 110) that '... instead of patronising young male students and treating them as cultural dopes, we need to devise classroom approaches and teaching methods ...' that recognise that boys themselves can demonstrate agency and knowledge about the sport which can be harnessed in order to challenge and contest present hegemonic practices. Researching this chapter has given us materials that can be further employed to examine and deconstruct the narrow and damaging discourse of 'macho man' that limits us all and damages the game itself. The process of making visible the conflicting and competing ideologies that operate under the umbrella of football itself and its associated fandom can open up sites for oppositional politics (Giroux, 1992). We hope this chapter will contribute to opening up a much needed debate concerning young boys, risk-taking, leisure and football. O'Donnell and Sharpe (2000, p. 164) ask whether boys': 'enthusiasm for football fuels intolerance for others such as ethnic minorities, or rather that the game channels aggression and competitiveness and opens up opportunity for tolerant and positive relationships'. Schools are places where hegemonic masculinities are reconstituted (Epstein, 1998); they can also be places where counter hegemonic practices can be explored and developed (Salisbury and Jackson, 1996a). The National Curriculum requirement for Citizenship at Key Stages three and four necessitates that 'pupils take part effectively in school and community-based activities, showing a willingness and commitment to evaluate such activities critically. They demonstrate personal and group responsibility in their attitudes to themselves and others.' Furthermore, Furlong *et al.* (1997b, p. 9) suggest that: 'the citizenship model of youth work could play a valid role in allowing young men to become "citizens within their society" '. The nature of the 'beautiful game' can invite 'the other' in and re-work the present hyper-masculine discourse into an enjoyable inclusionary game that does not celebrate white, hegemonic masculinity or economically exploit the less privileged.

References

Arnot, M., David, M. and Weiner, G. (1999) *Closing the Gender Gap*. London: Polity Press.

Bairner, A. (1999) 'Soccer, masculinity and violence in Northern Ireland'. *Men and Masculinity*, Vol. 1, No. 3, pp. 284–301.

Bennathan, J. (1999) *My England*. London: ARC Theatre Ensemble.

Blake, A. (1999) 'These sporting times'. *Soundings*, Issue 13, Autumn.

Brown, M. (1999) 'Community Leaders'. *When Saturday Comes*, Vol. 148, June.

Cohen, M. (1998) 'A habit of healthy idleness? Boys' underachievement in historical perspective' in Epstein, D., Elwood, J., Hey, V. and Maw, J. (eds) *Failing Boys: Issues in Gender and Achievement*. Buckingham: Open University Press.

Connolly, P. (1998) *Racism, Gender, Identities and Young Children*. London: Routledge.

Epstein, D. (1998) 'Real boys don't work' in Epstein, D., Elwood, J., Hey, V. and Maw, J. (eds) *Failing Boys: Issues in Gender and Achievement*. Buckingham: Open University Press.

Francis, B. (1998) *Power Plays*. Stoke on Trent: Trentham.

Furlong, A. and Cartmel, F. (1997a) *Young People and Social Change: Individualism and Risk in Late Modernity*. Buckingham: Open University Press.

Furlong, A., Cartmel, F., Powney, J. and Hall, S. (1997b) *Evaluating Youth Work with Vulnerable Young People*. Glasgow: The Scottish Council for Research in Education.

Giroux, H. (1992) *Border Crossings*. London: Routledge.

Hasbrook, C. and Harris, O. (1999) 'Wrestling with gender: physicality and masculinity(ies) among inner-city first and second graders'. *Men and Masculinities*, Vol. 1, No. 3, pp. 302–18.

Head, J. (1999) *Understanding the Boys*. London: Falmer.

Henry, J. (2000) 'A game for young hearts'. *The Times Educational Supplement*. 12 May, p. 15.

Hutchinson, R. (1996) *Empire Games*. Edinbrough: Mainstream Publishing.

Jackson, D. (1990) *Unmasking Masculinity: A Critical Autobiography*. London: Unwin Hyman.

Jackson, D. (1998) 'Breaking out of the binary trap: boys' underachievement, schooling, and gender relations' in Epstein, D., Elwood, J., Hey, V. and Maw, J. (eds) (1998) *Failing Boys: Issues in Gender and Achievement*. Buckingham: Open University Press.

Kehily, M. and Nayak, A. (1997) 'Lads and laughter: humour and production of heterosexual hierarchies'. *Gender and Education*, Vol. 9, No. 1, pp. 69–87.

Laberge, S. and Albert, M. (1999) 'Conceptions of masculinity and of gender transgressions in sport among adolescent boys'. *Men and Masculinities*, Vol. 1, No. 3, pp. 243–67.

Lenskyi, H. (1986) *Out of Bounds: Women, Sport and Sexuality*. Toronto: Women's Press.

Lorber, J. and Farrell, S. (1991) 'Principles of gender construction' in Lorber, J. and Farrell, S. (eds) *The Social Construction of Gender*. Newbury Park, CA: Sage, pp. 7–11.

McGavin, H. (2000) 'Field of dreams'. *The Times Educational Supplement*, 23 June, p. 14.

Mac An Ghaill, M. (1994) *The Making of Men: Masculinities, Sexualities and Schooling*. Buckingham: Open University Press.

Messner, M. (1990) 'Boyhood, organised sports and the construction of masculinities'. *Journal of Contemporary Ethnography*, Vol. 18, No. 4.

Messner, M. (1992) *Power at Play. Sport and the Problem of Masculinity*. Boston: Beacon.

Miller, J. (1996) *School for Women*. London: Virago.

Mills, M. (2001) 'Pushing it to the max: interrogating the risky business of being a boy' in Martino, W. and Meyenn, B. (eds) *What about the Boys?* Buckingham: Open University Press.

National Curriculum (1999) *Citizenship Key Stages 3 and 4*. London: DfEE.

National Numeracy Strategy (1999) London: DfEE.

O'Donnell, M. and Sharpe, S. (2000) *Uncertain Masculinities*. London: Routledge.

Orwell, G. (1950) 'Shooting an Elephant'. *The Sporting Spirit*. London: Lawrence and Wishart.

Parker, A. (1996) 'The construction of masculinity within boys' physical education'. *Gender and Education*, Vol. 8, No. 2, pp. 141–57.

Pettecrew, G. (2000) 'Whole new ball game'. *The Times Educational Supplement, Curriculum Special*, 19 May, p. 6.

Playing for Success (1997) www.dfes.gov.uk/playing for success/.

Pratt, S. (2000) 'Teenage kicks: a study of the construction and development of adolescent masculine identities in organised team sport' in Horne, J. and Fleming, S. (eds) *Masculinities: Leisure Cultures, Identities and Consumption*. Eastbourne: Leisure Studies Association.

Rafferty, C. (1997) 'Real maths wins praise'. *The Times Educational Supplement*, 12 December.

Raphael Reed, L. (1998) 'Zero tolerance: gender performance and school failure' in Epstein, D., Elwood, J., Hey, V. and Maw, J. (eds) *Failing Boys: Issues in Gender and Achievement*. Buckingham: Open University Press.

Ritzer, G. (1993) *The McDonaldisation of Society*. Newbury Park: Pine Forge.

Robson, G. (2000) 'Millwall football club' in Munt, S. (ed.) *Cultural Studies and the Working Class*. London: Cassell.

Sabo, D. (1985) 'Sport, patriarchy and male identity: new questions about men and sport'. *Arena Review*, Vol. 9, pp. 1–30.

Salisbury, J. and Jackson, S. (1996a) 'Why should secondary schools take working with boys seriously?' *Gender and Education*, Vol. 8, No. 1, pp. 103–15.

Salisbury, J. and Jackson, D. (1996b) *Challenging Macho Values*. London: Falmer Press.

Sewell, T. (1997) *Black Masculinities and Schooling*. Stoke on Trent: Trentham.

Shaw, D. and Shiels, J. (1999) *Football Maths*. Oxford: Oxford University Press.

Skelton, C. (1996) 'Learning to be tough? The fostering of maleness in one primary school'. *Gender and Education*, Vol. 8, No. 2, pp. 185–97.

Skelton, C. (1997) 'Primary Boys and Hegemonic Masculinity'. *British Journal of Sociology of Education*, Vol. 8, No. 2, pp. 185–97.

Teacher Training Agency (1999) Chelmsford, Essex.

Thornton, A. (1993) 'The accomplishment of masculinities: men and sports'. in Haddad, T. (ed.) *Men and Masculinities*. Toronto: Canadian Scholars Press Inc.

Thrupp, M. (2000) 'Compensating for class: are school improvement researchers being realistic?' *Education and Social Justice*, Vol. 2, No. 2, pp. 2–9.

Tulloch, J. (2000) *The Season Ticket*. London: Cape.

Weiner, G., Arnot, M. and David, M. (1997) 'Is the future female? Female success, male disadvantage and changing gender patterns in education' in Halsey, A., Brown, P., Lauder, H. and Stuart-Wells, A. (eds) *Education: Culture, Economy and Society*. Oxford: Oxford University Press.

Williams, E. (2000) 'Jane's bond'. *The Times Educational Supplement*, 25 February, p. 11.

Index